TOP STOCKS

STOCKS

THIRTIETH ANNIVERSARY EDITION

2024

MARTIN ROTH'S

BEST-SELLING ANNUAL

TOP
STOCKS

THIRTIETH ANNIVERSARY EDITION

2024

A SHAREBUYER'S GUIDE TO
LEADING AUSTRALIAN
COMPANIES

WILEY

The author and publisher would like to thank Alan Hull (author of *Active Investing*, Revised Edition, *Trade My Way* and *Invest My Way*; www.alanhull.com) for generating the five-year share-price charts.

This thirtieth edition first published in 2024 by Wrightbooks, an imprint of John Wiley & Sons Australia, Ltd

Level 4, 600 Bourke Street, Melbourne VIC 3000

Typeset Adobe Garamond Pro Regular by 10/12 pt

First edition published as *Top Stocks* by Wrightbooks in 1995

New edition published annually

© Martin Roth 2024

The moral rights of the author have been asserted

ISBN: 978-1-394-18867-3

Cover design: Wiley

Cover image: Stock market graph © EdNurg/Adobe Stock Photos

Charts created using MetaStock

Disclaimer
The material in this publication is of the nature of general comment only, and does not represent professional advice. It is not intended to provide specific guidance for particular circumstances and it should not be relied on as the basis for any decision to take action or not take action on any matter which it covers. Readers should obtain professional advice where appropriate, before making any such decision. To the maximum extent permitted by law, the author and publisher disclaim all responsibility and liability to any person, arising directly or indirectly from any person taking or not taking action based on the information in this publication.

Printed in Singapore
M124853_051023

Contents

PART I: the companies

PART II: the tables

Preface

Welcome to *Top Stocks 2024*, the 30th edition of the book. It is a milestone for a publication that was never envisaged as a series.

The first edition, published back in 1995, was intended as a one-off book, designed to help independent investors find a basket of secure and promising companies that they could then evaluate further, to see if they met the needs of their portfolios.

But, with the number of individual investors in Australia growing rapidly, the book struck a chord, and it became an annual publication, rewritten each year.

A wave of major new stock market listings was a primary incentive for the growth in share ownership. In 1991 the Commonwealth Bank of Australia was listed, creating many new first-time shareholders. It was followed by the insurance company GIO in 1992 and then by Woolworths in 1993 and Qantas in 1995.

A surge in share prices in 1993 was another incentive; at the same time, some companies actually tried to encourage individuals to buy their shares. One of these was Coles Myer, whose very generous shareholders' discount card led to a tripling of the number of holders of its shares over three years in the early 1990s.

By the end of 1994 some two million Australians owned shares directly (as opposed to indirectly through superannuation or some other kind of managed fund), nearly double the number of three years earlier.

Yet most investors still depended on the stockbroking industry for information about the market, with few outside sources providing independent and objective guidance. In addition, there were high levels of suspicion about financial markets. Several scandals, including the collapses of the State Bank of Victoria, Adelaide Steamship and the Bond Corporation, had soured the public. Many people — perhaps most — viewed the stock market as little more than a casino.

I saw a need for a book that could provide conservative investors with objective information on individual companies.

Birth of a series

I lived in Japan for 17 years until 1992, working first as a journalist and then as a securities analyst for British merchant banks. During the 1980s I witnessed first-hand what is now referred to as the Bubble Economy, when land prices soared into the stratosphere and the Nikkei stock market index more than tripled in just five years.

One consequence of this was an impressive infrastructure of Japanese investment publications that covered nothing but the stock market, including even several daily newspapers. There were also many regular books that introduced investors to the leading companies. I felt such a book might work well in Australia.

I approached Wrightbooks, then one of the leading publishers of investment and finance titles, and placed my proposal before them. The company saw promise in the idea, and *Top Stocks* was born.

My plan was to find 100 companies that met a range of financial criteria making them suitable for the conservative investor. In particular, each company should have strong profits and modest levels of debt (or no debt at all), and it should also have been listed for at least five years and have made a profit and paid a dividend for each of those five years.

In the event, I could find only 80 companies that more or less met the criteria, but I felt that was a sufficient number for a book.

The first three paragraphs of my preface for the initial edition summed up my intentions:

> Increasing numbers of people wish to take their own decisions on stock market investing, instead of feeling forced to rely on high-fee (and sometimes poorly performing) financial planners, investment advisers or fund managers. They know there are many excellent stocks out there; they're just not sure which ones they are, apart from a few obvious names like BHP. But they are also well aware that danger awaits the unwary, or the unskilled. They have read too many stories in recent years of the corporate high-fliers who went bust, taking down their shareholders with them.
>
> So they buy books that instruct them on the finer points of investment. But they find that somehow these books talk too much in generalities. They feel they are still sitting too far back in the investment arena; all the action in the centre is a little fuzzy.
>
> That, then, is a primary goal of this book. To try to bring you a little closer to the action, to help you learn which stocks are the potential winners and to let you eavesdrop on what insiders in the market say about them.

A little further on I wrote about the recession and financial turmoil of the early 1990s:

> Yet amidst the wreckage of plunging stock prices and spectacular corporate bankruptcies of that era there were a large number of quality companies that quietly continued to make good profits and to pay high dividends. Some of them were in businesses only marginally affected by the economic downturn; others used the problems to cut costs or to develop new export markets.
>
> It is these firms that form the core of this handbook. They are the real stars of the Australian stock market, the solid achievers that have weathered the worst of financial storms and come through even stronger. They should be at the heart of the share portfolio of any conservative investor, for whom this book is written.
>
> These companies are not run by flashy entrepreneurs. In fact, their general managers are for the most part little known to the general public. And though some of the firms are household names — like BHP, Woolworths and National Australia Bank — many ... are scarcely ever in the news, and do their work in relative anonymity.
>
> Do not expect their share prices to triple in a year. They are not that kind of company. Yet most of these recession-buster stocks delivered annual average returns (dividends plus capital gains) in double digits during the five years to mid-1995, and some have a substantially longer history of reward delivery.

That first edition sold just 2300 copies. Yet that was sufficient to make it one of the top books for several months on the bestseller lists of the Australian Stock Exchange bookstores and of *Personal Investment* magazine (neither the bookstores nor the magazine exists any longer).

A reprint was needed, but it seemed to make sense that I update all the figures first, as well as adding any new companies that now met the entry criteria, and removing those that did not match up any longer. The first edition of the book had been called simply *Top Stocks*. The new edition was called *Top Stocks '96*. And so the series came into existence.

A book for its time

It proved to be very much a book of its time. Certainly I had noted the rise in the number of independent investors, thanks especially to the stock market listings of Commonwealth Bank, GIO, Woolworths and Qantas. This had been one of the reasons I wrote the book. But this proved to be just a foretaste.

The partial float of Telstra in 1997 created 559000 first-time shareholders. Then in 1998 some 11 per cent of adult Australians received shares as part of the AMP demutualisation, including 730000 first-time shareholders. A further 500000 people entered the market in 2000 through receiving shares in the NRMA demutualisation.

A November 2000 survey found that around 40 per cent of adult Australians owned shares directly, one of the highest rates in the world. More than half of them had entered the market after 1995.

At the same time, Australians were being forced to make ever-growing contributions to their own superannuation. It led to a big increase in self-managed superannuation funds, along with the need for conservative investment advice.

Indeed, it is these two trends — the increase in individual share ownership and the growth in self-managed superannuation funds — that have helped spark the continuing strong demand each year for *Top Stocks*.

The book has certainly proven itself resilient. Each year, using roughly the same strict and objective entry criteria — my own subjective views count for nothing — the book fills, as if by magic, with between 80 and 115 companies.

It is surely a tribute to the strength of the Australian business world that we can boast so many strong companies, even in the midst of quite volatile economic conditions.

For example, COVID hit the world — and financial markets — in early 2020. Economies around the world wobbled, stock market indices plunged and Australia entered its first recession in 29 years. Yet the majority of companies in *Top Stocks* continued to report higher profits and in 2020 around half of them also boosted their dividend payouts.

Small stocks

Over the years the books have been able to help investors in many ways. For example, it is often useful to check out some of the new entries to the book each year. In some cases these are companies that are now big enough to be included among the 500 largest stocks in Australia (which is one of the criteria for entry to the book). However, they are still so small that they are not generally known by many investors, and are also too small to be of interest to fund managers.

The classic example, which I have cited several times in my introductions to the books, is that of the Perth engineering and mining support company Monadelphous. It first appeared in *Top Stocks '99*, at a share price (adjusted for a subsequent share split) of $0.66. It has subsequently been as high as $28.48.

Here are some more recent examples. Specialist software house Objective Corporation first appeared in *Top Stocks 2016* at a price of $1.61. It appears in the latest edition at $12.22.

In *Top Stocks 2017* medical imaging software specialist Pro Medicus entered at $6.29. In *Top Stocks 2024* it appears at $72.80. Also in *Top Stocks 2017* design software house Altium entered at $9.63. In the latest edition it is $48.00.

A final example: little-known truck components provider Supply Network first appeared in *Top Stocks 2020*, priced at $3.99. It is in *Top Stocks 2024* at $15.35.

Sectors

It is also possible to discern trends in sectors. For example, initial editions of the book contained very few companies in the high-tech or healthcare businesses. Computershare was one of the former; F.H. Faulding (a drugs manufacturer) was one of the latter. There were not many others.

But steadily a steam of such companies entered the book, often when they were still small and little known. Today they are strongly represented, and corporations like Cochlear, CSL and the aforementioned Pro Medicus, Objective and Altium have provided some superb returns to investors.

And though the book was always intended for the fairly conservative investor, an intriguing development is that it is also bought regularly by market traders. These are sometimes people who know little about the companies whose shares they are buying — they mainly examine charts for their guidance — but they do want companies that are safe and are unlikely to go bankrupt. So the companies in *Top Stocks* are very attractive to them for their trading activities.

What are the entry criteria?

The criteria for inclusion in *Top Stocks* are strict:

- All companies must be included in the All Ordinaries Index, which comprises Australia's 500 largest stocks (out of more than 2000). The reason for excluding smaller companies is that there is often little investor information available on them and some are so thinly traded as to be almost illiquid. In fact, the 500 All Ordinaries companies comprise, by market capitalisation, around 90 per cent of the entire market.
- It is necessary that all companies be publicly listed since at least the end of 2018, and have a five-year record of profits and dividend payments.
- All companies are required to post a return-on-equity ratio of at least 10 per cent in their latest financial year.
- No company should have a debt-to-equity ratio of more than 70 per cent.
- It must be stressed that share price performance is NOT one of the criteria for inclusion in this book. The purpose is to select companies with good profits and a strong balance sheet. These may not offer the spectacular share-price returns of a high-tech start-up or a promising lithium miner, but they should also present less risk.
- There are several notable exclusions. Listed managed investments are out, as these mainly buy other shares or investments. Examples are Australian Foundation Investment Company and all the real estate investment trusts.
- Foreign-registered stocks listed on the ASX are also excluded. There is sometimes a lack of information available about such companies. In addition, their stock prices tend to move on events and trends in their home countries, making it difficult at times for local investors to follow them.

Changes to this edition

A total of 13 companies from *Top Stocks 2023* have been omitted from this new edition.

Two corporations, OZ Minerals and Pendal Group, were acquired during the year.

Two other companies, IRESS and McMillan Shakespeare, saw their debt-to-equity ratios rise above the 70 per cent limit for this book.

The remaining nine excluded companies had return-on-equity ratios that fell below the required 10 per cent:

> Alumina
> Ansell
> AUB Group
> Aurizon Holdings
> Globe International
> Healius
> Perpetual
> Schaffer Corporation
> Sonic Healthcare

There are eight new companies in this book (although five of them have appeared in earlier editions of the book, but were not in *Top Stocks 2023*).

The new companies in this book are:

> Accent Group
> Coles Group*
> Insurance Australia Group
> Lindsay Australia*
> Lovisa Holdings*
> Lycopodium
> Santos
> Woodside Energy Group

* Companies that have not appeared in any previous edition of *Top Stocks*.

Company in every edition of *Top Stocks*

Just one company has appeared in all 30 editions: Commonwealth Bank of Australia.

Once again it is my hope that *Top Stocks* will serve you well.

Martin Roth
Melbourne
September 2023

Introduction

The 88 companies in this book have been placed as much as possible into a common format, for ease of comparison. Please study the following explanations in order to get as much as possible from the large amount of data.

The tables have been made as concise as possible, though they repay careful study, as they contain large amounts of information.

Note that the tables for the banks have been arranged a little differently from the others. Details of these are provided later in this Introduction.

Head
At the head of each entry is the company name, with its three-letter ASX code and the website address.

Share-price chart
Under the company name is a long-term share-price chart, to September 2023, provided by Alan Hull (www.alanhull.com), author of *Invest My Way*, *Trade My Way* and *Active Investing*.

Small table
Under the share-price chart is a small table with the following data.

Sector
This is the company's sector as designated by the ASX. These sectors are based on the Global Industry Classification Standard — developed by S&P Dow Jones Indices and Morgan Stanley Capital International — which was aimed at standardising global industry sectors. You can learn more about these on the ASX website.

Share price
This is the closing price on 4 September 2023. Also included are the 12-month high and low prices, as of the same date.

Market capitalisation

This is the size of the company, as determined by the stock market. It is the share price multiplied by the number of shares in issue. All companies in this book must be in the All Ordinaries Index, which comprises Australia's 500 largest stocks, as measured by market capitalisation.

Price-to-NTA-per-share ratio

The NTA-per-share figure expresses the worth of a company's net tangible assets — that is, its assets minus its liabilities and intangible assets — for each share of the company. The price-to-NTA-per-share ratio relates this figure to the share price.

A ratio of one means that the company is valued exactly according to the value of its assets. A ratio below one suggests that the shares are a bargain, though usually there is a good reason for this. Profits are more important than assets.

Some companies in this book have a negative NTA-per-share figure — as a result of having intangible assets valued at more than their net assets — and a price-to-NTA-per-share ratio cannot be calculated.

See Table M, in the second part of this book, for a little more detail on this ratio.

Five-year share price return

This is the approximate total return you could have received from the stock in the five years to September 2023. It is based on the share price appreciation or depreciation plus dividends, and is expressed as a compounded annual rate of return.

Dividend reinvestment plan

A dividend reinvestment plan (DRP) allows shareholders to receive additional shares in their company in place of the dividend. Usually — though not always — these shares are provided at a small discount to the prevailing price, which can make them quite attractive. And of course no broking fees apply.

Many large companies offer such plans. However, they come and go. When a company needs finance it may introduce a DRP. When its financing requirements become less pressing it may withdraw it. Some companies that have a DRP in place may decide to deactivate it for a time.

The information in this book is based on up-to-date information from the companies. But if you are investing in a particular company in expectation of a DRP, be sure to check that it is still on offer. The company's own website will often provide this information.

Price/earnings ratio

The price/earnings ratio (PER) is one of the most popular measures of whether a share is cheap or expensive. It is calculated by dividing the share price — in this case the closing price for 4 September 2023 — by the earnings per share figure. Obviously the share price is continually changing, so the PER figures in this book are for guidance only. Daily newspapers often publish each morning the latest PER for every stock.

Dividend yield

This is the latest full-year dividend expressed as a percentage of the share price. Like the price/earnings ratio, it changes as the share price moves. It is a useful figure, especially for investors who are buying shares for income, as it allows you to compare this income with alternative investments, such as a bank term deposit or a rental property.

Company commentary

Each commentary begins with a brief introduction to the company and its activities. Then follow the highlights of its latest business results. For the majority of the companies these are their June 2023 results, which were issued during July and August 2023. Finally, there is a section on the outlook for the company.

Main table

Here is what you can find in the main table.

Revenues

These are the company's revenues from its business activities, generally the sale of products or services. However, it does not usually include additional income from such sources as investments, bank interest or the sale of assets. If the information is available, the revenues figure has been broken down into the major product areas.

As much as possible, the figures are for continuing businesses. When a company sells a part of its operations the financial results for the sold activities are separated from the core results and reported as a separate item. This can mean that the previous year's results are restated—also excluding the sold business—to make year-on-year comparisons more valid.

Earnings before interest and taxation

Earnings before interest and taxation (EBIT) is the firm's profit from its operations before the payment of interest and tax. This figure is often used by analysts examining a company. The reason is that some companies have borrowed extensively to finance their activities, while others have opted for alternative means. By expressing profits before interest payments it is possible to compare more precisely the performance of these companies.

You will also find many companies using a measure called EBITDA, which is earnings before interest, taxation, depreciation and amortisation.

EBIT margin

This is the company's EBIT expressed as a percentage of its revenues. It is a gauge of a company's efficiency. A high EBIT margin suggests that a company is achieving success in keeping its costs low.

Gross margin

The gross margin is the company's gross profit as a percentage of its sales. The gross profit is the amount left over after deducting from a company's sales figure its cost of sales: that is, its manufacturing costs or, for a retailer, the cost of purchasing the goods it sells. The cost of goods sold figure does not usually include marketing or administration costs.

As there are different ways of calculating the cost of goods sold figure, this ratio is better used for year-to-year comparisons of a single company's efficiency, rather than in comparing one company with another.

Many companies do not present a cost of goods sold figure, so a gross margin ratio is not given for every stock in this book.

The revenues for some companies include a mix of sales and services. Where a breakdown is possible, the gross profit figure will relate to sales only.

Profit before tax/profit after tax

The profit before tax figure is simply the EBIT figure minus interest payments. The profit after tax figure is, of course, the company's profit after the payment of tax, and also after the deduction of minority interests. Minority interests are that part of a company's profit that is claimed by outside interests, usually the other shareholders in a subsidiary that is not fully owned by the company. Many companies do not have any minority interests, and for those that do it is generally a tiny figure.

As much as possible, I have adjusted the profit figures to exclude non-recurring profits and losses, which are often referred to as significant items. It is for this reason that the profit figures in *Top Stocks* sometimes differ from those in the financial media or on financial websites, where profit figures often include significant items.

Significant items are those that have an abnormal impact on profits, even though they happen in the normal course of the company's operations. Examples are the profit from the sale of a business, or expenses of a business restructuring, the write-down of property, an inventory write-down, a bad-debt loss or a write-off for research and development expenditure.

Significant items are controversial. It is often a matter of subjective judgement as to what is included and what excluded. After analysing the accounts of hundreds of companies while writing the various editions of this book, it is clear that different companies use varying interpretations of what is significant.

Further, when they do report a significant item there is no consistency as to whether they use pre-tax figures or after-tax figures. Some report both, making it easy to adjust the profit figures in the tables in this book. But difficulties arise when only one figure is given for significant items.

In normal circumstances most companies do not report significant items. But investors should be aware of this issue. It sometimes causes consternation for readers of *Top Stocks* to find that a particular profit figure in this book is substantially different from that given by some other source. My publisher occasionally receives emails from readers enquiring why a profit figure in this book is so different from that reported elsewhere. In virtually all cases the reason is that I have stripped out a significant item.

It is also worth noting my observation that a growing number of companies present what they call an underlying profit (called a cash profit for the banks), or even a so-called normalised profit, in addition to their reported (statutory) profit. This underlying profit will exclude not only significant items but also discontinued businesses and sometimes other related items. Where all the relevant figures are available, I have generally used these underlying figures for the tables in this book.

As already noted, when a company sells or terminates a significant business it will now usually report the profit or loss of that business as a separate item. It will also usually backdate its previous year's accounts to exclude that business, so that worthwhile comparisons can be made of continuing businesses.

The tables in this book usually refer to continuing businesses only.

Earnings per share
Earnings per share is the after-tax profit divided by the number of shares. Because the profit figure is for a 12-month period the number of shares used is a weighted average of those on issue during the year. This number is provided by the company in its annual report and its results announcements.

Cashflow per share
The cashflow per share ratio tells — in theory — how much actual cash the company has generated from its operations.

In fact, the ratio in this book is not exactly a true measure of cashflow. It is simply the company's depreciation and amortisation figures for the year added to the after-tax profit, and then divided by a weighted average of the number of shares. Depreciation and amortisation are expenses that do not actually utilise cash, so can be added back to after-tax profit to give a kind of indication of the company's cashflow.

By contrast, a true cashflow — including such items as newly raised capital and money received from the sale of assets — would require quite complex calculations based on the company's statement of cashflows.

However, many investors use the ratio as I present it, because it is easy to calculate, and it is certainly a useful guide to approximately how much funding the company has available from its operations.

Dividend
The dividend figure is the total for the year, interim and final. It does not include special dividends. The level of franking is also provided.

Net tangible assets per share
The NTA per share figure tells the theoretical value of the company — per share — if all assets were sold and then all liabilities paid. It is very much a theoretical figure, as there is no guarantee that corporate assets are really worth the price put on them in the balance sheet. Intangible assets such as goodwill and patent rights are excluded because of the difficulty in putting a sales price on them, and also because they may in fact not have much value if separated from the company.

As already noted, some companies in this book have a negative NTA, due to the fact that their intangible assets are so great, and no figure can be listed for them.

Where a company's most recent financial results are the half-year figures, these are used to calculate this ratio.

Interest cover

The interest cover ratio indicates how many times a company could make its interest payments from its pre-tax profit. A rough rule of thumb says a ratio of at least three times is desirable. Below that and fast-rising interest rates could imperil profits. The ratio is derived by dividing the EBIT figure by net interest payments. Some companies have interest receipts that are higher than their interest payments, which turns the interest cover into a negative figure, and so it is not listed.

Return on equity

Return on equity is the after-tax profit expressed as a percentage of the shareholders' equity. In theory, it is the amount that the company's managers have made for you—the shareholder—on your money. The shareholders' equity figure used is an average for the year.

Debt-to-equity ratio

This ratio is one of the best-known measures of a company's debt levels. It is total borrowings minus the company's cash holdings, expressed as a percentage of the shareholders' equity. Some companies have no debt at all, or their cash position is greater than their level of debt, which results in a negative ratio, so no figure is listed for them.

Where a company's most recent financial results are the half-year figures, these are used to calculate this ratio.

Current ratio

The current ratio is simply the company's current assets divided by its current liabilities. Current assets are cash or assets that can, in theory, be converted quickly into cash. Current liabilities are normally those payable within a year. Thus, the current ratio measures the ability of a company to repay in a hurry its short-term debt, should the need arise. The surplus of current assets over current liabilities is referred to as the company's working capital.

Where a company's most recent financial results are the half-year figures, these are used to calculate this ratio.

Banks

The tables for the banks are somewhat different from those for most other companies. EBIT and debt-to-equity ratios have little relevance for them, as they have such high interest payments (to their customers). Other differences are examined below.

Operating income

Operating income is used instead of sales revenues. Operating income is the bank's net interest income — that is, its total interest income minus its interest expense — plus other income, such as bank fees, fund management fees and income from activities such as corporate finance and insurance.

Net interest income

Banks borrow money — that is, they accept deposits from savers — and they lend it to businesses, homebuyers and other borrowers. They charge the borrowers more than they pay those who deposit money with them, and the difference is known as net interest income.

Operating expenses

These are all the costs of running the bank. Banks have high operating expenses, and one of the keys to profit growth is cutting these expenses.

Non-interest income to total income

Banks have traditionally made most of their income from savers and from lending out money. But they are also working to diversify into new fields, and this ratio is an indication of their success.

Cost-to-income ratio

As noted, the banks have high costs — numerous branches, expensive computer systems, many staff, and so on — and they are all striving to reduce these. The cost-to-income ratio expresses their expenses as a percentage of their operating income, and is one of the ratios most often used as a gauge of efficiency. The lower the ratio drops the better.

Return on assets

Banks have enormous assets, in sharp contrast to, say, a high-tech start-up whose main physical assets may be little more than a set of computers and other technological equipment. So the return on assets — the after-tax profit expressed as a percentage of the year's average total assets — is another measure of efficiency.

PART I
THE COMPANIES

Accent Group Limited

ASX code: AX1 www.accentgr.com.au

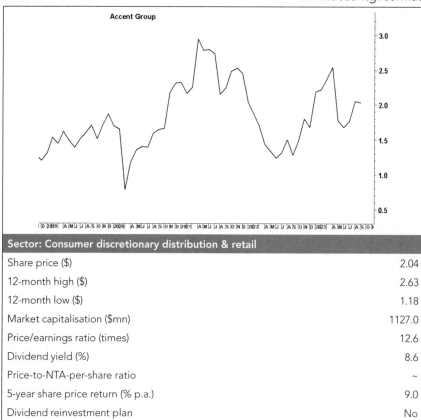

Sector: Consumer discretionary distribution & retail	
Share price ($)	2.04
12-month high ($)	2.63
12-month low ($)	1.18
Market capitalisation ($mn)	1127.0
Price/earnings ratio (times)	12.6
Dividend yield (%)	8.6
Price-to-NTA-per-share ratio	~
5-year share price return (% p.a.)	9.0
Dividend reinvestment plan	No

Sydney company Accent Group is a nationwide footwear wholesaler and retailer that has grown rapidly through a series of mergers and acquisitions. It owns nine brands and distributes 17 others. These include The Athlete's Foot—established in 1976—Hype DC, Platypus, Skechers, Merrell, CAT, Vans, Dr. Martens, Saucony, Timberland, Palladium and UGG. The company's wholesale division distributes footwear and apparel. Accent also operates in New Zealand.

Latest business results (July 2023, full year)

In an environment of subdued consumer discretionary spending, Accent produced an excellent result, with strength across all major brands, although with a slowdown towards the end of the financial year. Part of the growth came from the opening of new stores and the addition of the UGG brand to its portfolio, though on a like-for-like basis revenues were up 10.2 per cent. Total group sales, including franchisees, of $1.57 billion were up 24 per cent from the previous year. New Zealand sales, representing 11 per cent of the total, grew by 18 per cent. Even as growth was slowing towards the end of the financial year business remained strong for Skechers, The

Athlete's Foot and Hype DC. Apparel sales grew to represent around 7 per cent of total turnover. Digital sales edged down slightly to $260.5 million. Productivity benefits during the year boosted profit margins, despite unfavourable currency rate movements. During the year the company opened 80 new stores and closed 21, and at July 2023 it operated a network of 786 stores in Australia and New Zealand, along with 35 websites.

Outlook

Accent maintains its ambitious long-term growth strategy and expects profits to continue rising, although it is cautious about the near-term outlook as consumer spending continues to be hurt by inflationary pressures. It plans to open at least 50 new stores during the June 2024 year. It sees great potential in apparel sales, and has been achieving significant growth with its Nude Lucy women's lifestyle apparel brand, with 22 stores opened over 18 months. Its Glue Store and Stylerunner apparel brands are benefiting from operational improvements. Profits are growing for its key The Athlete's Foot brand, with a network of 92 corporate stores and 63 franchise stores. Accent's goal is that digital sales will eventually represent 30 per cent of total turnover, up from around 19 per cent at present. Its contactable customer database grew by 500 000 customers in the June 2023 year to 9.8 million customers, and the company is expanding its series of loyalty programs for them.

Year to 2 July*	2022	2023
Revenues ($mn)	1117.8	1409.0
Australia (%)	88	89
New Zealand (%)	12	11
EBIT ($mn)	63.1	140.2
EBIT margin (%)	5.6	10.0
Gross margin (%)	54.2	55.2
Profit before tax ($mn)	46.6	119.6
Profit after tax ($mn)	31.5	88.7
Earnings per share (c)	5.81	16.16
Cash flow per share (c)	32.30	45.22
Dividend (c)	6.5	17.5
Percentage franked	100	100
Net tangible assets per share ($)	~	~
Interest cover (times)	4.0	7.3
Return on equity (%)	7.2	20.1
Debt-to-equity ratio (%)	27.1	27.1
Current ratio	1.2	1.1

*26 June 2022

Adairs Limited

ASX code: ADH

investors.adairs.com.au

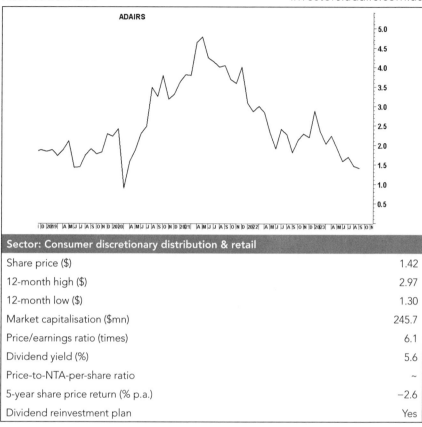

Sector: Consumer discretionary distribution & retail	
Share price ($)	1.42
12-month high ($)	2.97
12-month low ($)	1.30
Market capitalisation ($mn)	245.7
Price/earnings ratio (times)	6.1
Dividend yield (%)	5.6
Price-to-NTA-per-share ratio	~
5-year share price return (% p.a.)	−2.6
Dividend reinvestment plan	Yes

Melbourne-based home furnishings specialist Adairs dates back to 1918 and the opening of a store in Chapel Street in Prahran, Melbourne. It has since grown into a nationwide chain of stores specialising in bed linen, bedding, towels, homewares, soft furnishings, children's furnishings and some bedroom furniture. It has also expanded to New Zealand, and it manages a flourishing online business. It operates the Mocka online furniture business and Melbourne-based furniture and bedding retailer Focus on Furniture. At June 2023 it operated 171 Adairs stores and 23 Focus stores.

Latest business results (June 2023, full year)

Revenues rose, thanks especially to a full year's contribution from Focus, which was acquired in December 2021, but profits fell for the second straight year as consumer spending fell. In particular, the company experienced a sharp decline in customer traffic towards the end of the financial year as rising interest rates and cost-of-living pressures dented consumer sentiment. The company was also hurt by supply chain pressures, including rising delivery charges. Sales at Adairs stores rose 2.9 per cent, but higher costs meant underlying EBIT fell 37.1 per cent. Focus on Furniture saw sales up 5.3 per cent, with tight cost control delivering a small rise in EBIT. Though just 23 per cent of company turnover, the Focus business contributed 43 per cent of underlying EBIT. Mocka sales fell 24.1 per cent as customers returned to physical stores, with EBIT also down. Total company online sales of $175 million were down 10.5 per cent from the previous year.

Outlook

Adairs manages popular brands with high levels of customer recognition and loyalty. With an addressable Australian home furnishings market of some $12 billion it sees solid scope for growth. It sees great potential in its $80 million Focus acquisition, which significantly expands its exposure to the $8.3 billion bulky furniture sector. Adairs expects that through a modest investment in lighting, layout and styling it can boost sales at Focus stores, and has begun a refurbishment program. It believes that customer confidence is returning to Mocka, where supply delays had led to a series of order cancellations. Nevertheless, it is cautious about the near-term outlook, with discretionary consumer spending weak and the economic outlook uncertain. It is working to reduce its cost base and it is spending $20 million to take operational control from DHL of its underperforming National Distribution Centre. It believes it can reduce the Centre's annual operating costs by at least $4 million from 2024.

Year to 27 June*	2022	2023
Revenues ($mn)	564.5	621.3
Adairs (%)	74	69
Focus (%)	14	23
Mocka (%)	12	8
EBIT ($mn)	81.2	71.3
EBIT margin (%)	14.4	11.5
Gross margin (%)	54.7	45.9
Profit before tax ($mn)	73.3	57.6
Profit after tax ($mn)	51.6	40.2
Earnings per share (c)	30.32	23.35
Cash flow per share (c)	60.45	57.32
Dividend (c)	18	8
Percentage franked	100	100
Net tangible assets per share ($)	~	~
Interest cover (times)	10.2	5.4
Return on equity (%)	28.5	20.1
Debt-to-equity ratio (%)	47.1	36.4
Current ratio	1.2	1.0

*26 June 2022

Altium Limited

ASX code: ALU   www.altium.com

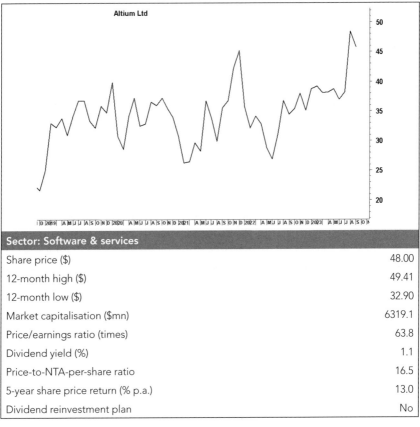

Sector: Software & services	
Share price ($)	48.00
12-month high ($)	49.41
12-month low ($)	32.90
Market capitalisation ($mn)	6319.1
Price/earnings ratio (times)	63.8
Dividend yield (%)	1.1
Price-to-NTA-per-share ratio	16.5
5-year share price return (% p.a.)	13.0
Dividend reinvestment plan	No

Sydney-based software company Altium was founded in Tasmania in 1985. It was originally named Protel. Its specialty is the provision of comprehensive and innovative software that allows engineers to design printed circuit boards (PCBs). Its core product is Altium Designer. A smaller division provides the Altium 365 cloud platform, an online collaboration platform that facilitates the manufacturing process. Altium has most of its operations abroad, with its headquarters in San Diego, but retains its Sydney office and its ASX listing.

Latest business results (June 2023, full year)

In an excellent result, Altium recorded its second consecutive year of double-digit increases in sales and profits. The core Design Software division, responsible for nearly 80 per cent of sales, saw revenues up 22 per cent, including a 32 per cent surge in demand from the Americas region. By contrast, China, which before COVID had been providing the company with some of its strongest growth, saw sales down 8 per cent. The Cloud Platform division achieved 17 per cent revenue growth. Thanks to strongly rising demand, Altium was able to benefit by pushing through price rises.

Note that Altium reports its finances in US dollars. All figures in this book are converted to Australian dollars using prevailing exchange rates and are for guidance only.

Outlook

PCBs are incorporated in most electronic devices, and demand for them continues to grow. Altium has a strong reputation for its PCB design software, with high profit margins and a growth rate higher than the industry average. The strong rise in smart electronic connected devices is partly behind this trend. The company claims that as smart products increase in complexity its multi-board design processes allow the creation of electronic systems comprising multiple PCBs, and it expects this will help drive significant future growth in demand. It also sees particular potential for its Altium 365 product, the world's first cloud platform for PCB design and realisation. It is expensive for a customer to switch once it makes a decision to employ Altium software. The company is working to transition to a subscription-based business, and recurring revenue grew to represent 77 per cent of total income in June 2023, up from 75 per cent in the prior year. For June 2024 it forecasts revenues of US$315 million to US$325 million, up from US$263.3 million in June 2023, and it has set itself a June 2026 target of US$500 million. At June 2023 Altium had no debt and more than US$200 million in cash holdings.

Year to 30 June	2022	2023
Revenues ($mn)	302.5	393.0
EBIT ($mn)	93.0	131.9
EBIT margin (%)	30.8	33.6
Profit before tax ($mn)	93.0	131.0
Profit after tax ($mn)	76.0	99.0
Earnings per share (c)	57.84	75.24
Cash flow per share (c)	70.06	86.14
Dividend (c)	47	54
Percentage franked	100	19
Net tangible assets per share ($)	2.46	2.92
Interest cover (times)	~	~
Return on equity (%)	20.6	23.0
Debt-to-equity ratio (%)	~	~
Current ratio	3.1	2.8

ANZ Group Holdings Limited

ASX code: ANZ

www.anz.com.au

Sector: Banks	
Share price ($)	25.19
12-month high ($)	26.08
12-month low ($)	22.21
Market capitalisation ($mn)	75551.6
Price/earnings ratio (times)	11.0
Dividend yield (%)	5.8
Price-to-NTA-per-share ratio	1.2
5-year share price return (% p.a.)	2.0
Dividend reinvestment plan	Yes

Melbourne-based ANZ has its roots in the establishment of the Bank of Australasia in London in 1835. It is today one of the country's four banking giants and one of the largest companies. It is a market leader in New Zealand banking, and it is also active in the Pacific region. It wishes to buy the banking business of Queensland-based Suncorp.

Latest business results (March 2023, half year)

ANZ posted a strong result, helped by rising interest rates and despite a highly competitive home loans business. The core Australia Retail division achieved an 11 per cent increase in revenues, thanks to new mortgage and savings account customers. However, intense competition led to just a small profit rise. The best result came from the Institutional division, which saw its profits nearly double, with rapid growth in payments and currency processing and a particularly strong contribution from international operations. The Australia Commercial division recorded higher revenues but a decline in profits, despite a good result from customers in agriculture, trade and manufacturing. The fourth major division, representing New Zealand operations, reported solid gains in revenues and profits.

Outlook

ANZ has restructured its operations into two broad groupings. The first of these manages the core banking businesses. The other is responsible for banking-adjacent businesses, including many with a focus on bringing technological innovations to the bank's customers. Above these two groups is the parent company, now known as ANZ Group Holdings, formerly Australia and New Zealand Banking Group. ANZ hopes to grow with the $4.9 billion acquisition of the banking business of Suncorp. However, the deal has been rejected by the Australian Competition and Consumer Commission, a decision that ANZ is appealing. The acquisition would add an estimated $47 billion in home loans to ANZ's portfolio, along with some $45 billion in deposits and $11 billion in commercial loans. It would also provide annual cost synergies of around $260 million, along with 1.2 million new customers. Nevertheless, the bank is wary about the near-term outlook for growth, as a result of higher interest rates and strong levels of competition among lenders. However, it believes that most borrowers—both home owners and businesses—are in a position to manage higher rates. The bank continues to invest in digital technology to reduce the processing time for home loan applications. This includes its new retail banking platform, ANZ Plus, which provides smoother customer transactions and boosts the personal banking business.

Year to 30 September	2021	2022
Operating income ($mn)	17420.0	19426.0
Net interest income ($mn)	14161.0	14874.0
Operating expenses ($mn)	9051.0	9579.0
Profit before tax ($mn)	8963.0	9200.0
Profit after tax ($mn)	6198.0	6515.0
Earnings per share (c)	216.52	228.80
Dividend (c)	142	146
Percentage franked	100	100
Non-interest income to total income (%)	18.7	23.4
Cost-to-income ratio (%)	52.0	49.3
Return on equity (%)	10.0	10.1
Return on assets (%)	0.6	0.6
Half year to 31 March	2022	2023
Operating income ($mn)	8948.0	10528.0
Profit before tax ($mn)	4441.0	5398.0
Profit after tax ($mn)	3113.0	3821.0
Earnings per share (c)	109.70	127.60
Dividend (c)	72	81
Percentage franked	100	100
Net tangible assets per share ($)	20.68	21.69

ARB Corporation Limited

ASX code: ARB   www.arb.com.au

ARB Corporation

Sector: Automobiles & components	
Share price ($)	33.89
12-month high ($)	34.64
12-month low ($)	25.21
Market capitalisation ($mn)	2782.3
Price/earnings ratio (times)	31.4
Dividend yield (%)	1.8
Price-to-NTA-per-share ratio	5.3
5-year share price return (% p.a.)	13.1
Dividend reinvestment plan	Yes

Melbourne-based ARB, founded in 1975, is a prominent manufacturer of specialty automotive accessories, and an international leader in the design, production and distribution of specialised equipment for four-wheel-drive vehicles. These include its Air Locker air-operated locking differential system, as well as a wide range of other products, including bull bars, roof racks, tow bars, canopies and the Old Man Emu range of suspension products. It operates a network of 74 ARB-brand stores throughout Australia, including 30 that are company-owned. It has established manufacturing facilities in Thailand and it exports to more than 100 countries.

Latest business results (June 2023, full year)

ARB's run of strong results came to an end, with sales down and a double-digit decline in profits, as the company was hit with rising costs and slowing demand. Exports represent more than a third of total turnover, and these were down 8.7 per cent, although this partially reflected disruption caused by restructuring at a major US customer. Also down were original equipment sales to local vehicle makers, although these comprise only 6 per cent of total company revenues. ARB's strongest and most profitable business is Australian aftermarket sales to its own stores and to other ARB stockists, and these grew 2.6 per cent for the year.

Outlook

ARB believes it can achieve higher sales and profits in the June 2024 year, even in an environment of slowing consumer spending. Branded ARB stores play a significant role in the company's domestic sales. It did not open any new stores during the June 2023 year, but plans three by June 2024 and upgrades to others. In addition, thanks to its strength in Australia it has been able to push through price increases to offset rising costs. A strategic partnership with Ford Australia provides it with early access to Ford vehicle designs and the opportunity to market a complete range of accessories as new vehicles are released. It was first to market with a complete range of over 160 accessories for the releases of the new Ford Ranger and Ford Everest models. It is implementing a number of growth initiatives in the key US market, including the launch of a flagship store in Seattle, a new direct-to-consumer eCommerce website and a new partnership with Toyota USA. It is seeing a recovery in OEM demand, with contracts in place that will underpin growth in the June 2024 and 2025 years. At June 2023 ARB had no debt and nearly $45 million in cash holdings.

Year to 30 June	2022	2023
Revenues ($mn)	694.5	671.2
EBIT ($mn)	167.7	123.8
EBIT margin (%)	24.2	18.4
Gross margin (%)	45.3	42.8
Profit before tax ($mn)	165.7	122.1
Profit after tax ($mn)	122.0	88.5
Earnings per share (c)	149.40	107.92
Cash flow per share (c)	180.00	139.50
Dividend (c)	71	62
Percentage franked	100	100
Net tangible assets per share ($)	5.62	6.40
Interest cover (times)	84.1	87.3
Return on equity (%)	23.4	15.2
Debt-to-equity ratio (%)	~	~
Current ratio	3.6	4.2

Aristocrat Leisure Limited

ASX code: ALL   ir.aristocrat.com

Sector: Consumer services	
Share price ($)	41.39
12-month high ($)	41.74
12-month low ($)	30.36
Market capitalisation ($mn)	27 142.0
Price/earnings ratio (times)	27.5
Dividend yield (%)	1.3
Price-to-NTA-per-share ratio	12.0
5-year share price return (% p.a.)	6.8
Dividend reinvestment plan	No

Sydney-based Aristocrat, founded in 1953, is one of the world's leading developers of hardware and software for the gaming industry. It divides its activities into three operating units. Aristocrat Gaming provides casino games to customers in more than 300 gaming jurisdictions around the world. Pixel United is involved in the development of games for electronic mobile devices. The third unit, Anaxi, provides customers with online gaming, known as real money gaming (RMG). In May 2023 Aristocrat agreed to acquire the Israeli-based RMG giant NeoGames.

Latest business results (March 2023, half year)

Aristocrat posted another solid result, assisted by dollar weakness, and building on the double-digit gains of the September 2022 year. The key North American casino market was particularly strong, with gaming machine unit sales up 27 per cent. The small European and Asian gaming machine business also achieved an increase in sales and profits, but the Australia/New Zealand segment was hurt by higher input costs and increased competition. Pixel United now represents more than 40 per cent of company turnover, but sales were largely flat, with profits down, reflecting an overall decline in the mobile games market and the cessation of gaming activities in Russia. Pixel United profitability remains substantially below that for the gaming business.

Outlook

Aristocrat enjoys a strong position in the global gaming industry, with high market shares in many regions. Nevertheless, this remains a competitive business, and the company is highly dependent on a continuing stream of attractive new and enhanced products. To develop these it must recruit and retain large numbers of highly skilled creative specialists and technology experts, and this has been one of its key challenges. Consequently, its design and development budget remains high at around 11 per cent to 12 per cent of annual revenues. Despite the recent slowdown, it expects continuing long-term expansion for Pixel United, and says it has been gaining market share, to be the fifth-largest mobile games publisher in major western markets. However, it sees some of the best growth potential from the RMG sector, which had a total addressable market of $121 billion in 2022 and is realising annual double-digit growth rates. With the planned NeoGames acquisition, for as much as $1.8 billion, Aristocrat has a target of eventually becoming the world's leading gaming platform for global online RMG. With much of its income coming from outside Australia, Aristocrat's earnings are heavily influenced by currency rate trends.

Year to 30 September	2021	2022
Revenues ($mn)	4736.6	5573.7
EBIT ($mn)	1154.6	1582.5
EBIT margin (%)	24.4	28.4
Profit before tax ($mn)	1016.8	1327.7
Profit after tax ($mn)	765.6	1000.9
Earnings per share (c)	120.11	150.77
Cash flow per share (c)	178.85	206.57
Dividend (c)	41	52
Percentage franked	100	100
Interest cover (times)	8.8	6.9
Return on equity (%)	21.8	20.2
Half year to 31 March	2022	2023
Revenues ($mn)	2745.4	3080.4
Profit before tax ($mn)	704.6	816.8
Profit after tax ($mn)	530.7	619.1
Earnings per share (c)	80.10	94.30
Dividend (c)	26	30
Percentage franked	100	100
Net tangible assets per share ($)	2.89	3.46
Debt-to-equity ratio (%)	~	~
Current ratio	3.8	3.3

ASX Limited

ASX code: ASX www.asx.com.au

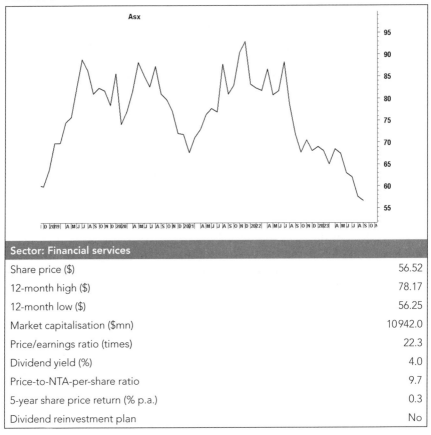

Sector: Financial services	
Share price ($)	56.52
12-month high ($)	78.17
12-month low ($)	56.25
Market capitalisation ($mn)	10942.0
Price/earnings ratio (times)	22.3
Dividend yield (%)	4.0
Price-to-NTA-per-share ratio	9.7
5-year share price return (% p.a.)	0.3
Dividend reinvestment plan	No

ASX (Australian Securities Exchange) was formed in 1987 through the amalgamation of six independent stock exchanges that formerly operated in the state capital cities. Each of those exchanges had a history of share trading dating back to the 19th century. Though originally a mutual organisation of stockbrokers, in 1998 ASX became a listed company, with its shares traded on its own market. It expanded in 2006 when it merged with the Sydney Futures Exchange. Today it provides primary, secondary and derivative market services, along with clearing, settlement and compliance services. It is also a provider of a range of comprehensive market data and technical services.

Latest business results (June 2023, full year)

Revenues and underlying profits fell back, with rising costs and weaker equity trading offsetting increased demand for information and technical services. ASX categorises its operations into four broad divisions. The best result came from the Technology and Data division, with revenues up 8.5 per cent, driven by growing demand for equities and futures market data. The Listings division achieved a 2.2 per cent rise in revenues, with just 57 new listings, compared to 217 in the June 2022 year. Growth in equity options was offset by a decline in cash market trading, and revenues fell 2.1 per cent for the Markets division. The Securities and Payments division recorded a 10.4 per cent fall in revenues, driven by a 22.2 per cent drop in issuer services business and an 11.9 per cent decline for equity post-trade services. ASX also reported a charge of $173.8 million — treated as a significant item — relating largely to costs associated with work on replacing its CHESS equities clearing and settlement system.

Outlook

ASX's profits are highly geared to levels of market activity. The company also enjoys a high degree of protection in its operations, with little effective competition for many of its businesses. It is working to control its expenses, which grew by 12.3 per cent in the June 2023 year and are forecast to grow by 12 per cent to 15 per cent in June 2024, though by a lesser amount in the June 2025 year. Much of this spending has been related to an ambitious project, now halted, to construct a major new platform to replace the CHESS system. ASX believes that easing inflation and a possible peaking of interest rates will boost cash market trading. In addition, it sees a solid pipeline of companies waiting to list as market conditions improve.

Year to 30 June	2022	2023
Revenues ($mn)	1022.7	1010.2
Markets (%)	29	29
Securities & payments (%)	29	26
Technology & data (%)	21	24
Listings (%)	21	21
EBIT ($mn)	744.1	1037.4
EBIT margin (%)	72.8	102.7
Profit before tax ($mn)	730.3	706.4
Profit after tax ($mn)	508.5	491.1
Earnings per share (c)	262.68	253.69
Cash flow per share (c)	289.75	273.89
Dividend (c)	236.4	228.3
Percentage franked	100	100
Net tangible assets per share ($)	5.73	5.80
Interest cover (times)	~	~
Return on equity (%)	13.5	13.2
Debt-to-equity ratio (%)	~	~
Current ratio	1.1	1.1

Australian Ethical Investment Limited

ASX code: AEF   www.australianethical.com.au

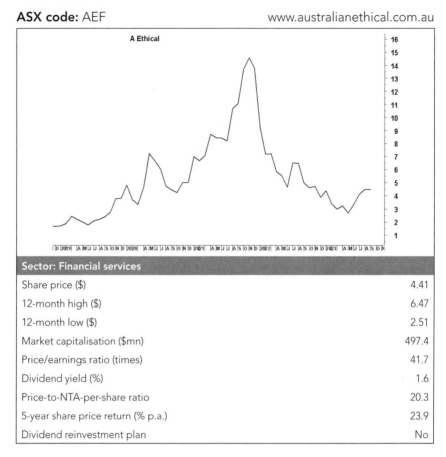

Sector: Financial services	
Share price ($)	4.41
12-month high ($)	6.47
12-month low ($)	2.51
Market capitalisation ($mn)	497.4
Price/earnings ratio (times)	41.7
Dividend yield (%)	1.6
Price-to-NTA-per-share ratio	20.3
5-year share price return (% p.a.)	23.9
Dividend reinvestment plan	No

Australian Ethical, based in Sydney, was founded in 1986. It is a wealth management company that specialises in investments in corporations that meet a set of ethical criteria. It operates a range of wholesale and retail funds — including superannuation — that incorporate Australian and international shares, emerging companies and fixed interest. It has launched an exchange traded fund. In 2023 it took over the funds of Christian Super. The company donates up to 10 per cent of its profits to charities and activist groups through its Australian Ethical Foundation.

Latest business results (June 2023, full year)

Revenues and underlying profits rose in an environment of volatile financial markets, boosted by the new business of Christian Super. Net inflows of $0.47 billion were down 50 per cent from the previous year, including a 20 per cent reduction in superannuation inflows. More than offsetting this was a solid investment performance for the year, which elevated funds by $0.61 billion. The addition of $1.93 billion from Christian Super meant that funds under management of $9.2 billion at June

2023 rose from $6.2 billion a year earlier. Increasing funds under management delivered higher revenues for the year, although the company did not receive performance fees, as funds did not reach their benchmarks. Careful cost management limited the growth in expenses to 15 per cent, roughly in line with revenue growth. Significant items—not included in the figures in this book—related to expenses for acquiring Christian Super's business and a write-down in an investment in the ethical investment firm Sentient Impact Group.

Outlook

Australian Ethical is a small company but is a leader in the trend towards ethical investment. In a growing marketplace, with many major financial institutions launching their own ESG (environmental, social and governance) funds, Australian Ethical has attracted attention because of its perceived independence. The company's pledge is that it seeks out positive investments that support its three pillars of people, planet and animals. Its Ethical Charter gives details of the criteria it uses for its investments, and it provides a public list of the companies in which it is prepared to invest. It believes that its larger scale, after acquiring the business of Christian Super, will help deliver solid profit growth in the June 2024 year. Nevertheless, Australian Ethical remains heavily exposed to volatile financial markets, and its businesses could be hurt in any sustained downturn. At June 2023 the company had no debt and more than $27 million in cash holdings.

Year to 30 June	2022	2023
Revenues ($mn)	70.8	81.1
EBIT ($mn)	14.6	15.9
EBIT margin (%)	20.6	19.6
Profit before tax ($mn)	14.5	15.8
Profit after tax ($mn)	10.3	11.8
Earnings per share (c)	9.26	10.57
Cash flow per share (c)	10.35	11.70
Dividend (c)	6	7
Percentage franked	100	100
Net tangible assets per share ($)	0.22	0.22
Interest cover (times)	~	~
Return on equity (%)	42.1	45.9
Debt-to-equity ratio (%)	~	~
Current ratio	1.9	2.0

Baby Bunting Group Limited

ASX code: BBN   investors.babybunting.com.au

Sector: Consumer discretionary distribution & retail	
Share price ($)	2.15
12-month high ($)	4.41
12-month low ($)	1.13
Market capitalisation ($mn)	290.0
Price/earnings ratio (times)	19.9
Dividend yield (%)	3.5
Price-to-NTA-per-share ratio	~
5-year share price return (% p.a.)	1.8
Dividend reinvestment plan	No

Melbourne retailer Baby Bunting started in 1979 with the opening of a store in the suburb of Balwyn. It has since grown into a nationwide chain of stores specialising in some 6000 lines of baby and nursery products, including prams, car seats, carriers, furniture, nursery items, safety goods, babywear, manchester, toys, feeding products and maternity wear. It has expanded to New Zealand.

Latest business results (July 2023, full year)

Sales edged up—though fell 3.6 per cent on a comparable store basis—and profits crashed, as households were hit by cost of living pressures and cut back their retail spending. Expenses rose as the company launched several growth initiatives, notably its Baby Bunting Marketplace online store and the opening of its first New Zealand store. The company also opened six new stores in Australia, and at July 2023 was managing a domestic network of 70 stores. Online sales, which had soared during the years of the COVID pandemic, fell 8.6 per cent to $103 million. As in the previous year, higher-margin private label and exclusive products represented about 45 per cent of total sales. Note that the July 2023 year represented 53 weeks, compared to 52 weeks for the June 2022 year.

Outlook

Baby Bunting occupies a strong position in the $3.5 billion Australian baby goods retail market. With the demise of some competitors, it is now the only specialist baby goods retailer with a national presence, and its major rivals are stores such as Kmart, Target and Big W. Though baby products to a certain extent are not discretionary items, the company is nevertheless feeling the pressures of reduced consumer spending. It has numerous strategies for growth. It plans to open two new Australian stores during the June 2024 year, and expects eventually to be operating a nationwide network of around 110 outlets. It sees great potential in the $450 million New Zealand baby product market, and plans to open three new stores there during the June 2024 year, with an eventual target of 10 stores. In June 2023 it launched Baby Bunting Marketplace, an online sales website that allows third-party sellers to offer a range of products. It expects to attract some 150 retail partners by June 2024, providing customers with 20 000 different products. It has introduced measures aimed at reducing overheads and managing cost inflation in stores and in its supply chain, and expects to generate $6 million to $8 million in savings during the June 2024 year.

Year to 2 July*	2022	2023
Revenues ($mn)	507.3	524.3
EBIT ($mn)	49.3	29.2
EBIT margin (%)	9.7	5.6
Gross margin (%)	38.6	37.4
Profit before tax ($mn)	42.3	20.5
Profit after tax ($mn)	29.6	14.5
Earnings per share (c)	22.53	10.83
Cash flow per share (c)	46.73	38.07
Dividend (c)	15.6	7.5
Percentage franked	100	100
Net tangible assets per share ($)	~	~
Interest cover (times)	7.1	3.3
Return on equity (%)	26.8	13.0
Debt-to-equity ratio (%)	0.6	5.8
Current ratio	1.3	1.2

*26 June 2022

Bapcor Limited

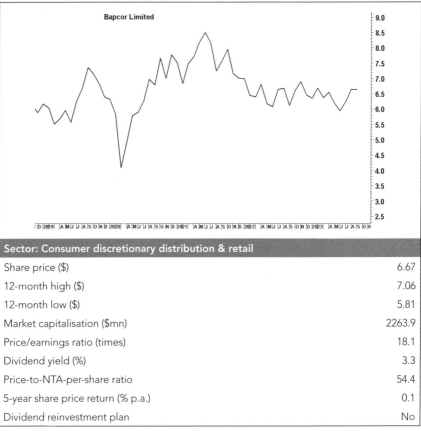

Sector: Consumer discretionary distribution & retail	
Share price ($)	6.67
12-month high ($)	7.06
12-month low ($)	5.81
Market capitalisation ($mn)	2263.9
Price/earnings ratio (times)	18.1
Dividend yield (%)	3.3
Price-to-NTA-per-share ratio	54.4
5-year share price return (% p.a.)	0.1
Dividend reinvestment plan	No

Melbourne company Bapcor started in 1971 as Burson Auto Parts, supplying a range of automotive products to workshops and service stations. It grew steadily, organically and by acquisition, opening stores throughout Australia, and taking its present name in 2016. It now services the automotive aftermarket under numerous brands, including Autobarn, Midas, Autopro and ABS. It has extensive operations in Australia and New Zealand, and in 2018 it opened its first stores in Thailand, in partnership with a local auto specialist company. It 2021 it acquired an equity stake in Singapore automotive parts distributor Tye Soon. Bapcor operates from around 1000 locations across Australia, New Zealand and Thailand.

Latest business results (June 2023, full year)

Revenues rose, thanks to both organic growth and the addition of 31 new stores, but rising costs sent profits down. The largest division, Specialist Wholesale, comprises a range of small outlets that focus on sourcing replacement parts for the wholesale automotive aftermarket. It achieved 9.5 per cent revenue growth, thanks especially to solid truck-related business, with profits edging up at the EBITDA level. The Trade division, comprising the Burson Auto Parts and the Precision Automotive Equipment business units, recorded solid growth in revenues and profits. The Retail division was hit by falling consumer discretionary spending, with sales up but profit margins down. New Zealand operations were weak, with a modest increase in sales but a drop in profits.

Outlook

Bapcor is a leader in the supply of a huge range of auto parts to more than 30 000 auto workshop customers, and this business is expected to continue to grow as the population increases and as the average age of cars in Australia slowly rises. It plans a steady rollout of new stores and is also seeking to continue growing through acquisition. Under its Better Than Before program it aims to reduce its annual cost base by $20 million to $30 million in the June 2024 year. It expects to benefit from the steady introduction of electric vehicles, which means the advent of new car makes and models requiring entire new lines of replacement parts. Under its Project Zero, Bapcor aspires to be a market leader in the supply of parts and technologies to zero-emission vehicles. It regards inventory availability as a key competitive advantage, and is investing in state-of-the-art centralised distribution centres in several locations. It has opened its first in Victoria, replacing 13 smaller regional centres, with significant cost benefits. A second centre is due to open in Queensland.

Year to 30 June	2022	2023
Revenues ($mn)	1841.9	2021.1
Specialist wholesale (%)	36	36
Trade (%)	35	36
Retail (%)	20	20
Bapcor New Zealand (%)	9	8
EBIT ($mn)	205.8	204.3
EBIT margin (%)	11.2	10.1
Gross margin (%)	46.7	46.7
Profit before tax ($mn)	186.5	175.4
Profit after tax ($mn)	131.6	125.3
Earnings per share (c)	38.77	36.92
Cash flow per share (c)	64.93	65.39
Dividend (c)	21.5	22
Percentage franked	100	100
Net tangible assets per share ($)	0.24	0.12
Interest cover (times)	10.8	7.1
Return on equity (%)	12.3	11.3
Debt-to-equity ratio (%)	24.4	22.4
Current ratio	2.4	2.3

Beach Energy Limited

ASX code: BPT   www.beachenergy.com.au

Sector: Energy	
Share price ($)	1.62
12-month high ($)	1.91
12-month low ($)	1.28
Market capitalisation ($mn)	3695.8
Price/earnings ratio (times)	9.6
Dividend yield (%)	2.5
Price-to-NTA-per-share ratio	1.0
5-year share price return (% p.a.)	−1.4
Dividend reinvestment plan	No

Adelaide-based Beach Energy, with a history dating back to 1961, is a major oil and gas producer, and a key supplier of gas to eastern states. Its operations are concentrated on five production hubs — the Cooper/Eromanga Basin region of South Australia and Queensland, the Bass Basin in the Bass Strait, the Otway Basin of Victoria and South Australia, the Perth Basin and the Taranaki Basin in New Zealand. It also maintains an active exploration and development program in other areas of Australia and New Zealand. Seven Group Holdings owns some 30 per cent of Beach's equity.

Latest business results (June 2023, full year)

Reduced oil and gas production and sales led to a fall in revenues and profits, with rising costs also hurting the result. Total production of 19.5 million barrels of oil equivalent (boe) fell from 21.8 million barrels in the previous year. The average realised oil price of $138 per barrel was slightly down from the previous year, with the average realised gas/ethane price up 9 per cent.

Outlook

Beach is working to boost its output, but for the June 2024 year has a production target of a relatively modest 18 billion boe to 21 million boe, with much depending on the timing of major projects. It has initiated a new Perth Basin gas exploration project. However, it is also being hurt there by delays and cost overruns at its major Waitsia Gas Project. Thanks to this scheme, which is being developed in a joint venture with Mitsui E&P Australia, Beach will become a participant in the global liquefied natural gas market. The first gas was planned to flow during 2023 but is now not expected until mid 2024. Beach is also investing in the development of new gas supply in the Otway Basin, in order to support the East Coast market. In the Bass Basin it is engaged in development planning with a view to boosting production and also extending asset life. In the Taranaki Basin it has secured approvals and a rig for the Kupe South 9 development well. The company also plans continuing oil and gas exploration and development in the Cooper Basin. In addition, Beach is moving into new energy opportunities. It is a partner with Belgium's Parkwind for a possible offshore wind project in Victoria. It is also investigating wind energy opportunities at the Taranaki Basin in New Zealand. In addition, it has conducted pre-feasibility studies into the potential for hydrogen production and storage in South Australia and Victoria.

Year to 30 June	2022	2023
Revenues ($mn)	1771.4	1646.4
EBIT ($mn)	730.3	590.7
EBIT margin (%)	41.2	35.9
Gross margin (%)	43.8	35.9
Profit before tax ($mn)	716.6	559.3
Profit after tax ($mn)	504.0	384.8
Earnings per share (c)	22.11	16.88
Cash flow per share (c)	38.60	34.57
Dividend (c)	2	4
Percentage franked	100	100
Net tangible assets per share ($)	1.52	1.67
Interest cover (times)	54.1	21.9
Return on equity (%)	15.2	10.4
Debt-to-equity ratio (%)	~	4.2
Current ratio	1.4	1.5

Beacon Lighting Group Limited

ASX code: BLX   www.beaconlighting.com.au

Sector: Consumer discretionary distribution & retail	
Share price ($)	1.82
12-month high ($)	2.49
12-month low ($)	1.36
Market capitalisation ($mn)	408.8
Price/earnings ratio (times)	12.1
Dividend yield (%)	4.6
Price-to-NTA-per-share ratio	15.0
5-year share price return (% p.a.)	6.6
Dividend reinvestment plan	Yes

Melbourne-based lighting specialist Beacon dates back to the launch of the first Beacon Lighting store in 1967. It steadily expanded throughout Australia, and today has 119 stores — two of them franchised — supplying a wide range of lighting fixtures and light globes, as well as ceiling fans. Its Beacon Commercial division supplies many commercial projects, including volume residential developments, apartment complexes, aged care facilities, hotels and retail fit-outs, with five sales offices around Australia. The Beacon International business operates sales offices in Hong Kong, Germany and the US, with a support office in China.

Latest business results (June 2023, full year)

Buoyant demand from trade customers made up for declining retail consumer confidence and delays in planned new store openings, and total sales edged up, though with a marked slowdown in the second half. Rising costs hurt profits, which were down. Following the relaunch of the Beacon Trade Club loyalty program during the year, total trade sales were up 21.6 per cent. Only two new stores were opened and two others were closed. The small Beacon International division saw a significant jump in sales in the June 2022 year, but a slight decline in June 2023, as online demand in the US fell, offsetting strong European growth.

Outlook

Beacon's business is closely linked to trends in the housing market. With renovation activity in decline the company could suffer, as households are hit by cost-of-living pressures and cut back on discretionary spending. Much of its product range is imported, so it is also vulnerable to currency fluctuations and supply chain disruptions. In response, Beacon has a variety of strategies for growth. Following delays in new store openings during the June 2023 year it now expects to open eight new stores by June 2024. It will continue its focus on boosting services to trade customers, estimating the trade market in Australia for its products as worth $2.1 billion annually. Initiatives include the rollout of further trade-specific products, dedicated trade rooms at its stores, trade seminars, a trade training program and enhanced internet platforms to facilitate online business from trade customers. Despite a dip in sales in the June 2023 year, the Beacon International division continues to expand its marketing efforts in North America, Europe and Asia for Beacon's fan and lighting products. Three small specialist businesses, the Custom Lighting division, the Connected Light Solutions outdoor lighting division and the Masson for Light designer lighting division for architects, all continue to do well.

Year to 25 June*	2022	2023
Revenues ($mn)	304.8	312.0
EBIT ($mn)	63.8	54.8
EBIT margin (%)	20.9	17.6
Gross margin (%)	69.1	67.7
Profit before tax ($mn)	58.0	48.2
Profit after tax ($mn)	40.7	33.6
Earnings per share (c)	18.24	15.05
Cash flow per share (c)	31.18	28.82
Dividend (c)	9.3	8.3
Percentage franked	100	100
Net tangible assets per share ($)	0.07	0.12
Interest cover (times)	11.4	8.5
Return on equity (%)	33.1	23.8
Debt-to-equity ratio (%)	~	1.2
Current ratio	1.5	1.7

*26 June 2022

BHP Group Limited

ASX code: BHP　　　　　　　　　　　　　　　　www.bhp.com

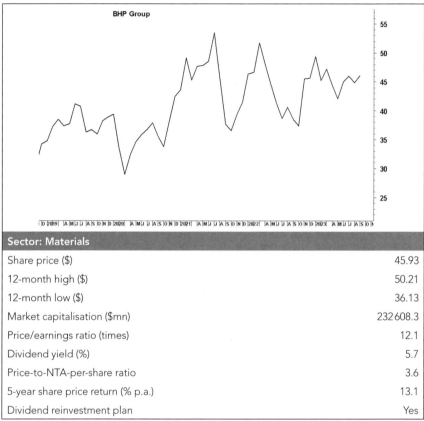

Sector: Materials	
Share price ($)	45.93
12-month high ($)	50.21
12-month low ($)	36.13
Market capitalisation ($mn)	232608.3
Price/earnings ratio (times)	12.1
Dividend yield (%)	5.7
Price-to-NTA-per-share ratio	3.6
5-year share price return (% p.a.)	13.1
Dividend reinvestment plan	Yes

Melbourne-based resources giant BHP was founded as Broken Hill Proprietary in 1885. In 2001 it merged with another resources major, Billiton, which dated back to 1851. Today it segments its operations into five broad product areas—iron ore, copper, coal, nickel and potash—with activities in many countries. In May 2023 it acquired South Australian copper miner OZ Minerals.

Latest business results (June 2023, full year)

Falling iron ore and copper prices more than offset increased production, and company revenues and profits fell sharply. The mainstay iron ore business saw revenues down 19 per cent and profits falling 23 per cent, despite record production in Western Australia. Nevertheless, such is the company's strength in iron ore, including its low production costs, that it still contributed more than 60 per cent of BHP's total EBIT. Copper revenues fell 5 per cent and profits were down 22 per cent, with inflationary pressures at its mines forcing costs higher. The coal business, which in the previous year had generated a substantial boost to company profits, this time reported a 30 per cent drop in revenues, with profits nearly halving, as prices fell and steel production declined in many countries. BHP's nickel business made a very small contribution to sales and profits. Note that BHP reports its results in US dollars. The Australian dollar figures in this book—converted at prevailing exchange rates—are for guidance only.

Outlook

BHP is restructuring its operations in order to gain greater exposure to what it believes are mega-trends of decarbonisation and electrification, with an exploration program that is focused on copper and nickel. It is boosting copper production at its Escondida and Spence projects in Chile. Its acquisition of OZ Minerals has also enhanced its copper exposure. It is developing a major new copper province in South Australia and forecasts synergies of up to US$50 million annually from the OZ Minerals acquisition. It forecasts long-term escalating demand for nickel from the electric vehicle industry and is exploring ways to boost output. It also expects over the medium term to increase its Western Australian iron ore production. It is investing heavily in its Jansen potash project in Canada, with initial production now expected by the end of 2026, in order to meet global fertiliser demand that the company believes could double from present levels by the 2040s. Nevertheless, with 58 per cent of its June 2023 revenues deriving from sales to China, BHP remains heavily influenced by economic trends in that country.

Year to 30 June	2022	2023
Revenues ($mn)	89175.3	80323.9
Iron ore (%)	47	44
Copper (%)	26	30
Coal (%)	24	20
EBIT ($mn)	46831.5	35016.4
EBIT margin (%)	52.5	43.6
Profit before tax ($mn)	45393.2	31941.8
Profit after tax ($mn)	30684.9	19285.1
Earnings per share (c)	606.30	380.83
Cash flow per share (c)	760.12	529.99
Dividend (c)	463.14	261.43
Percentage franked	100	100
Net tangible assets per share ($)	12.48	12.83
Interest cover (times)	35.3	15.3
Return on equity (%)	46.0	29.1
Debt-to-equity ratio (%)	~	20.4
Current ratio	1.7	1.2

BlueScope Steel Limited

ASX code: BSL
www.bluescope.com

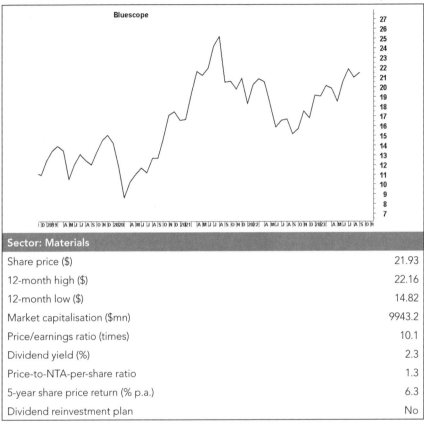

Bluescope

Sector: Materials	
Share price ($)	21.93
12-month high ($)	22.16
12-month low ($)	14.82
Market capitalisation ($mn)	9943.2
Price/earnings ratio (times)	10.1
Dividend yield (%)	2.3
Price-to-NTA-per-share ratio	1.3
5-year share price return (% p.a.)	6.3
Dividend reinvestment plan	No

Melbourne-based BlueScope Steel, originally a division of BHP, was established as an independent company in 2002. It is a major international producer of steel products for a wide variety of industrial applications. It is one of the world's largest manufacturers of painted and coated steel products. The company is structured into five businesses. Australian Steel Products operates the country's largest steelworks at Port Kembla, with a focus on the building and construction industry. Buildings and Coated Products North America services low-rise non-residential customers. North Star BlueScope Steel is a leading American producer of hot rolled coil. Coated Products Asia produces metal coated and painted steel building products for the Asia-Pacific region. The New Zealand and Pacific Islands division operates production facilities in New Zealand, Fiji, New Caledonia and Vanuatu.

Latest business results (June 2023, full year)

Falling steel prices and rising costs sent profits crashing. In the previous year they had more than doubled. The core Australian Steel Products division saw revenues edge down, but with underlying EBIT plummeting 59 per cent, despite record sales for Colorbond steel products. North Star BlueScope Steel had a dreadful year, with sales down 23.5 per cent and EBIT falling 77 per cent as a significant fall in the benchmark hot rolled coil price easily offset rising production. By contrast, the Buildings & Coated Products North America division enjoyed a positive result, with double-digit increases in sales and profits, due mainly to margin expansion in the engineered buildings systems business. A record result in China was more than offset by weakness elsewhere, and Asian revenues and profit fell. New Zealand business was hurt by a weak economy and declining demand, along with supply and cost constraints.

Outlook

BlueScope occupies a solid position within the Australian economy, and to a lesser extent within the economies of the US and Asia. Its fortunes will be greatly affected by economic trends in these regions. It is also influenced by global steel prices, currency rate trends and raw material prices. It is planning further expansions to its operations, particularly in the US, where it benefits from energy costs substantially below those in Australia and where it makes more than half its profits. In Australia it is benefiting from continuing strong demand for its Colorbond steel products, and it plans a major $1.15 billion upgrade of its Port Kembla Steelworks. In New Zealand it has initiated a feasibility study for the construction of a NZ$300 million electric arc furnace at its Glenbrook plant.

Year to 30 June	2022	2023
Revenues ($mn)	19029.9	18242.5
Australian steel products (%)	42	42
Buildings & coated products North America (%)	16	20
North Star BlueScope Steel (%)	23	19
Coated products Asia (%)	14	14
New Zealand & Pacific Islands (%)	5	5
EBIT ($mn)	3800.5	1516.8
EBIT margin (%)	20.0	8.3
Profit before tax ($mn)	3729.2	1444.4
Profit after tax ($mn)	2701.1	1009.2
Earnings per share (c)	549.36	217.42
Cash flow per share (c)	661.12	358.90
Dividend (c)	50	50
Percentage franked	0	100
Net tangible assets per share ($)	14.83	16.69
Interest cover (times)	65.5	41.2
Return on equity (%)	31.0	10.0
Debt-to-equity ratio (%)	~	~
Current ratio	1.7	1.9

Breville Group Limited

ASX code: BRG www.brevillegroup.com

Sector: Consumer durables & apparel	
Share price ($)	24.28
12-month high ($)	27.07
12-month low ($)	17.61
Market capitalisation ($mn)	3466.7
Price/earnings ratio (times)	31.4
Dividend yield (%)	1.3
Price-to-NTA-per-share ratio	11.5
5-year share price return (% p.a.)	13.8
Dividend reinvestment plan	No

Sydney-based Breville Group traces its origins to the production of the first Breville radio in 1932. It later moved into the home appliance business and was subsequently acquired by Housewares International. In 2008 Housewares changed its name to Breville Group, and today the company is a leading designer and distributor of kitchen home appliances under various brands, including Breville, Sage, Baratza, Polyscience and Kambrook. Breville sells its products in some 80 countries, and international business is responsible for around 80 per cent of company turnover. Premier Investments hold 28 per cent of Breville's equity. In July 2022 the company acquired the Italian premium coffee-making equipment manufacturer Lelit.

Latest business results (June 2023, full year)

Revenues and profits continued to grow, but at a slower pace than in previous years as a slowdown in consumer spending in many countries hurt demand. The company also benefited from dollar weakness during the year. Breville segments its operations into two broad divisions, Global Product and Distribution. The former is now responsible for more than 85 per cent of company turnover, with revenues up 8.5 per cent, thanks especially to new product launches and strong sales for coffee and cooking equipment. The Distribution division sells products designed and developed by third parties, and sales fell 17 per cent — having risen 18 per cent in the previous year — driven notably by weaker demand for Nespresso coffee products.

Outlook

Breville has been achieving great success with its strategy of developing its own lines of premium home appliances for the North American, European and Asia-Pacific markets. North America alone now represents half of company revenues and Europe has passed the Asia-Pacific region as the second-largest market. The company continues steadily to enter new markets and is now realising strong demand from countries it entered during the COVID period, including Portugal, Spain, France, Italy, Poland, Mexico and South Korea. It also plans to step up the pace of new product launches, with an increased budget, and expects growing sales for advanced products that include its Barista Impress range of espresso machines and its Joule range of specialist cooking equipment. It regards coffee in particular as offering great potential, and its $169 million acquisition of Lelit follows the purchase in 2020 of coffee grinder manufacturer Baratza, making Breville a force in the international specialty coffee equipment sector. It believes its popular range of innovative products and strong brand image will help protect it against inflationary forces, cost-of-living pressures and currency rate fluctuations.

Year to 30 June	2022	2023
Revenues ($mn)	1418.4	1478.6
EBIT ($mn)	156.7	172.7
EBIT margin (%)	11.0	11.7
Gross margin (%)	34.3	35.0
Profit before tax ($mn)	147.8	151.0
Profit after tax ($mn)	105.7	110.2
Earnings per share (c)	75.89	77.23
Cash flow per share (c)	97.77	109.57
Dividend (c)	30	30.5
Percentage franked	100	100
Net tangible assets per share ($)	2.36	2.11
Interest cover (times)	18.4	8.2
Return on equity (%)	18.9	15.9
Debt-to-equity ratio (%)	0.7	15.8
Current ratio	2.5	2.6

Brickworks Limited

ASX code: BKW   investors.brickworks.com.au

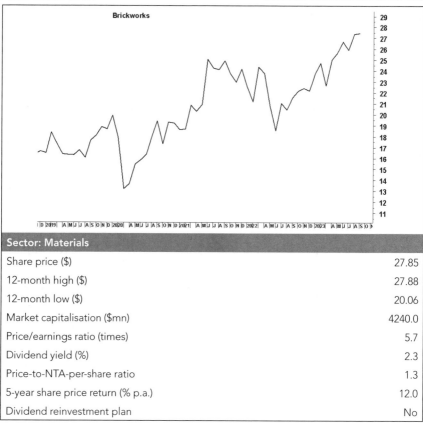

Sector: Materials	
Share price ($)	27.85
12-month high ($)	27.88
12-month low ($)	20.06
Market capitalisation ($mn)	4240.0
Price/earnings ratio (times)	5.7
Dividend yield (%)	2.3
Price-to-NTA-per-share ratio	1.3
5-year share price return (% p.a.)	12.0
Dividend reinvestment plan	No

Sydney-based Brickworks, founded in 1934, is one of Australia's largest manufacturers of building products used especially in the home construction sector. Its brands include Austral Bricks, Austral Masonry, Bristile Roofing, Bowral Bricks, Nubrik, GB Masonry and UrbanStone. Since 2018 it has been building up a portfolio of American brick-making assets, and it is now also a leading producer of bricks in the north-east United States. In Australia it manages an extensive land portfolio, based on surplus and redundant building product sites, and with Goodman Group it operates the Brickworks Manufacturing Trust and the Industrial JV Trust. In a cross-shareholding arrangement, it owns 26 per cent of the equity of Washington H. Soul Pattinson, while Soul Pattinson owns more than 40 per cent of the equity in Brickworks. In addition, Brickworks holds 18 per cent of the equity in ASX-listed FBR, developer of a brick-laying robot.

Latest business results (January 2023, half year)

Most of the company's sales revenues derived from its building products businesses, but around 90 per cent of the profit came from its property and investments operations. Building product demand in Australia remained firm, with sales up, despite a decline in residential commencements. However, a sharp drop in building activity in Western Australia during the period meant that domestic profits fell. North American building product sales — about 35 per cent of total turnover — rose, with profits also higher, although profit margins remained low. Property delivered EBIT of $453 million, up 26 per cent from a year earlier, thanks especially to a $263 million profit from the sale of the Oakdale East Stage Two property in Sydney. EBIT from investments of $100 million was up 37 per cent, thanks to a strong contribution from the Washington H. Soul Pattinson shareholding.

Outlook

With inflation and interest rates rising, Brickworks expects a slowing in house construction and renovation activity by the end of 2023, although a backlog of work, sparked in part by tradie shortages, could provide a short-term buffer. Price rises are intended to help mitigate the impact of rising costs. It is working to boost the profitability and long-term earnings of US operations through strategies of rationalisation, plant upgrades and premium product positioning. Nevertheless, the company's investment and property arms are likely to have the biggest near-term impact on profit trends. In particular, its moves into industrial property trusts present a significant opportunity to benefit from fast-rising rentals, with the average rent achieved by its Industrial JV Trust still below market averages.

Year to 31 July	2021	2022
Revenues ($mn)	850.9	1093.2
EBIT ($mn)	350.7	993.9
EBIT margin (%)	41.2	90.9
Gross margin (%)	29.5	31.2
Profit before tax ($mn)	328.9	962.2
Profit after tax ($mn)	242.8	746.1
Earnings per share (c)	160.68	491.71
Cash flow per share (c)	207.24	543.24
Dividend (c)	61	63
Percentage franked	100	100
Interest cover (times)	16.3	31.6
Return on equity (%)	9.9	26.0
Half year to 31 January	2022	2023
Revenues ($mn)	514.7	583.9
Profit before tax ($mn)	440.5	546.0
Profit after tax ($mn)	330.5	410.0
Earnings per share (c)	217.85	269.52
Dividend (c)	22	23
Percentage franked	100	100
Net tangible assets per share ($)	16.75	22.27
Debt-to-equity ratio (%)	20.9	16.7
Current ratio	2.3	2.0

Carsales.com Limited

ASX code: CAR

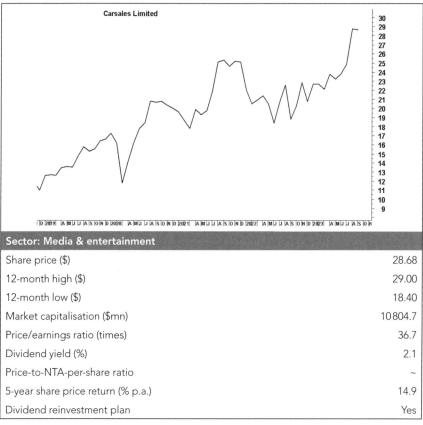

Sector: Media & entertainment	
Share price ($)	28.68
12-month high ($)	29.00
12-month low ($)	18.40
Market capitalisation ($mn)	10 804.7
Price/earnings ratio (times)	36.7
Dividend yield (%)	2.1
Price-to-NTA-per-share ratio	~
5-year share price return (% p.a.)	14.9
Dividend reinvestment plan	Yes

Carsales.com was founded in Melbourne in 1997 and has grown to become the market leader in online automotive advertising. It also operates specialist websites for the sale of a variety of other goods, including boats, motorcycles, trucks, construction equipment, farm machinery, caravans and tyres. It has expanded abroad, with interests in automotive businesses in the US, Asia and Latin America, and these operations now generate more than half of company turnover. A smaller division provides a diverse range of data services for customers, including software as a service, research and reporting, valuations, appraisals, website development and photography services.

Latest business results (June 2023, full year)

Revenues and profits grew, with another solid domestic performance and a big contribution from overseas businesses. The core Australian online advertising services business continued to benefit from post-COVID volatility, with shortages of some new vehicles still forcing buyers to turn to secondhand models. The September 2022 acquisition by Carsales.com of the remaining 51 per cent interest in Trader Interactive in the US generated a substantial boost to company revenues and profits. In May 2023 it took its ownership of Brazil's Webmotors from 30 per cent to 70 per cent, and this business too made a solid contribution. Asian revenues and profits rose 9 per cent.

Outlook

Carsales.com operates domestically in a largely mature market in which it has a dominant market share. It believes underlying market conditions remain solid, and it continues to tweak its products. It expects the increased penetration of premium products to contribute to stronger revenues and profits in the June 2024 year. However, it now sees much of its growth coming from its moves overseas. Trader Interactive—acquired for nearly $2 billion—is an American leader in the provision of digital markets for commercial and recreational vehicles and industrial equipment. Carsales.com is already generating synergies from this business through introducing its own technology, developing new products and acquiring more customers. Carsales.com is also introducing new systems and technology to Webmotors, which is the leading automotive digital marketplace in Brazil, and is realising significant growth in dealer numbers. It also expects continuing strong progress in its Korean Encar business—which is that country's leader in automotive classifieds—thanks especially to increased uptake of the company's Guarantee vehicle inspection service. Carsales.com calculates that it operates in four regions—Australia, the US, Brazil and South Korea—with a total addressable market of some $10.3 billion annually, and it sees significant scope for long-term growth.

Year to 30 June	2022	2023
Revenues ($mn)	509.1	781.2
Australia—online advertising services (%)	60	45
North America (%)	0	23
Asia (%)	19	13
Australia—carsales investments (%)	11	8
Australia—data, research & services (%)	9	6
EBIT ($mn)	317.2	416.0
EBIT margin (%)	62.3	53.3
Profit before tax ($mn)	299.5	360.1
Profit after tax ($mn)	194.8	278.2
Earnings per share (c)	68.96	78.11
Cash flow per share (c)	85.49	108.16
Dividend (c)	50	61
Percentage franked	100	73
Net tangible assets per share ($)	1.24	~
Interest cover (times)	18.4	8.7
Return on equity (%)	20.0	13.6
Debt-to-equity ratio (%)	52.5	31.2
Current ratio	1.7	1.8

Clinuvel Pharmaceuticals Limited

ASX code: CUV   www.clinuvel.com

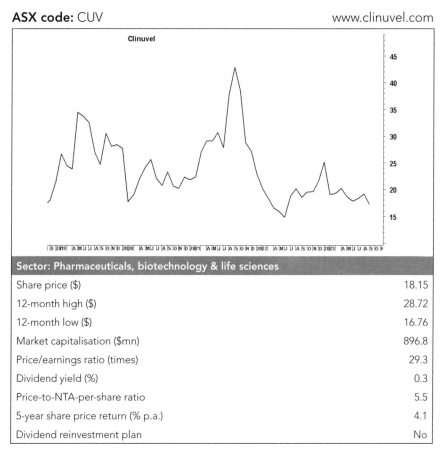

Clinuvel

Sector: Pharmaceuticals, biotechnology & life sciences	
Share price ($)	18.15
12-month high ($)	28.72
12-month low ($)	16.76
Market capitalisation ($mn)	896.8
Price/earnings ratio (times)	29.3
Dividend yield (%)	0.3
Price-to-NTA-per-share ratio	5.5
5-year share price return (% p.a.)	4.1
Dividend reinvestment plan	No

Melbourne-based biopharmaceutical company Clinuvel dates back to 1987, when scientists devised technologies for the protection of skin using human hormones. Today it is a global company with a focus on developing drugs for the treatment of various skin disorders. Its lead therapy afamelanotide, known as Scenesse, has been shown to be effective in treating severe phototoxicity—intolerance of light—in many badly affected patients. It has been approved by regulators for commercial distribution in Europe, the US, Canada, Israel and Australia. The company is also developing other drugs.

Latest business results (June 2023, full year)

Revenues and profits rose again in a pleasing result for the company, thanks to fast-growing demand for Scenesse in the markets where it has been approved. The company reported that a growing number of treatment centres were prescribing the drug, along with high patient retention. Most sales were overseas, so there was also a benefit from the weaker dollar. Profits rose at a faster pace than revenues, and profit margins were up. With no debt, and cash holdings at June 2023 of more than

$156 million, Clinuvel also benefited from rising interest rates, with its interest income rising from $0.4 million to $3.9 million.

Outlook

Scenesse reduces the severity of phototoxic skin reactions in patients with a rare light intolerance condition known as erythropoietic protoporphyria. Such patients can experience severe pain from sun exposure, as well as swelling and scarring of exposed areas of the body such as the face and hands, with hospitalisation and powerful pain killers sometimes necessary. Scenesse is the first drug developed for this condition. Following regulatory approval it was launched in Europe in 2016 and in the US in 2020, and the company is actively seeking to have it approved in other countries. It is also working to have it approved for adolescents. In addition, Clinuvel is involved in a series of drug trials. It has launched tests in the US to determine whether Scenesse can be used to treat vitiligo, a skin disorder where patches of skin become pale or white. It is also working on the development of a range of over-the-counter skin protection products based on Scenesse. In 2020 it announced the development of a new drug, Prénumbra, a liquid formulation of Scenesse, and has begun studies on using this drug in the treatment of arterial ischaemic stroke. It is developing a third drug, Neuracthel, which it believes could have applications in the treatment of neurological, endocrinological and degenerative diseases.

Year to 30 June	2022	2023
Revenues ($mn)	65.7	78.3
EBIT ($mn)	34.4	45.6
EBIT margin (%)	52.3	58.2
Profit before tax ($mn)	34.3	45.6
Profit after tax ($mn)	20.9	30.6
Earnings per share (c)	42.25	61.94
Cash flow per share (c)	43.79	63.54
Dividend (c)	4	5
Percentage franked	100	100
Net tangible assets per share ($)	2.51	3.31
Interest cover (times)	~	~
Return on equity (%)	18.6	21.1
Debt-to-equity ratio (%)	~	~
Current ratio	10.2	7.4

Clover Corporation Limited

ASX code: CLV　　　　　　　　　　　　　www.clovercorp.com.au

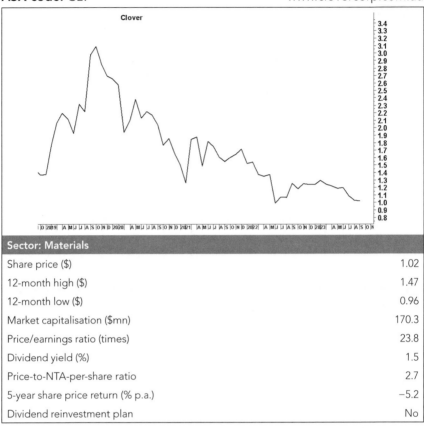

Sector: Materials

Share price ($)	1.02
12-month high ($)	1.47
12-month low ($)	0.96
Market capitalisation ($mn)	170.3
Price/earnings ratio (times)	23.8
Dividend yield (%)	1.5
Price-to-NTA-per-share ratio	2.7
5-year share price return (% p.a.)	−5.2
Dividend reinvestment plan	No

Melbourne-based Clover, founded in 1988 as a family-owned company, develops value-added nutrients for use in foods or as nutritional supplements. Its key product is docosahexaenoic acid (DHA), a form of omega 3. It sells this under the Nu-Mega and Ocean Gold range of tuna oils. It also markets nutritional oil powders, based on technology developed by the Commonwealth Scientific and Industrial Research Organisation (CSIRO). In addition, the company has developed technology that allows nutritional oils to be added to infant formula, foods and beverages. Overseas customers account for around two-thirds of company sales.

Latest business results (January 2023, half year)

Strong global demand for its products generated an excellent result for Clover, thanks to a mix of new customers and new products. Revenues from external customers in Europe and the Middle East more than doubled from the January 2022 period, and these regions now represent more than a quarter of total company turnover. The key Asian market—more than one-third of turnover—achieved a 28 per cent gain in sales, with Chinese customers stocking up on the company's products in advance of new licensing requirements concerning the sale of infant formula in that country. The Australia/New Zealand segment was also buoyant, with sales up 55 per cent.

Outlook

Clover expects some near-term volatility in sales, following a build-up in inventory by Chinese customers, in advance of new licensing standards, which require a minimum level of DHA in some infant formula products. It is working with manufacturers to help them meet the new conditions. The ending of COVID restrictions has enabled Clover to boost its global marketing efforts, with the aim of seeking out new business opportunities overseas, and it has been achieving a steady increase in demand for its products from many regions. It has also been placing new products on trial with target customers with the aim of expanding markets it already serves in the medical foods, general food and drinks and nutraceuticals segments. It has begun to achieve sales in the US for its new Gelphorm product, which allows users to fortify ultra-heat treatment drinks with omega 3, and it has Gelphorm on trial with additional customers. It sees particular potential for its Premneo omega 3 product for pre-term babies. A five-year clinical trial found that Premneo can boost the IQ of these infants and Clover is now seeking regulatory registration and approval in key markets for this product. Improvements to the company's Melody Dairies production facility in New Zealand have boosted productivity.

Year to 31 July	2021	2022
Revenues ($mn)	60.5	70.7
EBIT ($mn)	8.6	10.3
EBIT margin (%)	14.2	14.6
Profit before tax ($mn)	8.2	9.8
Profit after tax ($mn)	6.0	7.1
Earnings per share (c)	3.61	4.29
Cash flow per share (c)	4.04	4.72
Dividend (c)	1	1.5
Percentage franked	100	100
Interest cover (times)	21.4	22.6
Return on equity (%)	10.4	11.7
Half year to 31 January	2022	2023
Revenues ($mn)	29.7	44.4
Profit before tax ($mn)	2.8	5.1
Profit after tax ($mn)	2.0	3.6
Earnings per share (c)	1.21	2.18
Dividend (c)	0.5	0.75
Percentage franked	100	100
Net tangible assets per share ($)	0.34	0.38
Debt-to-equity ratio (%)	7.0	5.7
Current ratio	6.9	4.5

Cochlear Limited

ASX code: COH   www.cochlear.com

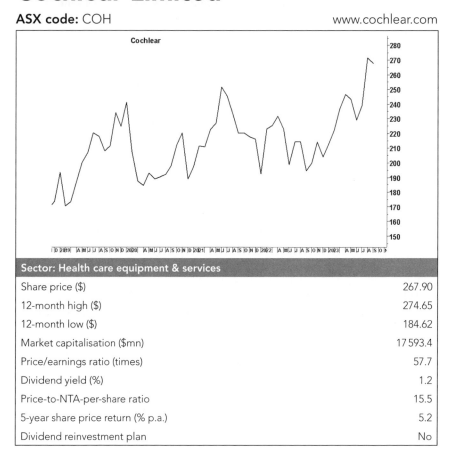

Sector: Health care equipment & services	
Share price ($)	267.90
12-month high ($)	274.65
12-month low ($)	184.62
Market capitalisation ($mn)	17 593.4
Price/earnings ratio (times)	57.7
Dividend yield (%)	1.2
Price-to-NTA-per-share ratio	15.5
5-year share price return (% p.a.)	5.2
Dividend reinvestment plan	No

Sydney-based Cochlear, founded in 1981, has around 60 per cent of the world market for cochlear bionic-ear implants, which are intended to assist the communication ability of people suffering from severe hearing impediments. It also sells the Baha bone-anchored hearing implant, as well as a range of acoustic products. With manufacturing facilities and technology centres in Australia, Sweden, Belgium, China and the US, it has sales in over 180 countries, and overseas business accounts for more than 90 per cent of revenues and profits.

Latest business results (June 2023, full year)

Sales and profits rose again in a good result. Cochlear implant sales rose 16 per cent to 44 156 units, with revenues up 21 per cent. The rollout of the Nucleus 8 sound processor in the US and Western Europe contributed to the good result, and the company also benefited from a steady easing of COVID-era hospital constraints. Emerging markets were also strong. Service revenues grew by 16 per cent, with particularly strong demand in the second half as the Nucleus 8 unit became available. Acoustics sales rose 19 per cent, having jumped 28 per cent in the previous year, with solid demand across all regions. There was strong demand for the Osia 2 system and the company also benefited from a recovery in surgery volumes following COVID-related delays.

Outlook

Cochlear continues to launch new products at an impressive rate, with a high level of research and development spending, and this is helping it maintain its market leadership. It expects sales to continue to grow for the Nucleus 8 sound processor, which is 15 per cent smaller and 13 per cent lighter than its predecessor. A particular recent marketing focus has been adults and seniors in developed markets, which it regards as its biggest opportunity, given the large and growing market size and a current penetration rate of only about 3 per cent. The company points to research suggesting that good hearing is an important contributor to healthy ageing. In particular, it notes a July 2023 report that found cognitive decline slowing by 48 per cent for a group of older adults with a degree of hearing loss and at risk of cognitive decline, after they had worn hearing aids for three years. At June 2023 Cochlear had no debt and cash holdings of more than $555 million. The company's early June 2024 forecast is for strong growth in sales, as well as margin improvement, and an after-tax profit of $355 million to $375 million.

Year to 30 June	2022	2023
Revenues ($mn)	1648.3	1936.1
Cochlear implants (%)	57	58
Services (%)	31	30
Acoustics (%)	12	12
EBIT ($mn)	385.1	412.6
EBIT margin (%)	23.4	21.3
Gross margin (%)	74.6	74.3
Profit before tax ($mn)	376.5	403.2
Profit after tax ($mn)	277.0	305.2
Earnings per share (c)	421.16	464.09
Cash flow per share (c)	532.15	587.11
Dividend (c)	300	330
Percentage franked	19	54
Net tangible assets per share ($)	16.94	17.27
Interest cover (times)	62.1	~
Return on equity (%)	16.4	17.8
Debt-to-equity ratio (%)	~	~
Current ratio	2.5	2.4

Codan Limited

ASX code: CDA   www.codan.com.au

Sector: Technology hardware & equipment

Share price ($)	7.91
12-month high ($)	8.41
12-month low ($)	3.64
Market capitalisation ($mn)	1433.0
Price/earnings ratio (times)	21.1
Dividend yield (%)	2.3
Price-to-NTA-per-share ratio	15.2
5-year share price return (% p.a.)	22.8
Dividend reinvestment plan	No

Adelaide electronics company Codan was founded in 1959. It is a leading world manufacturer of metal-detecting products, including Minelab metal detectors for hobbyists, gold detectors for small-scale miners and landmine detectors for humanitarian applications. The second major division produces high-frequency communication equipment for military and humanitarian use. Codan sells to more than 150 countries, and overseas sales represent around 90 per cent of company revenues. In August 2023 it acquired the British emergency services software supplier Eagle NewCo.

Latest business results (June 2023, full year)

Another drop in sales of its high-margin metal detectors led to a decline in revenues and profits for Codan. In the June 2022 year metal detector sales fell 20 per cent, and this year they dropped by a further 33 per cent, due mainly to significant disruptions experienced in African markets, and with profits crashing by more than 50 per cent. This business also suffered from the company's withdrawal from the Russian market. Other regions were generally positive. By contrast, Communications division sales rose by 14 per cent. This division benefited from the company's growing moves into public safety and military and law enforcement. It also benefited from one significant contract worth $20 million. Profits for the division rose by more than 35 per cent as margins expanded, and for the first time the Communications division generated more company profit than the Metal Detection division.

Outlook

Codan is a significant force in two niche high-tech product areas. Its metal detectors dominate the African artisanal gold mining sector, and it is also a significant force in recreational markets. However, with turmoil continuing in its most profitable African markets it is cautious about the outlook, although it is experiencing some solid sales growth in other regions, with a particular contribution from a range of newly released models that have been well received. It is also achieving strong demand for landmine detecting equipment and is involved in humanitarian efforts in Ukraine. The Communications division held an order book of $163 million at June 2023, up 9 per cent from a year earlier, and the company's early forecast was for revenues growth for this division of 10 per cent to 15 per cent in the June 2024 year. The $22 million acquisition of Eagle NewCo delivers to Codan some strategically important technology that is highly complementary to its existing technology and will help Codan gain access to the British public safety market. It will also provide a platform for expansion across European and Middle Eastern markets.

Year to 30 June	2022	2023
Revenues ($mn)	506.1	456.5
Communications (%)	48	60
Metal detection (%)	52	39
EBIT ($mn)	137.4	88.0
EBIT margin (%)	27.1	19.3
Gross margin (%)	56.6	54.6
Profit before tax ($mn)	135.7	82.6
Profit after tax ($mn)	100.7	67.8
Earnings per share (c)	55.71	37.46
Cash flow per share (c)	69.31	53.42
Dividend (c)	28	18.5
Percentage franked	100	100
Net tangible assets per share ($)	0.51	0.52
Interest cover (times)	79.2	16.5
Return on equity (%)	30.0	17.5
Debt-to-equity ratio (%)	8.0	12.7
Current ratio	1.7	1.7

Coles Group Limited

ASX code: COL   www.colesgroup.com.au

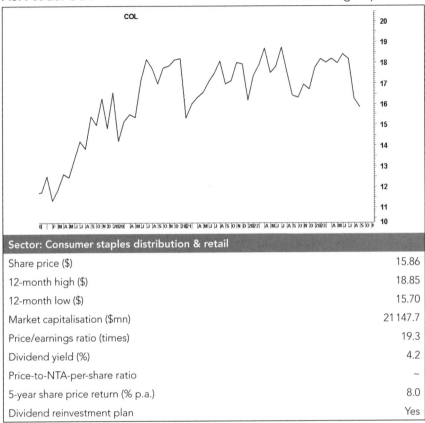

Sector: Consumer staples distribution & retail

Share price ($)	15.86
12-month high ($)	18.85
12-month low ($)	15.70
Market capitalisation ($mn)	21 147.7
Price/earnings ratio (times)	19.3
Dividend yield (%)	4.2
Price-to-NTA-per-share ratio	~
5-year share price return (% p.a.)	8.0
Dividend reinvestment plan	Yes

Melbourne-based Coles Group dates back to 1914 and the opening of the first Coles store in the Melbourne suburb of Collingwood. Over many years it evolved from a single variety store to a chain of supermarkets, then expanded further with the acquisition of the Myer department store business. In 2006 the company sold Myer and in 2007 Coles was acquired by Wesfarmers. In 2018 it was demerged from Wesfarmers as, once again, an independent company. At June 2023 it operated 846 supermarkets nationwide and 957 liquor stores, the latter under the Liquorland, Vintage Cellars and First Choice banners. It is a 50 per cent shareholder of the Flybuys loyalty program. In May 2023 it sold its Coles Express petrol and convenience retail operation.

Latest business results (June 2023, full year)

In a difficult year, with customers facing rising cost-of-living pressures, Coles saw revenues and profits generally higher. The Supermarkets division achieved sales growth of 6.1 per cent, including a notable 9.6 per cent rise in sales of Coles own-brand items. Liquor division sales were flat for the year, having risen solidly during the period of COVID, though with 8.5 per cent growth in exclusive Coles products.

Profits did not grow at the same pace as sales. Supermarkets division EBIT rose 2.9 per cent. Liquor division EBIT was down 3.7 per cent. The company faced a variety of higher costs during the year, including higher salaries, increased investment in digital and technology assets and a rising wave of shoplifting. During the year Coles opened 17 new supermarkets and 35 new liquor stores.

Outlook

The big supermarket chains are generally immune to declines in discretionary consumer spending. However, it is noteworthy that consumers are trading down to cheaper home brands. Coles has made a substantial investment in these products over many years and has become a beneficiary of this move, with more than 6000 own-brand products, and these have grown to represent around a third of total sales. It expects that the steady expansion of Australia's population will underpin its long-term growth. It is developing major new automated customer fulfillment centres in Sydney and Melbourne, but has been struggling with project delays and cost overruns. It is concerned that extreme weather events, including floods, cyclones and bushfires, will increasingly disrupt its supply chains. Four fresh produce categories are considered to be at medium risk—lettuces, strawberries, other berries and bananas—and consequently Coles is working with suppliers to move some growing to new regions.

Year to 25 June*	2022	2023
Revenues ($mn)	38 237.0	40 483.0
Supermarkets (%)	91	91
Liquor (%)	9	9
EBIT ($mn)	1827.0	1859.0
EBIT margin (%)	4.8	4.6
Gross margin (%)	25.7	25.8
Profit before tax ($mn)	1467.0	1465.0
Profit after tax ($mn)	1048.0	1098.0
Earnings per share (c)	78.80	82.31
Cash flow per share (c)	186.47	196.48
Dividend (c)	63	66
Percentage franked	100	100
Net tangible assets per share ($)	~	~
Interest cover (times)	5.1	4.7
Return on equity (%)	35.3	33.9
Debt-to-equity ratio (%)	16.2	15.5
Current ratio	0.6	0.6

*26 June 2022

Collins Foods Limited

ASX code: CKF

www.collinsfoods.com

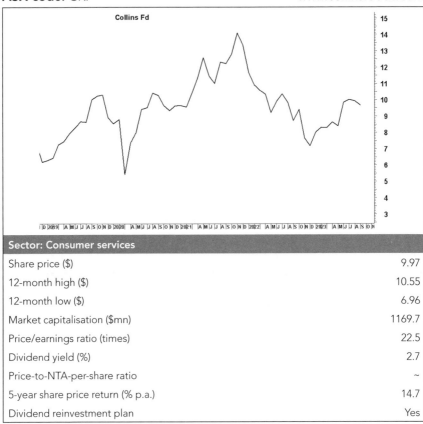

Collins Fd

Sector: Consumer services

Share price ($)	9.97
12-month high ($)	10.55
12-month low ($)	6.96
Market capitalisation ($mn)	1169.7
Price/earnings ratio (times)	22.5
Dividend yield (%)	2.7
Price-to-NTA-per-share ratio	~
5-year share price return (% p.a.)	14.7
Dividend reinvestment plan	Yes

Collins Foods, based in Brisbane, dates back to 1968, when it obtained the KFC fried chicken franchise for Queensland. Today it operates KFC outlets across Australia and is the country's largest KFC franchisee. It also manages the Taco Bell Mexican restaurant brand in Australia. It operates KFC stores in Germany and the Netherlands. It has closed its Sizzler restaurant business in Australia and in 2023 sold its Asian Sizzler franchise operation.

Latest business results (April 2023, full year)

Sales rose but profits fell, in a challenging year for the company's businesses. Domestic KFC operations achieved a 10 per cent increase in revenues, driven by same-store sales growth of 5.8 per cent and the opening of new stores. However, profits fell, hit by supply chain issues and higher-than-expected inflationary pressures. By contrast, European operations saw sales and profits up, with same-store growth of 13.9 per cent. Taco Bell revenues rose significantly, thanks to the opening of new stores, but same-store sales fell for the second straight year and this business remained in the red. The small Sizzler Asia franchise business made a profit, before being sold in July 2023.

On a statutory basis the company also recorded non-recurring charges of more than $40 million, related mainly to impairment provisions for Taco Bell. At the end of the period the company operated 272 franchised KFC restaurants in Australia, up from 261 a year earlier, with a further 48 in the Netherlands and 16 in Germany, compared respectively to 45 and 17 a year earlier. It also ran 28 Taco Bell restaurants in Australia, up from 20.

Outlook

Collins continues to face supply chain problems and inflationary pressures, and has been raising menu prices in response. Nevertheless, it believes the longer-term outlook is positive and plans a steady roll-out of new restaurants in Australia, with up to 12 more in the April 2024 year. It has been experiencing a satisfying increase in business as many Australian households deal with a degree of cost-of-living pressures. It also continues to enjoy solid same-store growth in Europe. It has become the largest KFC franchisee in the Netherlands and expects to launch as many as 130 new restaurants in that country over the next 10 years. In May 2023 its Dutch subsidiary acquired eight new KFC restaurants, and this is expected to deliver further economies of scale. However, it has paused the roll-out of new Taco Bell outlets in Australia while it works to move this business into profit.

Year to 30 April*	2022	2023
Revenues ($mn)	1188.1	1348.6
KFC restaurants Australia (%)	81	78
KFC restaurants Europe (%)	16	18
Taco Bell restaurants (%)	3	4
EBIT ($mn)	110.9	110.9
EBIT margin (%)	9.3	8.2
Gross margin (%)	52.4	50.1
Profit before tax ($mn)	80.7	77.5
Profit after tax ($mn)	54.8	51.9
Earnings per share (c)	46.96	44.29
Cash flow per share (c)	126.73	128.06
Dividend (c)	27	27
Percentage franked	100	100
Net tangible assets per share ($)	~	~
Interest cover (times)	3.7	3.4
Return on equity (%)	14.5	13.3
Debt-to-equity ratio (%)	44.2	55.0
Current ratio	0.7	0.7

*1 May 2022

Commonwealth Bank of Australia

ASX code: CBA   www.commbank.com.au

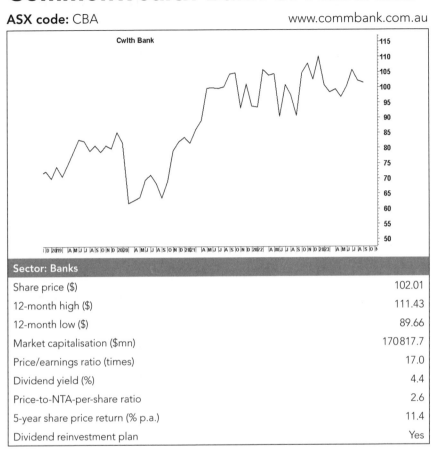

Sector: Banks	
Share price ($)	102.01
12-month high ($)	111.43
12-month low ($)	89.66
Market capitalisation ($mn)	170817.7
Price/earnings ratio (times)	17.0
Dividend yield (%)	4.4
Price-to-NTA-per-share ratio	2.6
5-year share price return (% p.a.)	11.4
Dividend reinvestment plan	Yes

The Commonwealth Bank, based in Sydney, was founded in 1911. It is today one of Australia's largest banks, and one of the country's top providers of home loans, personal loans and credit cards, as well as the largest holder of deposits, while its Commonwealth Securities business is a prominent online stockbroker. It has significant interests in New Zealand, through ASB Bank. It owns Bankwest in Western Australia.

Latest business results (June 2023, full year)

In another good result, the cash profit rose for a third successive year, after three straight years of decline, thanks especially to rising interest rates, which led to a higher net interest margin over the 12-month period. The core Retail Banking Services division enjoyed a 5 per cent rise in profits, the same increase as in the previous year, thanks especially to the higher net interest margin, though partially offset by a lower home loan lending margin. The best result came from the Business Banking division, with profits jumping 32 per cent as the bank saw a substantial increase in the division's net interest margin, along with growing business from customers and flat operating expenses. By contrast, the smaller Institutional Banking and Markets division, which in the previous year has achieved a double-digit profit increase, this time experienced a small dip, as expenses rose at a faster pace than income. New Zealand profits continued to rise. Productivity benefits of some $200 million partially offset both inflationary pressures and higher spending on new technology, and operating expenses grew by just 5 per cent.

Outlook

Commonwealth Bank occupies a powerful position in the domestic economy as well as in the local banking industry. Thanks to a large branch network, offering many cross-selling opportunities, it has pricing power that has generally enabled it to maintain a cost advantage over some of its rivals. It is cautious about the near-term economic outlook, noting that all its customers are being affected by a rising cost of living, and with younger Australians in particular now reducing the savings buffers they had built up during the COVID pandemic. In addition, reduced discretionary spending is hurting the bank's small and medium-sized business customers. It has warned that profits in both Australia and New Zealand are also under threat from highly competitive mortgage markets. Nevertheless, the bank's view is that inflationary and interest rate pressures will ease during 2024. It continues to roll out a range of new products that are designed to boost customer engagement. It sees particular potential in its new Powerboard payment service, which helps businesses manage their payment collections.

Year to 30 June	2022	2023
Operating income ($mn)	24935.0	27530.0
Net interest income ($mn)	19473.0	23056.0
Operating expenses ($mn)	11039.0	11646.0
Profit before tax ($mn)	13618.0	14271.0
Profit after tax ($mn)	9595.0	10164.0
Earnings per share (c)	557.20	601.42
Dividend (c)	385	450
Percentage franked	100	100
Non-interest income to total income (%)	21.9	16.3
Net tangible assets per share ($)	38.79	38.58
Cost-to-income ratio (%)	44.3	42.3
Return on equity (%)	12.7	14.0
Return on assets (%)	0.8	0.8

Computershare Limited

ASX code: CPU www.computershare.com

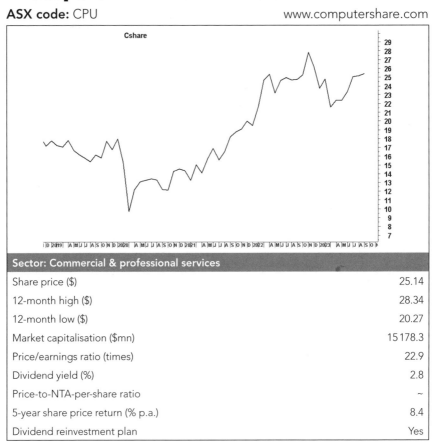

Sector: Commercial & professional services	
Share price ($)	25.14
12-month high ($)	28.34
12-month low ($)	20.27
Market capitalisation ($mn)	15 178.3
Price/earnings ratio (times)	22.9
Dividend yield (%)	2.8
Price-to-NTA-per-share ratio	~
5-year share price return (% p.a.)	8.4
Dividend reinvestment plan	Yes

Melbourne-based Computershare, established in 1978, is one of the world's leading financial services and technology providers for the global securities industry, offering services to listed companies, investors, employees, exchanges and other financial institutions. These offerings include share registration, employee equity plans, corporate governance, class action administration and other specialised financial, governance and stakeholder communication services. Its Computershare Corporate Trust (CCT) business helps administer debt securities in the US. The company manages more than 75 million customer records for more than 25 000 clients across all major financial markets, with significant market shares in many countries. More than 90 per cent of revenues come from abroad, including around 64 per cent from the US.

Latest business results (June 2023, full year)

Rising interest rates and a full year's contribution from CCT—acquired in November 2021—combined to generate an excellent result. CCT revenues of $848 million were more than 150 per cent up from the previous year, with profits surging more than fivefold. The company's largest operating segment, Issuer Services, benefited from higher interest rates, more than offsetting a dip in fee and transaction income, with double-digit gains in revenues and profits. CCT and the Issuer Services division together now represent more than three-quarters of total company profit. The employee share plans business benefited from fee growth, offsetting adverse foreign exchange movements. But the low-margin mortgage services operation suffered from reduced fee income, and revenues and profits fell. Note that Computershare reports its results in US dollars. The Australian dollar figures in this book—converted at prevailing exchange rates—are for guidance only.

Outlook

Computershare is a beneficiary of robust worldwide equity markets, and can suffer in periods of volatility. It is also hurt by rising inflation. Nevertheless, it continues to gain market share in its issuer services and employee share plan operations, and it is actively working on new technological innovations. It holds a considerable amount of clients' funds in various forms, and is a notable beneficiary of rising interest rates. However, to protect itself from looming downward moves in rates it plans to lock in a total of US$1.5 billion of future interest-related income. It sees particular potential for CCT, which it says has already exceeded expectations. It is evaluating strategic options for its underperforming mortgage services unit, including a possible sale of the business. Recognising that interest rates may be close to peaking in its regions of operation, Computershare is forecasting EPS growth for the June 2024 year of just 7.5 per cent.

Year to 30 June	2022	2023
Revenues ($mn)	3509.7	4726.5
Issuer services (%)	38	34
Computershare Corporate Trust (%)	13	26
Mortgage & property rental services (%)	23	17
Employee share plans & voucher services (%)	13	11
Business services (%)	7	6
EBIT ($mn)	506.1	1121.7
EBIT margin (%)	14.4	23.7
Profit before tax ($mn)	423.9	921.9
Profit after tax ($mn)	311.9	663.8
Earnings per share (c)	51.66	109.95
Cash flow per share (c)	94.56	156.08
Dividend (c)	54	70
Percentage franked	18	0
Net tangible assets per share ($)	~	~
Interest cover (times)	6.4	7.2
Return on equity (%)	10.1	20.8
Debt-to-equity ratio (%)	64.9	56.8
Current ratio	1.6	1.7

Credit Corp Group Limited

ASX code: CCP www.creditcorpgroup.com.au

Sector: Financial services	
Share price ($)	21.24
12-month high ($)	24.80
12-month low ($)	15.00
Market capitalisation ($mn)	1445.7
Price/earnings ratio (times)	15.8
Dividend yield (%)	3.3
Price-to-NTA-per-share ratio	1.9
5-year share price return (% p.a.)	1.0
Dividend reinvestment plan	No

Sydney-based Credit Corp was formed in 1992, although it has its origins in companies that started in the early 1970s. It engages in debt collection activity, through the acquisition of defaulted consumer debt for companies in numerous industries, notably the banking, finance, telecommunications and utility sectors. It has operations in Australia, New Zealand and the United States, as well as a large call centre in the Philippines. It maintains an agency collection service, under the brands National Credit Management, Baycorp and Collection House, for clients who wish to outsource debt collections without actually selling the debt. It also operates a fast-growing consumer lending business with brands that include CarStart and Wallet Wizard.

Latest business results (June 2023, full year)

Revenues made a solid gain, bolstered by the 2022 acquisition of rival Collection House, but profits dipped. The company's core Australian debt collection businesses saw revenues edge down, in a constrained market environment for its products, and with profits falling a sharp 27 per cent. By contrast, the American operation continued to grow, with revenues up 15 per cent, although rising costs and increased repayment plan delinquency caused profits to decline. The standout performer for the company was its high-margin consumer lending operation, with continuing strong demand for the Wallet Wizard product. Consumer lending revenues rose more than 50 per cent with profits surging 83 per cent. At June 2023 Credit Corp's loan book of $358 million was up from $251 million a year earlier, and consumer lending now represents around a third of company revenues and profits.

Outlook

Credit Corp's main business effectively involves buying consumer debt at a discount to its face value, and then seeking to recover an amount in excess of the purchase price. Often this recovery takes the form of phased payments over an extended period, and Credit Corp thus has substantial recurring income. Setting an appropriate price for the acquisition of parcels of debt is one of the keys to success, and Credit Corp has acquired considerable expertise in this. It has achieved success with its drive into the American market, and expects earnings progress there, thanks to expanded collection capacity and operational improvements. It believes US profitability will eventually equal that for Australian business. It also expects continuing strong consumer lending growth. Nevertheless, the company's early forecast is that further weakness in domestic debt-collection operations will hold back earnings, with a predicted June 2024 after-tax profit of some $90 million to $100 million.

Year to 30 June	2022	2023
Revenues ($mn)	411.2	473.4
EBIT ($mn)	148.2	145.3
EBIT margin (%)	36.0	30.7
Profit before tax ($mn)	143.0	128.4
Profit after tax ($mn)	100.7	91.3
Earnings per share (c)	148.89	134.22
Cash flow per share (c)	164.43	150.64
Dividend (c)	74	70
Percentage franked	100	100
Net tangible assets per share ($)	10.51	11.43
Interest cover (times)	28.9	9.0
Return on equity (%)	14.3	11.7
Debt-to-equity ratio (%)	13.4	30.4
Current ratio	6.2	5.7

CSL Limited

ASX code: CSL

investors.csl.com

Sector: Pharmaceuticals, biotechnology & life sciences	
Share price ($)	268.43
12-month high ($)	314.28
12-month low ($)	255.87
Market capitalisation ($mn)	129 482.4
Price/earnings ratio (times)	33.2
Dividend yield (%)	1.4
Price-to-NTA-per-share ratio	~
5-year share price return (% p.a.)	4.3
Dividend reinvestment plan	No

Melbourne-based CSL, formerly the state-owned Commonwealth Serum Laboratories, was founded in 1916. It has grown organically and through acquisition to become a major global biotechnology company, with operations in numerous countries — with particular strength in the US, Australia, Germany, the UK, China and Switzerland — and more than 90 per cent of revenues derive from outside Australia. Its principal business now, through its CSL Behring division, is the provision of plasma-derived coagulation therapies for the treatment of a range of medical conditions. The CSL Seqirus division is one of the world's largest influenza vaccine companies and a producer of other prescription medicines and pharmaceutical products. CSL enjoys high margins and high market shares for many of its products. In August 2022 it acquired Swiss biotech company Vifor Pharma.

Latest business results (June 2023, full year)

A post-COVID recovery in its blood plasma business and an 11-month contribution from the Vifor acquisition helped deliver a satisfying increase in sales and underlying profits. The COVID pandemic had sparked a sharp decline in blood donations, but in this period the core CSL Behring division achieved revenue growth of 12 per cent, with solid demand for all main products and plasma collection volumes at record levels. The CSL Seqirus division continued to benefit from firm demand for seasonal influenza vaccines, including an impressive 30 per cent jump in sales for the innovative Flucelvax vaccine. The new CSL Vifor division posted an 11-month revenue contribution of US$2 billion, which the company said was 14 per cent higher than in the previous year, before CSL ownership. Note that CSL reports its results in US dollars. The figures in this book have been converted to Australian dollars based on prevailing exchange rates.

Outlook

CSL remains a powerhouse biotechnology company, with an impressive research and development capability and a solid pipeline of potential new products. It expects the recovery in plasma collections to lead to strong growth in sales of related products. In addition, it expects continuing robust influenza vaccine demand. It sees great potential for its $16.7 billion Vifor Pharma acquisition, one of the largest-ever acquisitions by an Australian company. Vifor boasts a world-leading iron replacement platform for treatment of diseases such as iron deficiency anaemia and through its extensive dialysis portfolio has built a strong presence in renal diseases. The company's early June 2024 forecast is for revenue growth of 9 per cent to 11 per cent, with rising margins delivering after-profit growth of 13 per cent to 17 per cent.

Year to 30 June	2022	2023
Revenues ($mn)	14468.5	19865.7
EBIT ($mn)	4246.8	5514.9
EBIT margin (%)	29.4	27.8
Gross margin (%)	54.3	51.4
Profit before tax ($mn)	4020.5	4852.2
Profit after tax ($mn)	3261.6	3895.5
Earnings per share (c)	695.81	807.91
Cash flow per share (c)	854.20	1065.14
Dividend (c)	318.12	362.92
Percentage franked	5	6
Net tangible assets per share ($)	32.03	~
Interest cover (times)	21.0	9.1
Return on equity (%)	20.2	17.3
Debt-to-equity ratio (%)	~	59.9
Current ratio	2.3	2.0

CSR Limited

ASX code: CSR

Sector: Materials	
Share price ($)	6.08
12-month high ($)	6.08
12-month low ($)	4.25
Market capitalisation ($mn)	2902.5
Price/earnings ratio (times)	13.0
Dividend yield (%)	6.0
Price-to-NTA-per-share ratio	2.6
5-year share price return (% p.a.)	12.3
Dividend reinvestment plan	Yes

Sydney-based CSR, founded in 1855 as a sugar refiner, is now a leading manufacturer of building products for residential and commercial construction, with distribution throughout Australia and New Zealand. Its brands include Gyprock plasterboard, Bradford insulation products, Monier roof tiles, Hebel concrete products and PGH bricks and pavers. It is also a joint venture partner in Australia's largest aluminium smelter at Tomago. In addition, it operates a residential and industrial property development business, based on former industrial sites.

Latest business results (March 2023, full year)

CSR delivered another solid result, with strong demand for its building products more than offsetting a slump in aluminium profits, and with a further boost from property developments. All the company's diverse Building Products division units achieved growth, with a particularly strong result for the largest business, Gyprock. CSR also benefited from price rises and operational improvements, and EBIT for the division was up 20 per cent. By contrast, the aluminium business was hit by higher energy and raw material costs, and EBIT slumped from $39.7 million to $8 million, despite stronger sales and higher aluminium prices. The Property division enjoyed an excellent year, thanks to six major transactions, with EBIT of $71.7 million, up from $46.9 million.

Outlook

Inflationary pressures and rising interest rates could put a significant dent in the detached housing construction market. Nevertheless, CSR has pointed to a higher-than-average pipeline of homes awaiting construction—due especially to tradie shortages—and expects firm demand for its building products to continue at least until the end of 2023. It continues to raise prices to offset rising costs, and with a network of over 170 manufacturing and distribution sites, it believes it has the flexibility to meet evolving trends in demand. It is also working to diversify into new market segments, particularly in non-residential construction sectors, where demand continues to rise, and believes this will help drive future growth. Its Aluminium division has locked in prices with an extensive hedging program that extends to 2027, although it remains vulnerable to rising energy costs. Property will also continue to make a solid contribution. CSR owns almost 1400 hectares of land across Australia at some 50 property sites, including more than 1000 hectares in urban areas, with a value of some $1.5 billion. Major projects are under way at Darra in Queensland and at Schofields and Badgerys Creek in NSW, and CSR has already entered into property sales contracts that will generate more than $100 million in EBIT by March 2025.

Year to 31 March	2022	2023
Revenues ($mn)	2311.6	2613.3
Building products (%)	70	70
Aluminium (%)	30	30
EBIT ($mn)	296.9	337.5
EBIT margin (%)	12.8	12.9
Gross margin (%)	30.3	29.0
Profit before tax ($mn)	281.9	315.0
Profit after tax ($mn)	192.6	225.0
Earnings per share (c)	39.74	46.89
Cash flow per share (c)	57.99	64.59
Dividend (c)	31.5	36.5
Percentage franked	100	100
Net tangible assets per share ($)	1.93	2.30
Interest cover (times)	20.5	16.9
Return on equity (%)	18.1	20.7
Debt-to-equity ratio (%)	~	~
Current ratio	1.3	1.7

Data#3 Limited

ASX code: DTL   investor.data3.com

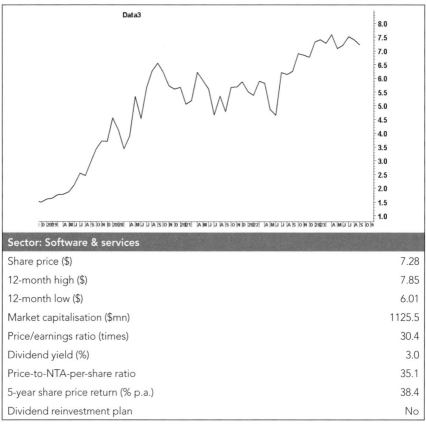

Sector: Software & services	
Share price ($)	7.28
12-month high ($)	7.85
12-month low ($)	6.01
Market capitalisation ($mn)	1125.5
Price/earnings ratio (times)	30.4
Dividend yield (%)	3.0
Price-to-NTA-per-share ratio	35.1
5-year share price return (% p.a.)	38.4
Dividend reinvestment plan	No

Brisbane-based IT consultant Data#3 was formed in 1984 from the merger of computer software consultancy Powell, Clark and Associates with IBM typewriter dealer Albrand Typewriters and Office Machines. Today it operates from offices around Australia and in Fiji, providing information and communication technology services to a wide range of sectors that include banking and finance, mining, tourism and leisure, legal, health care, manufacturing, distribution, government and utilities.

Latest business results (June 2023, full year)

Data#3 achieved a fifth straight year of higher sales and profits in a strong result, as corporate and government IT spending generally returned to normal patterns after the disruptions of COVID. An easing of supply constraints during the year meant the company was able to clear much of the backlog that had developed in the previous year. Data#3 divides its activities into three broad divisions. The first of these, Software Solutions, involves managing clients' software investments. Strength in the public sector and new contracts from commercial clients helped boost revenues by 15.3 per cent to $1653 million. A second division, Infrastructure Solutions, helps clients maximise returns from infrastructure investments in servers, storage, networks and devices. This business rebounded from the previous year, when supply chain delays hurt sales, and revenues jumped 28.6 per cent to $566 million. The small Services division also enjoyed a good year, with particularly strong demand once again for the company's Microsoft Azure Managed Services work.

Outlook

Technology investment continues to grow in Australia, even as the economy slows. Data#3 expects IT, and particularly digital transformation, to play a leading role in the country's economic future, with strong demand for cybersecurity, multi-cloud and artificial intelligence services. With an expanding pipeline of large integration project opportunities among its public sector and commercial clients, Data#3 is optimistic about the near-term outlook. A key competitive advantage is the strength of its partnerships with major vendors, notably Microsoft, Cisco and Hewlett Packard, with each of whom it claims to be the leading Australian partner. It is enjoying particularly strong growth in its high-margin managed services and consulting businesses. It is also working to boost recurring income, currently around two-thirds of total revenues. Although the problems of global computer chip shortages and supply chain constraints have largely eased, the company still faces a backlog in its infrastructure business. It must also address the issue of staff shortages and rapid wage growth within the IT industry. At June 2023 Data#3 had no debt and cash holdings of more than $400 million.

Year to 30 June	2022	2023
Revenues ($mn)	2192.4	2560.7
EBIT ($mn)	45.5	54.5
EBIT margin (%)	2.1	2.1
Profit before tax ($mn)	44.1	53.2
Profit after tax ($mn)	30.3	37.0
Earnings per share (c)	19.61	23.96
Cash flow per share (c)	23.61	28.59
Dividend (c)	17.9	21.9
Percentage franked	100	100
Net tangible assets per share ($)	0.13	0.21
Interest cover (times)	41.2	~
Return on equity (%)	51.3	57.0
Debt-to-equity ratio (%)	~	~
Current ratio	1.1	1.1

Elders Limited

ASX code: ELD   www.elders.com.au

Sector: Food, beverage & tobacco	
Share price ($)	6.38
12-month high ($)	13.45
12-month low ($)	5.99
Market capitalisation ($mn)	998.6
Price/earnings ratio (times)	5.9
Dividend yield (%)	8.8
Price-to-NTA-per-share ratio	2.3
5-year share price return (% p.a.)	3.2
Dividend reinvestment plan	Yes

Adelaide-based agribusiness giant Elders dates back to 1839, when Scotsman Alexander Elder established a store in South Australia. It has expanded and undergone many transformations, until today it is a leader in a range of businesses serving rural Australia. It is a prominent supplier of agricultural products, including seeds, fertilisers, chemicals and animal health products. It is a leading agent for the sale of wool, grain and livestock. It is also a major provider of financial and real estate services to the rural sector. An operation in China imports, processes and distributes Australian meat.

Latest business results (March 2023, half year)

Strong demand for retail products boosted revenues, but profits fell sharply as the company was hit by falling crop and livestock prices and by some unseasonably wet weather. In addition, the March 2022 period had seen farmers purchasing higher-than-normal amounts of fertiliser and crop chemicals due to concerns of supply chain disruptions. The key Agency Services division saw an especially large decline, with lower prices for cattle, sheep and wool, combined with reduced cattle sales. The company's real estate business was also hit, as rising interest rates led to a decline in property sales, partially offset by a continued improvement in property management earnings. The insurance business was also strong. A large recruiting drive, intended to facilitate a series of growth projects, led to higher staffing costs.

Outlook

As one of Australia's agribusiness leaders, Elders is heavily geared to the rural economy, which can be volatile. The weather, interest rates, supply chains and commodity prices are all important influences, along with trends in the domestic and global economies. At present the company holds just 7.3 per cent of the estimated $48 billion annual Australian farm costs market and it sees significant scope for expansion. It has developed an ambitious eight-point plan aimed at winning market share across all its products and services, along with higher profits and moves into new product lines, notably in crop protection and animal health. It is also working to deepen its customer relationships, streamline its supply chains and upgrade its technological systems. The company is particularly interested in growing through acquisition, and recent staff recruitment efforts have partially been aimed at facilitating this. It sees a strong pipeline of potential bolt-on acquisitions aimed at expanding its geographic reach, and it is also exploring greenfield locations where it sees opportunities for boosting market shares. It is developing an innovative $25 million automated wool handling facility in Victoria.

Year to 30 September	2021	2022
Revenues ($mn)	2548.9	3445.3
EBIT ($mn)	165.4	246.3
EBIT margin (%)	6.5	7.1
Gross margin (%)	20.3	18.6
Profit before tax ($mn)	157.7	237.7
Profit after tax ($mn)	151.1	170.0
Earnings per share (c)	96.67	108.65
Cash flow per share (c)	122.85	138.84
Dividend (c)	42	56
Percentage franked	20	30
Interest cover (times)	32.2	34.8
Return on equity (%)	20.9	20.9
Half year to 31 March	2022	2023
Revenues ($mn)	1514.8	1657.3
Profit before tax ($mn)	129.4	70.3
Profit after tax ($mn)	91.2	48.8
Earnings per share (c)	58.30	31.20
Dividend (c)	28	23
Percentage franked	30	30
Net tangible assets per share ($)	2.58	2.72
Debt-to-equity ratio (%)	32.1	49.6
Current ratio	1.3	1.2

Enero Group Limited

ASX code: EGG

Sector: Media & entertainment	
Share price ($)	1.60
12-month high ($)	3.40
12-month low ($)	1.33
Market capitalisation ($mn)	148.1
Price/earnings ratio (times)	6.1
Dividend yield (%)	6.9
Price-to-NTA-per-share ratio	~
5-year share price return (% p.a.)	12.7
Dividend reinvestment plan	No

Sydney marketing and communications services specialist Enero, formerly known as Photon Group, was founded in 2000. It has expanded greatly through a flurry of acquisitions, mergers and divestments, and today divides its activities into three broad segments — creative and content; integrated communications and PR; and digital, data, analytics and technology. Its brands include Hotwire, BMF, CPR, OB Media and Orchard. It operates from three key locations — Australia, America and the UK — with offices in 16 cities and business in many countries. More than 70 per cent of company income comes from overseas operations, including over half from the US.

Latest business results (June 2023, full year)

Two July 2022 acquisitions by Enero's Hotwire business helped boost revenues, with profits generally also higher, although the after-tax profit fell, as a subdued environment within the marketing and communications services sector caused the delay or scope reduction of some projects. The company divides its operations into two broad segments. The larger of these, Creative Technology and Data, enjoyed a strong year, with double-digit gains in sales and profits and another good performance from the high-margin OB Media, which functions as a digital platform, connecting publishers with the world's largest search engines. The Orchard business experienced weakness in the US health sector but with strength in Australia and some key client wins. The second segment, Brand Transformation, benefited from the Hotwire acquisitions and revenues rose. However, profits fell as the company struggled with a slowdown in some areas. The strongest growth for the company came once again from its American operations, where profit margins remain superior to those elsewhere.

Outlook

Enero occupies strong positions in niche areas of the marketing, PR, communications and advertising sectors. More than 40 per cent of its revenues now derive from clients in the technology sector, predominantly in high-growth areas such as cloud computing and cyber-security. Other specialties are providing communications and marketing services to the digital media, retail and healthcare sectors. It expects technology clients to return to more normalised trading during the June 2024 year. Thanks also to recent cost-cutting initiatives it is expecting improved margins and further profit growth. It sees great long-term potential in its two 2022 acquisitions. The first of these, the American business-to-business sales and marketing agency ROI DNA, has delivered a significant portfolio of technology clients, boosting Enero's exposure to this sector. The second acquisition, the Singapore-based business-to-business technology marketing agency GetIT, will help the Hotwire business expand in Asia.

Year to 30 June	2022	2023
Revenues ($mn)	522.1	740.2
Creative technology & data (%)	73	76
Brand transformation (%)	27	24
EBIT ($mn)	59.3	69.0
EBIT margin (%)	11.4	9.3
Gross margin (%)	37.4	32.6
Profit before tax ($mn)	58.3	64.6
Profit after tax ($mn)	27.1	24.4
Earnings per share (c)	30.88	26.38
Cash flow per share (c)	38.79	37.27
Dividend (c)	12.5	11
Percentage franked	100	100
Net tangible assets per share ($)	0.46	~
Interest cover (times)	61.1	16.7
Return on equity (%)	19.7	13.6
Debt-to-equity ratio (%)	~	~
Current ratio	1.8	1.2

Fiducian Group Limited

ASX code: FID www.fiducian.com.au

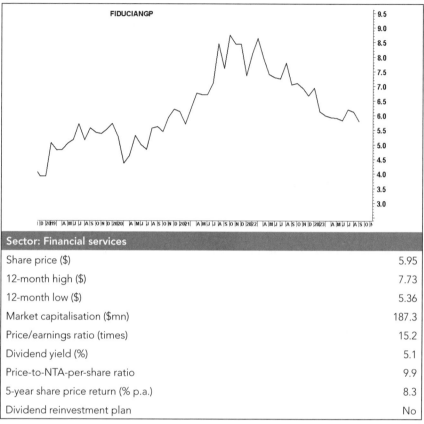

Sector: Financial services	
Share price ($)	5.95
12-month high ($)	7.73
12-month low ($)	5.36
Market capitalisation ($mn)	187.3
Price/earnings ratio (times)	15.2
Dividend yield (%)	5.1
Price-to-NTA-per-share ratio	9.9
5-year share price return (% p.a.)	8.3
Dividend reinvestment plan	No

Sydney financial services company Fiducian Group was founded in 1996 by executive chairman Indy Singh, who owns more than a third of the company equity. Initially it specialised in the provision of masterfund, client administration and financial planning services to financial advisory groups. It has since expanded and is now a holding company with five divisions—Fiducian Portfolio Services is in charge of trustee and superannuation services; Fiducian Investment Management Services operates the company's managed funds; Fiducian Services is the administration service provider for all the company's products; Fiducian Financial Services manages the company's financial planning businesses; and Fiducian Business Services provides accounting and business services.

Latest business results (June 2023, full year)

Revenues rose as the company continued to expand its activities, but volatile financial markets drove profits down. For reporting purposes the company divides its operations into broad segments. The largest of these is now financial planning, which enjoyed strong growth, thanks in large part to the February 2022 acquisition of the financial planning business of the People's Choice Credit Union of South Australia (PCCUSA). Funds under advice rose to $4.6 billion, from $4.4 billion in June 2022. By contrast, revenues and profits for the funds management segment edged down in line with a slight decline in average funds under management for the year. A third segment, platform administration, offers portfolio wrap administration services to financial planners, and this business too reported a drop in revenues and profits. At June 2023 the total funds under management, advice and administration of $12.3 billion was up from $10.9 billion a year earlier.

Outlook

Fiducian managed 45 financial planning offices across Australia at June 2023, both company-owned and franchised, with a total of 80 financial advisers. It is continually seeking new offices to join the group, and it has also been achieving solid organic growth. At the same time, Fiducian itself has been named as a possible takeover target for a larger financial institution. The funds management business offers a suite of funds from various asset managers, and the company believes that its method of choosing managers with differing investment styles offers the ability to deliver above-average returns with greater diversification and reduced risk. Fiducian management have stated that, thanks especially to the PCCUSA acquisition, they now see excellent growth prospects in South Australia. However, the company is vulnerable to any major downturn in financial markets. At June 2023 it had no debt and cash holdings of more than $19 million.

Year to 30 June	2022	2023
Revenues ($mn)	69.3	72.4
Financial planning (%)	34	38
Funds management (%)	39	36
Platform administration (%)	27	26
EBIT ($mn)	19.1	17.7
EBIT margin (%)	27.5	24.4
Profit before tax ($mn)	19.1	17.7
Profit after tax ($mn)	13.3	12.3
Earnings per share (c)	42.31	39.14
Cash flow per share (c)	55.31	54.31
Dividend (c)	29.7	30.3
Percentage franked	100	100
Net tangible assets per share ($)	0.31	0.60
Interest cover (times)	~	~
Return on equity (%)	29.3	25.1
Debt-to-equity ratio (%)	~	~
Current ratio	1.7	2.5

Fortescue Metals Group Limited

ASX code: FMG

fortescue.com

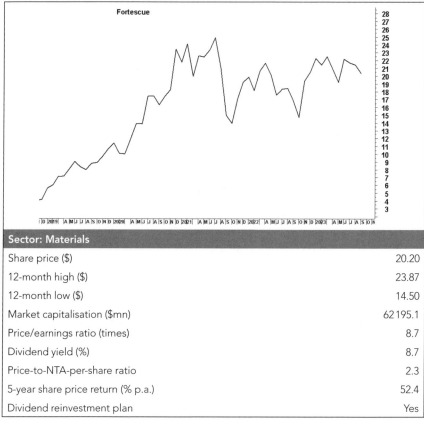

Sector: Materials	
Share price ($)	20.20
12-month high ($)	23.87
12-month low ($)	14.50
Market capitalisation ($mn)	62 195.1
Price/earnings ratio (times)	8.7
Dividend yield (%)	8.7
Price-to-NTA-per-share ratio	2.3
5-year share price return (% p.a.)	52.4
Dividend reinvestment plan	Yes

Perth-based Fortescue was founded in 2003. It has been responsible for discovering and developing some of the largest iron ore mines in the world and is today one of the world's largest iron ore producers, with operations at the Chichester Hub, the Solomon Hub and the Western Hub, all in the Pilbara region. Its Iron Bridge Magnetite Project has also begun production. It operates its own heavy-haul railway between its mines and Port Hedland. In addition, it is involved in the Belinga Iron Ore Project in Gabon. It is engaged in exploration work at sites in Western Australia, New South Wales and South Australia, with other ventures in South America and Kazakhstan. Nearly 90 per cent of its iron ore sales are to China.

Latest business results (June 2023, full year)

A lower iron ore price meant a further decline in revenues and profits for Fortescue, although because it reports its results in US dollars the revenues figure rose when converted to Australian dollars. Sales of 192 million tonnes were up 2 per cent from the previous year, but the average price received of US$95 per tonne was 5 per cent lower. Average production costs of US$17.54 per tonne were up 10 per cent, due especially to an increase in energy prices and other consumables and a rising wages bill. As noted, Fortescue reports its results in US dollars. The Australian dollar figures in this book—converted at prevailing exchange rates—are for guidance only.

Outlook

Fortescue is responsible for major iron ore developments. Its three primary production hubs, Chichester, Solomon and Western, have a combined annual production capacity of up to 200 million tonnes. Its US$4 billion Iron Bridge Magnetite Project, a joint venture with Formosa Steel, signifies Fortescue's entry into the high-grade segment of the iron ore market. It has begun production, with the first concentrate shipped in July 2023, and with forecast output of some 22 million tonnes annually. In February 2023 Fortescue entered into its first iron ore project outside Australia, with the Belinga development in Gabon. The initial shipment is expected by the end of 2023, and Fortescue has reported that the project has the potential to be of significant scale. With its new Fortescue Energy division the company is involved in a diverse flurry of green energy projects in many countries. Among these are green hydrogen and green ammonia schemes in Australia, the United States, Norway and Brazil and a green fertiliser project in Kenya.

Year to 30 June	2022	2023
Revenues ($mn)	23 821.9	25 180.6
EBIT ($mn)	12 323.3	10 688.1
EBIT margin (%)	51.7	42.4
Gross margin (%)	56.0	53.7
Profit before tax ($mn)	12 117.8	10 277.6
Profit after tax ($mn)	8489.0	7161.2
Earnings per share (c)	275.92	232.81
Cash flow per share (c)	343.95	317.43
Dividend (c)	207	175
Percentage franked	100	100
Net tangible assets per share ($)	8.05	8.71
Interest cover (times)	66.1	56.8
Return on equity (%)	34.8	27.3
Debt-to-equity ratio (%)	5.1	5.7
Current ratio	2.9	2.5

Grange Resources Limited

ASX code: GRR www.grangeresources.com.au

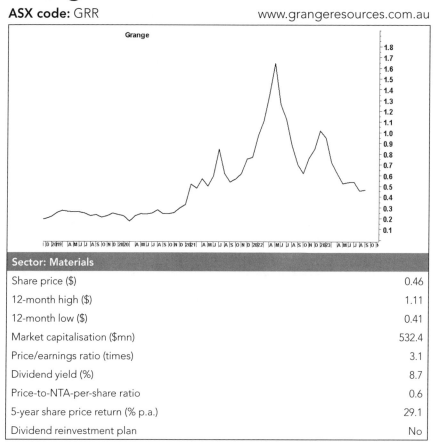

Sector: Materials	
Share price ($)	0.46
12-month high ($)	1.11
12-month low ($)	0.41
Market capitalisation ($mn)	532.4
Price/earnings ratio (times)	3.1
Dividend yield (%)	8.7
Price-to-NTA-per-share ratio	0.6
5-year share price return (% p.a.)	29.1
Dividend reinvestment plan	No

Based in Burnie, Tasmania, Grange Resources is an iron ore producer. It dates back to the 1980s when it was a Western Australian gold–copper miner with the name Sabminco. It is today involved in three major projects — the Savage River magnetite iron ore mine and the Port Latta pellet plant and port facility, both in Tasmania, and the Southdown Magnetite Project in Western Australia's Great Southern region.

Latest business results (June 2023, half year)

A weakened iron ore price and rising costs once again sent revenues and profits down. The company produced 1.19 million tonnes of iron ore pellets, down from 1.22 million tonnes in the June 2022 period and sold 1.21 million tonnes, up from 1.18 million tonnes. Lower iron ore prices were only partially offset by a favourable currency exchange rate, and it received an average price of $198.14 per tonne, down from $241.59 in the June 2022 half and $339.21 in June 2021. Production costs of $137.41 per tonne were up from $113.66, due mainly to lower concentrate production and higher energy costs.

Outlook

Grange's fortunes are quite dependent on movements in the iron ore market, which in turn have become fairly reliant on Chinese political and economic trends. The company's business involves the mining of magnetite from its Savage River mine and then refining it at the Port Latta plant into an iron ore concentrate that can be used for steel production. Its output is sold through a combination of long-term supply contracts and a spot sales tendering and contracting process. It estimates that Savage River has a mine life that will extend into the 2030s, and it is involved in a feasibility study of its North Pit Underground Development, with the company believing this project has the potential to deliver 6 million tonnes of ore annually for more than 10 years. Port Latta can produce more than 2 million tonnes annually of iron ore pellets and Grange plans to boost this. It is carrying out a feasibility study regarding its Southdown Magnetite Project in Western Australia, with a view to initiating mining operations. It believes the mine could be capable of an annual output of 5 million tonnes of high-quality magnetite concentrate, and in July 2023 it moved from 70 per cent to 100 per cent ownership of this asset. It may seek strategic partners to join it in the development of the mine. At June 2023 Grange had net cash holdings of more than $105 million.

Year to 31 December	2021	2022
Revenues ($mn)	781.7	594.6
EBIT ($mn)	462.1	252.3
EBIT margin (%)	59.1	42.4
Gross margin (%)	56.9	43.8
Profit before tax ($mn)	460.9	248.8
Profit after tax ($mn)	322.3	171.7
Earnings per share (c)	27.84	14.84
Cash flow per share (c)	34.99	19.64
Dividend (c)	12	4
Percentage franked	100	100
Interest cover (times)	~	~
Return on equity (%)	40.7	19.3
Half year to 30 June	2022	2023
Revenues ($mn)	341.1	278.4
Profit before tax ($mn)	191.9	101.0
Profit after tax ($mn)	132.2	70.4
Earnings per share (c)	11.42	6.08
Dividend (c)	2	0
Percentage franked	100	~
Net tangible assets per share ($)	0.74	0.82
Debt-to-equity ratio (%)	~	~
Current ratio	5.1	7.8

GUD Holdings Limited

ASX code: GUD   www.gud.com.au

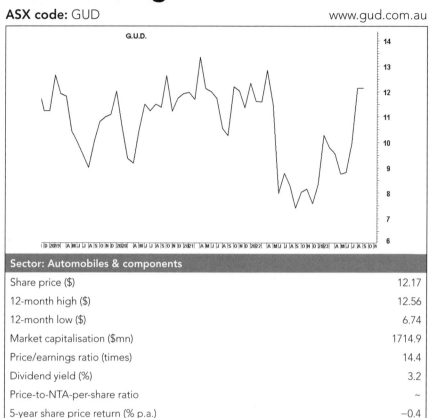

Sector: Automobiles & components	
Share price ($)	12.17
12-month high ($)	12.56
12-month low ($)	6.74
Market capitalisation ($mn)	1714.9
Price/earnings ratio (times)	14.4
Dividend yield (%)	3.2
Price-to-NTA-per-share ratio	~
5-year share price return (% p.a.)	−0.4
Dividend reinvestment plan	No

GUD, based in Melbourne and founded in 1940, is a manufacturer and distributor of a diversified range of auto and industrial products. Its main automotive brands include Ryco, Wesfil, Goss, Brown and Watson International—incorporating the Narva and Projecta brands—Griffiths Equipment, Innovative Mechatronic Group, AA Gaskets, Disc Brakes Australia and Hayman Reese. It has sold its Davey water pumps and water treatment products business.

Latest business results (June 2023, full year)

Continuing strength in its core auto parts businesses and a full year's contribution from AutoPacific Group (APG)—acquired in 2021 for $745 million—generated a solid result. The core Automotive division realised sales and profit growth, with a good performance from both existing businesses and several new acquisitions. New products and price rises contributed to the result. APG, a leader in the manufacture of towing and trailering accessories for four-wheel drives, utes and SUVs, has been classified as a separate division. Thanks to a full year's contribution, it reported sales and profits more than double the figures for the previous year. The small Davey business, which has since been sold, saw revenues fall but profits were up.

Outlook

The $65 million sale of Davey to ASX-listed Waterco, finalised in September 2023, transforms GUD into a pure-play automotive products company. It is now seeking to boost its exposure to the electric vehicle sector, with a view to becoming a leader in the electric vehicle aftermarket in Australia and New Zealand. However, it also maintains a broader vision, with the goal of becoming a front-runner in selected sectors of the automotive aftermarket. Growth in the aftermarket business is driven by the number of cars in Australia and their average age. According to the company, the number of cars in Australia grew from 19.1 million in 2021 to 19.6 million in 2022, with 22.4 million forecast for 2028. The average vehicle age of 11.1 years in 2022 is forecast to rise to 11.4 years by 2028. GUD sees its APG acquisition as part of its growth strategy, helping the company become one of the leaders in four-wheel-drive accessories and trailers domestically, with exports also a goal. However, with much of APG's production going to new-car buyers, sales have been held back by supply constraints for new vehicles. GUD also aims to become a global leader in specialist automotive lighting, and it has been achieving success with innovative new products from its Brown and Watson International and Vision X businesses.

Year to 30 June	2022	2023
Revenues ($mn)	826.8	1036.9
Automotive (%)	69	61
APG (%)	16	27
Davey (%)	15	12
EBIT ($mn)	147.8	183.8
EBIT margin (%)	17.9	17.7
Gross margin (%)	40.5	41.7
Profit before tax ($mn)	129.8	152.5
Profit after tax ($mn)	89.3	118.7
Earnings per share (c)	74.77	84.25
Cash flow per share (c)	105.34	121.30
Dividend (c)	39	39
Percentage franked	100	100
Net tangible assets per share ($)	~	~
Interest cover (times)	8.2	6.1
Return on equity (%)	14.4	13.7
Debt-to-equity ratio (%)	55.1	45.2
Current ratio	2.2	2.3

GWA Group Limited

ASX code: GWA   www.gwagroup.com.au

Sector: Capital goods	
Share price ($)	1.93
12-month high ($)	2.26
12-month low ($)	1.60
Market capitalisation ($mn)	511.8
Price/earnings ratio (times)	11.6
Dividend yield (%)	6.7
Price-to-NTA-per-share ratio	~
5-year share price return (% p.a.)	−2.5
Dividend reinvestment plan	No

Brisbane-based GWA is a prominent designer, importer and distributor of residential and commercial bathroom, laundry and kitchen products, marketed under brands that include Caroma, Dorf, Fowler, Methven, Stylus and Clark. About 10 per cent of its sales are in New Zealand, with 8 per cent to other countries, primarily the United Kingdom.

Latest business results (June 2023, full year)

Sales and profits fell, as the company was hit by a sluggish housing market. The first half was particularly weak, due to a decline in activity in the residential renovation and replacement segment, along with unexpected higher domestic freight rates. The company managed an improved domestic performance in the second half, thanks to disciplined cost management and a price increase, though with weakness in New Zealand hurting the result. For the full year, Australian revenues fell 1.2 per cent, with a 4.4 per cent decline in New Zealand. Other international markets saw sales revenues rise on a constant currency basis, but with a decline when converted to Australian dollars.

Outlook

After a long series of restructurings GWA is now almost completely exposed to a bathroom, laundry and kitchen fixtures market that in Australia is worth more than $2 billion annually. It claims market shares as high as 50 per cent for some of its products, with an overall share of about 23 per cent. Around 61 per cent of its sales go to the residential renovation and replacement market, and with households cutting back on discretionary spending it expects subdued activity in this sector for the near term. The commercial segment represents a further 21 per cent of sales, and the company forecasts increased demand for commercial projects, and especially for new health and aged care facilities. It also foresees continuing firm demand for commercial repair and renovation work. Residential detached housing is around 12 per cent of sales. Demand is easing, but the company notes that there can be a 15-month time lag between building approval and construction completion, and this will help sustain it at least until 2024. It is also optimistic about the outlook for multi-residential developments, although these represent just 6 per cent of sales. It has a solid pipeline of new products, including its Livewell range for the aged care sector and a series of commercial tapware products intended to capitalise on growing demand in the education and public amenities sectors. Products introduced in the previous two years now comprise more than 10 per cent of total sales.

Year to 30 June	2022	2023
Revenues ($mn)	418.7	411.8
EBIT ($mn)	74.8	70.4
EBIT margin (%)	17.9	17.1
Gross margin (%)	38.6	38.4
Profit before tax ($mn)	67.6	61.6
Profit after tax ($mn)	47.3	44.1
Earnings per share (c)	17.84	16.63
Cash flow per share (c)	25.39	23.66
Dividend (c)	15	13
Percentage franked	100	100
Net tangible assets per share ($)	~	~
Interest cover (times)	10.3	8.7
Return on equity (%)	15.8	14.5
Debt-to-equity ratio (%)	45.1	37.9
Current ratio	2.0	1.8

Hansen Technologies Limited

ASX code: HSN   www.hansencx.com

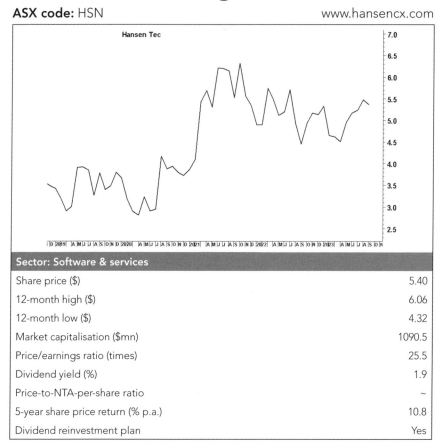

Sector: Software & services

Share price ($)	5.40
12-month high ($)	6.06
12-month low ($)	4.32
Market capitalisation ($mn)	1090.5
Price/earnings ratio (times)	25.5
Dividend yield (%)	1.9
Price-to-NTA-per-share ratio	~
5-year share price return (% p.a.)	10.8
Dividend reinvestment plan	Yes

Melbourne company Hansen Technologies dates back to an IT business launched in 1971. It later moved into the development of billing software systems and is today a significant global provider of these services, specialising in the electricity, gas, water, pay television and telecommunications sectors. Its Hansen Suite is a set of modular software products aimed at providing corporate customers with a diverse range of capabilities in evolving markets. Hansen has offices around the world, and services some 600 customers across 16 product lines in over 80 countries.

Latest business results (June 2023, full year)

Revenues and profits bounced back modestly, after falling in the previous year, although on an underlying basis profits edged down slightly. The company benefited from a stream of contract renewals and expansions from its customers, along with new business and price increases. The energy sector — mainly gas, electricity and water — represented 53 per cent of total income, with revenues up 11.5 per cent for the year. Communications businesses contributed the remaining 47 per cent of company turnover, with revenues flat for the year. A reduction in debt led to reduced borrowing costs.

Outlook

Though a small company, Hansen has developed a high reputation for its services. Its billing software enables its customers to create, sell and deliver new products and services, as well as manage and analyse customer data and control critical revenue management and customer support processes. Once it does business with a customer it stands to benefit further from a long-term stream of recurring revenue. Some 95 per cent of June 2023 revenue was recurring in nature, and the company experienced an attrition rate of less than 2 per cent. It views moves by its customers into renewable energy and 5G telecommunications as growth opportunities. Hansen's particular strategy is growth by acquisition, and with the billing services industry still fragmented and largely regionalised, it expects further attractive acquisition opportunities to present themselves. In particular, it is aiming at assets that own intellectual property and with recurring revenue streams that will help Hansen move into new regions or market segments. It is also seeking acquisitions in new businesses that complement or leverage its existing strengths. It has a dedicated mergers and acquisitions team, which has developed a proactive relationship with many brokers and bankers around the world, and with the ability to move quickly if it finds the right opportunities. It has also been building up its sales teams and expects continuing growth in the June 2024 year.

Year to 30 June	2022	2023
Revenues ($mn)	296.5	311.8
EBIT ($mn)	55.5	57.8
EBIT margin (%)	18.7	18.6
Profit before tax ($mn)	51.0	54.3
Profit after tax ($mn)	41.9	42.8
Earnings per share (c)	20.91	21.14
Cash flow per share (c)	41.91	43.03
Dividend (c)	12	10
Percentage franked	42	15
Net tangible assets per share ($)	~	~
Interest cover (times)	12.5	17.0
Return on equity (%)	13.9	13.1
Debt-to-equity ratio (%)	9.0	~
Current ratio	1.8	1.9

Harvey Norman Holdings Limited

ASX code: HVN www.harveynormanholdings.com.au

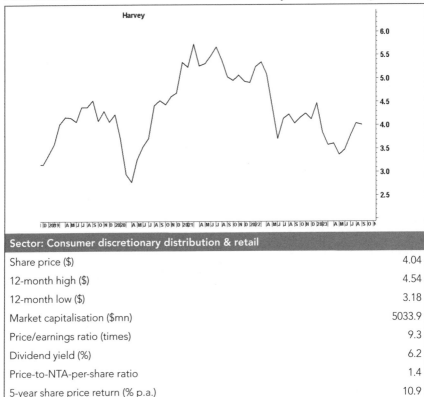

Sector: Consumer discretionary distribution & retail	
Share price ($)	4.04
12-month high ($)	4.54
12-month low ($)	3.18
Market capitalisation ($mn)	5033.9
Price/earnings ratio (times)	9.3
Dividend yield (%)	6.2
Price-to-NTA-per-share ratio	1.4
5-year share price return (% p.a.)	10.9
Dividend reinvestment plan	No

Sydney-based Harvey Norman, established in 1982, operates a chain of 308 retail stores specialising in electrical and electronic goods, home appliances, furniture, flooring, carpets and manchester items, throughout Australia, New Zealand, Ireland, Northern Ireland, Singapore, Malaysia, Slovenia and Croatia, under the Harvey Norman, Domayne and Joyce Mayne banners. The 197 Australian stores are independently held as part of a franchise operation, from which Harvey Norman receives income for advisory and advertising services. It also receives a considerable amount of income from its own stores, from its $4.1 billion property portfolio and from the provision of finance to franchisees and customers.

Latest business results (June 2023, full year)

Sales and profits fell in an environment of rising costs and weakening consumer spending. Total store sales—franchise and company-owned—fell 4 per cent to $9.19 billion, having edged down 2 per cent in the previous year. Revenues from the company's overseas stores of $2.6 billion was down 1.3 per cent. New Zealand, where the company operates 45 stores, was particularly weak. Franchise income received by Harvey Norman fell 10.7 per cent to $1.07 billion. Though only a quarter of company turnover, franchise revenue represents more than half of total profit, if property revaluations are excluded. Property revenue of $423 million was down 14.4 per cent. The company said that, excluding the impact of property revaluations, its after-tax profit was $471.9 million, down from $673.6 million.

Outlook

Harvey Norman is highly exposed to economic conditions. A rising wage bill and a continuing slowdown in discretionary consumer spending are particular challenges. It has high fixed costs, so even a modest decline in sales can translate to a larger fall in earnings. However, the company has pointed to a low jobless rate and rising immigration levels as reasons for optimism about future demand. In addition, it benefits from continuing technological innovation that induces customers to upgrade to large-screen and smart TVs and to the latest mobile phones and accessories. It plans to open two new franchised stores in Australia. Overseas, it sees particular potential in Malaysia. The opening of two new stores in July and August 2023 brought its total there to 30, and it expects to be operating 50 stores in the country by mid 2025 and up to 80 by the end of 2028. It also intends to expand in Croatia and is eyeing an entry to Hungary during the June 2025 year. It has postponed two store openings in New Zealand due to the sluggish economy there.

Year to 30 June	2022	2023
Revenues ($mn)	4505.7	4275.2
Retail (%)	63	65
Franchising operations (%)	26	24
Property (%)	11	10
EBIT ($mn)	1192.6	867.7
EBIT margin (%)	26.5	20.3
Gross margin (%)	33.4	32.1
Profit before tax ($mn)	1140.4	776.1
Profit after tax ($mn)	811.5	539.5
Earnings per share (c)	65.13	43.30
Cash flow per share (c)	72.40	50.63
Dividend (c)	37.5	25
Percentage franked	100	100
Net tangible assets per share ($)	2.83	2.94
Interest cover (times)	26.4	11.4
Return on equity (%)	20.0	12.4
Debt-to-equity ratio (%)	10.5	14.1
Current ratio	1.9	2.5

IDP Education Limited

ASX code: IEL   investors.idp.com

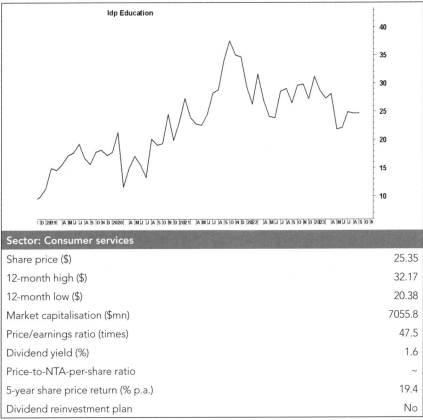

Sector: Consumer services	
Share price ($)	25.35
12-month high ($)	32.17
12-month low ($)	20.38
Market capitalisation ($mn)	7055.8
Price/earnings ratio (times)	47.5
Dividend yield (%)	1.6
Price-to-NTA-per-share ratio	~
5-year share price return (% p.a.)	19.4
Dividend reinvestment plan	No

Melbourne-based IDP Education dates back to 1969 and the launch of the Australian Asian Universities Cooperation Scheme, aimed at helping Asian students study in Australia. In 1981 it changed its name to the International Development Program (IDP) and opened a series of offices throughout Asia. It has since expanded through acquisition and organic growth, and today helps students from around the world find placements in higher education programs in English-speaking countries. It also works with University of Cambridge ESOL Examinations and the British Council to administer worldwide testing for the International English Language Testing System (IELTS). About 25 per cent of IDP's equity is held by 38 Australian universities.

Latest business results (June 2023, full year)

IDP enjoyed another excellent year as business continued to recover from pandemic-related lockdowns and travel restrictions that had severely hurt its activities. Revenue growth of 63 per cent for student placement services was the primary driver. This resulted from a 77 per cent increase in the numbers of Australian student placements and a 39 per cent rise in the company's other markets. By contrast, IDP's other main business, language testing, was hit by weakness in the key Indian market. Revenue growth of just 7 per cent for the year was mainly thanks to price increases. On a geographic basis, Asian revenues grew by 24 per cent, with Indian student placement revenues more than offsetting the decline there in language testing. Australasian revenues grew by 15 per cent, thanks especially to the big increase in student placements in Australia. The company's Rest of World segment includes some 40 countries and recorded a 26 per cent growth in revenues.

Outlook

IDP is investing heavily in transforming itself into a company with significant digital capabilities. It has helped develop a new English language testing platform that supports the delivery of the IELTS online. Its student placement operation now includes a technology platform that delivers a range of digital services to students. Its new FastLane app allows students to get an indicative placement offer from an institution instantly, and is achieving wide acceptance by universities and students. The company's strategy is to expand its physical network and complement this with digital platforms, and it believes this is already helping it gain market share. A new acquisition, Intake Education, should boost the company's business in Africa. However, IDP could be hurt by new Canadian student placement regulations that have significantly opened up the English testing market in Canada to some of its rivals.

Year to 30 June	2022	2023
Revenues ($mn)	793.3	981.9
Asia (%)	74	74
Rest of World (%)	21	21
Australasia (%)	5	5
EBIT ($mn)	159.7	223.5
EBIT margin (%)	20.1	22.8
Profit before tax ($mn)	152.1	207.3
Profit after tax ($mn)	102.6	148.5
Earnings per share (c)	36.86	53.36
Cash flow per share (c)	50.60	71.49
Dividend (c)	27	41
Percentage franked	12	21
Net tangible assets per share ($)	~	~
Interest cover (times)	23.7	16.7
Return on equity (%)	24.3	30.5
Debt-to-equity ratio (%)	~	8.2
Current ratio	1.6	1.3

IGO Limited

ASX code: IGO

www.igo.com.au

Sector: Materials	
Share price ($)	14.27
12-month high ($)	17.32
12-month low ($)	11.64
Market capitalisation ($mn)	10 806.2
Price/earnings ratio (times)	7.1
Dividend yield (%)	4.1
Price-to-NTA-per-share ratio	2.9
5-year share price return (% p.a.)	28.4
Dividend reinvestment plan	No

Perth company IGO, formerly known as Independence Group, was established in 2000 to explore for gold and nickel. Today it has operations at a number of sites in Western Australia. It mines for nickel, copper and cobalt at its Nova development. Following the 2022 acquisition of Western Areas it is also mining for nickel at the Forrestania and Cosmos projects. It holds a 49 per cent stake in Tianqi Lithium Energy Australia (TLEA), which itself has a 51 per cent holding of the Greenbushes Lithium Mine, the world's largest hard rock lithium mine, and 100 per cent ownership of the Kwinana Lithium Hydroxide Refinery.

Latest business results (June 2023, full year)

A sharply increased contribution from its TLEA lithium business saw underlying profits surge for IGO. Because of the company's 49 per cent equity holding in TLEA, its contribution was not included in the revenues figure, so profits were substantially higher than revenues. In addition, IGO reported a $979 million impairment charge, not included in the figures in this book, due to a write-down of its newly acquired Western Areas assets, and on a statutory basis the after-tax profit was $549 million. There was a 32 per cent increase in spodumene production from Greenbushes and

IGO's share of TLEA's profits rose from $177 million to $1.6 billion. During the year it produced 34 846 tonnes of nickel, up from 26 675 tonnes, thanks to the addition of the Forrestania mine. However, production problems at its Nova mine meant that copper and cobalt production fell. Having repaid a substantial amount of debt, IGO at June 2023 had net cash holdings of some $417 million.

Outlook

IGO has been working to transform itself into a major producer of commodities related to clean energy, thanks to its stake in TLEA and its acquisition of Western Areas. It expects Greenbushes June 2024 production to be roughly in line with June 2023. However, TLEA has been struggling at its Kwinana refinery, where full commercial production of battery-grade lithium hydroxide has been delayed by engineering challenges. Nickel production has expanded with the addition of the Forrestania project, though with a big jump in costs, and the Nova mine is believed to have only about three years of reserves remaining. IGO is developing a new mine at its Cosmos nickel project, but cost blowouts led to the big impairment write-down in the June 2023 accounts. It is considering the development of a nickel processing operation to produce battery-grade nickel sulphate for the lithium-ion battery industry.

Year to 30 June	2022	2023
Revenues ($mn)	900.6	1014.7
EBIT ($mn)	542.6	1709.0
EBIT margin (%)	60.2	168.4
Profit before tax ($mn)	536.6	1665.0
Profit after tax ($mn)	404.0	1528.0
Earnings per share (c)	53.35	201.78
Cash flow per share (c)	76.54	239.69
Dividend (c)	10	58
Percentage franked	100	100
Net tangible assets per share ($)	4.45	4.92
Interest cover (times)	142.8	49.1
Return on equity (%)	12.2	42.3
Debt-to-equity ratio (%)	15.2	~
Current ratio	1.6	2.8

Iluka Resources Limited

ASX code: ILU   www.iluka.com

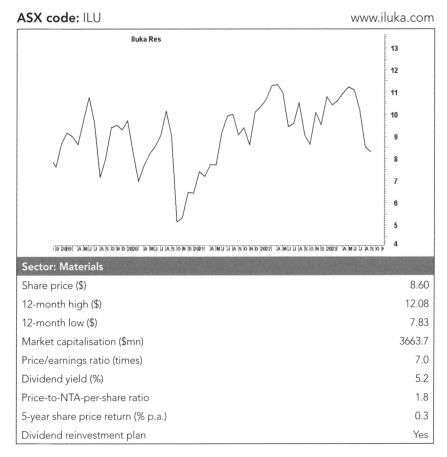

Sector: Materials	
Share price ($)	8.60
12-month high ($)	12.08
12-month low ($)	7.83
Market capitalisation ($mn)	3663.7
Price/earnings ratio (times)	7.0
Dividend yield (%)	5.2
Price-to-NTA-per-share ratio	1.8
5-year share price return (% p.a.)	0.3
Dividend reinvestment plan	Yes

Perth resources company Iluka started in 1954 as Westralian Sands, before merging in 1998 with the titanium mineral business of RGC and subsequently taking its present name. It is today a global leader in the mining and processing of mineral sands and rare earths. It has four operations in Western Australia: it manages the Cataby mine, a large ilmenite deposit with associated zircon and rutile; its Eneabba development involves the reclaiming and processing of a strategic stockpile high in monazite; its Narngulu mineral separation plant produces zircon, rutile and ilmenite products; and the Capel operation incorporates two synthetic rutile kilns. In South Australia it operates the world's largest zircon mine, Jacinth-Ambrosia, and it is involved in exploration and development work in other states. It holds a 20 per cent holding in ASX-listed Deterra Royalties, a company that receives royalties from certain BHP iron ore tenements.

Latest business results (June 2023, half year)

Weakening global demand for mineral sands saw revenues and profits down, despite prices generally rising a little. The company arranges its sales profile into four products—zircon volume sales were down 28 per cent from the June 2022 half;

ilmenite sales were down 16 per cent; synthetic rutile sales were down 14 per cent; and rutile sales were down 5 per cent. Profits were hurt by rising production costs, particularly for fuel and labour. In addition, the June 2022 result was more heavily weighted to higher-margin zircon sales. The company benefited from a weaker dollar during the period.

Outlook

Rare earth minerals are a key component for a growing number of high-tech industries. They are essential for the creation of powerful magnets for wind turbines and electric vehicles. They are also needed in vehicle emission control units and in modern rechargeable batteries, as well as for many defence industry applications, including jet engines and drones. Consequently, they are in growing demand globally. However, with some 80 per cent of the world's supply now coming from China, countries in the West have been urging Australia, which has large-scale reserves of rare earths, to boost output. In 2022 Iluka received a $1.2 billion loan from the government to build Australia's first rare earth refinery at its Eneabba operation, with production expected from 2025. In February 2023 it decided to proceed with its rutile-rich critical minerals development at Balranald in New South Wales. Also in February 2023 it initiated a detailed feasibility study into a possible new rare earths and zircon development at Wimmera in Victoria.

Year to 31 December	2021	2022
Revenues ($mn)	1316.1	1611.3
EBIT ($mn)	494.1	736.1
EBIT margin (%)	37.5	45.7
Profit before tax ($mn)	488.9	730.1
Profit after tax ($mn)	354.3	517.3
Earnings per share (c)	83.90	122.48
Cash flow per share (c)	112.09	155.89
Dividend (c)	24	45
Percentage franked	100	100
Interest cover (times)	105.1	~
Return on equity (%)	24.6	29.7
Half year to 30 June	2022	2023
Revenues ($mn)	836.6	745.4
Profit before tax ($mn)	404.3	291.4
Profit after tax ($mn)	286.0	203.8
Earnings per share (c)	67.80	48.30
Dividend (c)	25	3
Percentage franked	100	100
Net tangible assets per share ($)	4.46	4.69
Debt-to-equity ratio (%)	~	~
Current ratio	3.0	5.0

Insurance Australia Group Limited

ASX code: IAG　　　　　　　　　　　　　　　www.iag.com.au

Sector: Insurance	
Share price ($)	5.79
12-month high ($)	6.10
12-month low ($)	4.33
Market capitalisation ($mn)	14 127.6
Price/earnings ratio (times)	17.1
Dividend yield (%)	2.6
Price-to-NTA-per-share ratio	5.3
5-year share price return (% p.a.)	−2.6
Dividend reinvestment plan	Yes

Sydney-based Insurance Australia Group (IAG), formerly NRMA Insurance, dates back to 1925, when the National Roads and Motorists' Association began providing insurance to its members in New South Wales and the Australian Capital Territory. It subsequently demutualised and listed on the ASX. It has grown through acquisition, and is now the largest general insurance group in Australia and New Zealand. Its brands include NRMA Insurance, CGU, SGIO, SGIC, WFI and Swann Insurance, all in Australia, as well as NZI, State and AMI in New Zealand. In Victoria it provides general insurance products under the RACV brand through a distribution and underwriting relationship with RACV, and it underwrites the Coles Insurance brand nationally through a distribution agreement with Coles. It operates a reinsurance partnership with Berkshire Hathaway, the American company associated with famed investor Warren Buffett, and Berkshire Hathaway owns 4 per cent of IAG's equity.

Latest business results (June 2023, full year)

Revenues rose and profits more than doubled in a good result. However, a large part of the profit increase came from the release of $392 million that had been kept as a provision for pandemic-related claims that did not occur. The company also benefited from higher returns on its investment portfolio. Nevertheless, the general insurance business was also solid, with gross written premium growth of 10.6 per cent, which was due mainly to the company's success in pushing through premium increases. The underlying insurance margin — insurance and investment profits as a percentage of premiums, a key measure of profitability — fell from 14.6 per cent to 12.6 per cent, with inflation driving higher the average size of motor and homes claims. New Zealand business, representing about a quarter of company income, benefited from premium increases, but the insurance margin was hit badly by some 50 000 claims lodged due to flooding in Auckland and the impact of Cyclone Gabrielle.

Outlook

IAG occupies a strong position in the Australian and New Zealand general insurance business, giving it considerable pricing power. But the insurance business is inherently volatile, and any unforeseen major natural disaster has the capacity to take a big chunk from the company's earnings. It is benefiting from moves taken in 2021 to reset its business, with a simpler operating model and a greater focus on its core activities. It believes it can continue to raise premiums and achieve gross written premium growth in the low double-digits in the June 2024 year, with an insurance margin of 13.5 per cent to 15.5 per cent.

Year to 30 June	2022	2023
Revenues ($mn)	18 347.0	19 851.0
Profit before tax ($mn)	564.0	1354.0
Profit after tax ($mn)	347.0	832.0
Earnings per share (c)	14.09	33.92
Cash flow per share (c)	19.74	41.46
Dividend (c)	11	15
Percentage franked	32	30
Net tangible assets per share ($)	0.95	1.09
Return on equity (%)	5.6	13.0
Debt-to-equity ratio (%)	26.2	23.6

IPH Limited

ASX code: IPH   www.iphltd.com.au

Sector: Commercial & professional services	
Share price ($)	7.75
12-month high ($)	10.12
12-month low ($)	7.09
Market capitalisation ($mn)	1820.1
Price/earnings ratio (times)	17.7
Dividend yield (%)	4.3
Price-to-NTA-per-share ratio	~
5-year share price return (% p.a.)	10.6
Dividend reinvestment plan	Yes

Sydney-based IPH, formed in 2014 but with roots that stretch back to 1887, is a holding company for a group of businesses offering a wide range of intellectual property services and products. These include the filing, prosecution, enforcement and management of patents, designs, trademarks and other intellectual property. IPH incorporates six brands: AJ Park, Griffith Hack, Smart & Biggar, Spruson & Ferguson, Pizzeys and Applied Marks. It operates from 25 offices in Australia, Canada, China, Hong Kong, Indonesia, Malaysia, New Zealand, the Philippines, Singapore and Thailand. In August 2023 it announced the acquisition of Canadian intellectual property firm Ridout & Maybee.

Latest business results (June 2023, full year)

Revenues and profits grew, thanks especially to a notable contribution from Canada's Smart & Biggar, acquired in October 2022. The result also benefited from dollar weakness during the year. Australian and New Zealand business declined slightly, with a second-half recovery unable to offset first-half weakness, as patent market filing volumes fell. Nevertheless, IPH said it remained the market leader in Australia for this business, with patent market share for the year of 32.4 per cent. In Asia the company enjoyed good business in Singapore. However, this was partially offset by a significant decline in patent and trade market revenue in China and Hong Kong. In particular, the company suffered as a large client chose to exit from the Chinese market, part of a recent trend of Western enterprises seeking alternative manufacturing locations to China. The company also incurred costs from a cyber-attack on its computer systems during the year.

Outlook

IPH has established itself as one of the leaders in Australia, New Zealand, Canada and South-East Asia in the intellectual property business. It has expanded steadily, through organic growth and acquisition. As it grows it achieves economies of scale that boost margins. It is achieving success with its strategy of leveraging its network of companies, with a growing number of referrals between member companies in different regions. In May 2023 it opened its first office in the Philippines. It continues to seek out further acquisition opportunities, with the stated goal of becoming the leading intellectual property services group in markets outside the US, EU or Japan. It regards its $387 million acquisition of Smart & Biggar—a leader in Canada's intellectual property sector—as transformational for the company. The subsequent acquisition for approximately $74 million of Ridout & Maybee will further consolidate IPH's position in Canada, and it has been actively pursuing further Canadian acquisition opportunities.

Year to 30 June	2022	2023
Revenues ($mn)	385.1	490.1
Australia & New Zealand (%)	73	57
Asia (%)	27	24
Canada (%)	0	19
EBIT ($mn)	115.8	155.5
EBIT margin (%)	30.1	31.7
Profit before tax ($mn)	111.1	135.3
Profit after tax ($mn)	82.4	99.0
Earnings per share (c)	37.77	43.90
Cash flow per share (c)	55.90	67.56
Dividend (c)	30.5	33
Percentage franked	45	37
Net tangible assets per share ($)	~	~
Interest cover (times)	24.8	8.5
Return on equity (%)	19.2	19.7
Debt-to-equity ratio (%)	7.0	51.0
Current ratio	2.8	3.2

JB Hi-Fi Limited

ASX code: JBH   investors.jbhifi.com.au

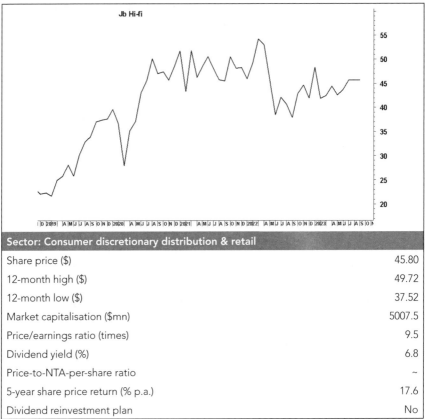

Sector: Consumer discretionary distribution & retail	
Share price ($)	45.80
12-month high ($)	49.72
12-month low ($)	37.52
Market capitalisation ($mn)	5007.5
Price/earnings ratio (times)	9.5
Dividend yield (%)	6.8
Price-to-NTA-per-share ratio	~
5-year share price return (% p.a.)	17.6
Dividend reinvestment plan	No

Melbourne-based JB Hi-Fi dates back to the opening in 1974 of a single recorded music store in the Melbourne suburb of East Keilor. It has since grown into a nationwide chain of home electronic and home appliance products outlets, and it has also expanded to New Zealand. In Australia it operates The Good Guys chain of home appliance stores, as well as specialised divisions that sell to the commercial and educational sectors. The company also maintains an online presence. At the end of June 2023 it operated 202 JB Hi-Fi and JB Hi-Fi Home stores in Australia, 14 JB Hi-Fi stores in New Zealand and 106 The Good Guys stores in Australia.

Latest business results (June 2023, full year)

In a volatile and competitive consumer goods market JB Hi-Fi was able to boost sales and its market share, but profits were down. JB Hi-Fi Australia enjoyed a sales increase of 5.6 per cent, or 4.8 per cent on a same-store basis, with pre-tax profit edging up, and particular strength in communications, audio, accessories, games hardware and services. The Good Guys achieved a 0.8 per cent rise in revenues, with strength in refrigeration, laundry, floorcare, personal care and audio, but profits fell by 12 per cent. The small New Zealand operation actually enjoyed the best sales growth — up 11.3 per cent — but with profits plunging, and New Zealand profit margins remain substantially below those for Australian operations. Total company online sales fell, having soared during the COVID pandemic period.

Outlook

JB Hi-Fi has a strong brand image throughout Australia and great customer loyalty. It has shown an impressive ability to contain costs. It continues to open new stores, though at a slower pace than in previous years. It is boosting floor space at its stores for growth categories such as mobile phones, gaming and connected technology. It is also working to strengthen its online operations. It is realising continuing strong demand for items that include mobile phones, gaming consoles and small kitchen appliances, such as coffee machines. It is also boosting its commercial side, and sees considerable potential for growth, especially among small and medium-sized businesses. It is working to boost its limping New Zealand operations, with new personnel, store upgrades, the opening of three to five new stores annually over three years and the development of commercial sales. However, as long as Australian consumer spending remains subdued, the company could be forced to discount more in order to maintain sales, cutting into profit margins.

Year to 30 June	2022	2023
Revenues ($mn)	9232.0	9626.4
JB Australia (%)	67	68
The Good Guys (%)	30	29
JB New Zealand (%)	3	3
EBIT ($mn)	795.4	773.4
EBIT margin (%)	8.6	8.0
Gross margin (%)	22.5	22.7
Profit before tax ($mn)	775.3	747.1
Profit after tax ($mn)	544.9	524.6
Earnings per share (c)	479.24	479.96
Cash flow per share (c)	668.16	683.35
Dividend (c)	316	312
Percentage franked	100	100
Net tangible assets per share ($)	~	~
Interest cover (times)	41.2	35.3
Return on equity (%)	42.1	38.9
Debt-to-equity ratio (%)	~	~
Current ratio	1.1	1.2

Johns Lyng Group Limited

ASX code: JLG   investors.johnslyng.com.au

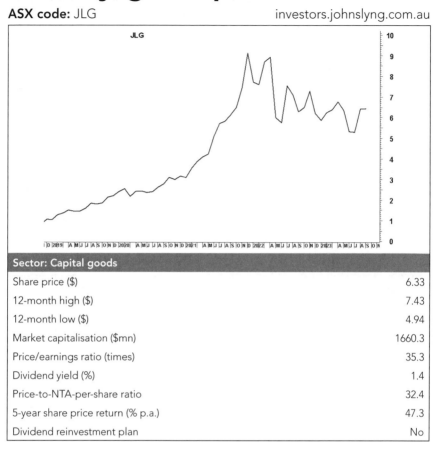

Sector: Capital goods	
Share price ($)	6.33
12-month high ($)	7.43
12-month low ($)	4.94
Market capitalisation ($mn)	1660.3
Price/earnings ratio (times)	35.3
Dividend yield (%)	1.4
Price-to-NTA-per-share ratio	32.4
5-year share price return (% p.a.)	47.3
Dividend reinvestment plan	No

Specialist Melbourne building company Johns Lyng Group was established in 1953 as Johns & Lyng Builders. It has a particular specialty in building and restoration work for insurance claims, with operations nationwide under various brands, and its clients include most of Australia's leading insurance companies. It also undertakes a range of commercial construction work and operates a fast-growing strata services business. The company has grown substantially through acquisition and at June 2023 operated from 109 offices in Australia under the Johns Lyng, Steamatic and Bright & Duggan brands and from 51 offices in the United States under the Steamatic and Reconstruction Experts brands.

Latest business results (June 2023, full year)

Another strong result from its core Insurance Building and Restoration Services division, compounded by a further series of acquisitions during the year, generated a solid rise in revenues and profits. Revenues for this division rose 53 per cent, with EBITDA up 61 per cent. Johns Lyng has a particular specialty in repair work related to major weather disasters, mainly storms and floods, and this business contributed a third of the division's income. American revenues rose 25 per cent to represent nearly

20 per cent of the total. The small Commercial Building Services division, which is engaged in flooring work, emergency repairs, retail shop fitting and heating and air conditioning services, enjoyed another year of double-digit growth in revenues and profits. But the Commercial Construction division remained in the red.

Outlook

Johns Lyng has developed a high reputation for its insurance-related work and it continues to expand, with major new clients in recent years and market share gains. It sees particular potential in its strata management activities, with substantial cross-selling opportunities for its building work. Thanks to a series of acquisitions in this highly fragmented sector it now manages some 95 000 strata lots at around 3800 properties, and it expects this number will continue to grow as it rolls out its Strata Building Services division. Following the 2019 acquisition of the US-based fire and flood restoration business Steamatic, the company has been researching the American market. It believes that the US can become a key pillar of long-term future growth, leading to the US$145 million acquisition in 2022 of insurance repair services provider Reconstruction Experts. The July 2023 acquisitions of Smoke Alarms Australia and Link Fire Holdings are intended to lay the foundations for a new Essential Home Services division. The company's early June 2024 forecast is for continuing double-digit growth in revenues and profits.

Year to 30 June	2022	2023
Revenues ($mn)	895.0	1281.3
Insurance building & restoration (%)	84	89
Commercial building services (%)	6	6
Commercial construction (%)	10	5
EBIT ($mn)	59.1	97.2
EBIT margin (%)	6.6	7.6
Gross margin (%)	22.0	21.5
Profit before tax ($mn)	56.9	93.4
Profit after tax ($mn)	25.1	46.8
Earnings per share (c)	10.34	17.94
Cash flow per share (c)	16.55	26.05
Dividend (c)	5.7	9
Percentage franked	100	100
Net tangible assets per share ($)	0.09	0.20
Interest cover (times)	28.1	80.1
Return on equity (%)	13.0	13.8
Debt-to-equity ratio (%)	~	~
Current ratio	1.2	1.3

Jumbo Interactive Limited

ASX code: JIN www.jumbointeractive.com

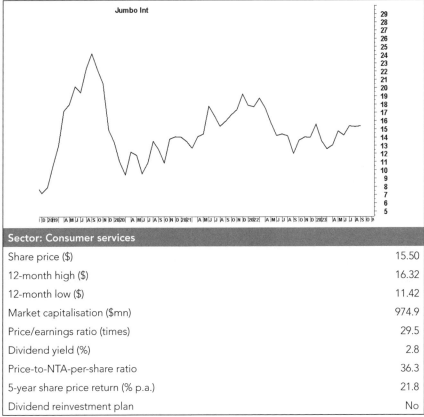

Sector: Consumer services	
Share price ($)	15.50
12-month high ($)	16.32
12-month low ($)	11.42
Market capitalisation ($mn)	974.9
Price/earnings ratio (times)	29.5
Dividend yield (%)	2.8
Price-to-NTA-per-share ratio	36.3
5-year share price return (% p.a.)	21.8
Dividend reinvestment plan	No

Jumbo Interactive was founded in Brisbane in 1995 as an internet service provider, but has since evolved into a major operator of internet services for lotteries. Its core business, Oz Lotteries, involves the provision of lottery services for The Lottery Corporation — which was formerly a part of Tabcorp — at its ozlotteries.com website. These lotteries include OzLotto, Powerball, Lotto Strike and Lucky Lotteries. It has introduced a software-as-a-service (SaaS) business, called Powered by Jumbo, that manages lotteries for charitable organisations and other institutions. It also runs a Managed Services division to provide lottery management services to charities and other organisations on an international basis. Through this division it has entered the British market with the acquisition of Gatherwell and StarVale and the Canadian market with the acquisition of Stride Management.

Latest business results (June 2023, full year)

Revenues and profits were up, but this reflected the acquisitions of Stride in June 2022 and StarVale in November 2022. Excluding their contributions, the performance was mixed. Large Powerball and OzLotto jackpots are an important stimulus to sales, and the company was hurt by a decline in these from the previous year. Total lottery transaction value for the company of $441.6 million was down 2.3 per cent, although price increases meant that actual company revenues from its lottery activities edged up from the previous year. The number of active online lottery customers fell 0.5 per cent to 914 215, with an average spend per active lottery customer of $467.12, down 1.7 per cent. Revenues slipped 0.7 per cent for the SaaS business, with profits also down. However, the Managed Services division saw revenues and profits up substantially, thanks to the 2022 overseas acquisitions.

Outlook

Jumbo is a significant beneficiary of the Australian love of gambling, although its rate of growth has slowed considerably compared to some earlier years. A new software platform and a vigorous marketing campaign have helped stimulate its recent growth. It is also enjoying success with new apps for mobile devices, and reports that these have succeeded in attracting a new demographic of younger customers. Its lottery business is benefiting from price increases implemented in May 2023, helping offset increases in the service fees it pays to The Lottery Corporation. It sees good potential in its overseas businesses, with modest investments expected to generate steady growth. The acquisitions have also delivered a significant increase in the number of the company's active customers, and it regards active customers as the foundation for future expansion.

Year to 30 June	2022	2023
Revenues ($mn)	104.3	118.7
EBIT ($mn)	46.5	48.2
EBIT margin (%)	44.6	40.6
Profit before tax ($mn)	46.3	47.4
Profit after tax ($mn)	32.2	33.1
Earnings per share (c)	51.50	52.60
Cash flow per share (c)	65.48	70.55
Dividend (c)	42.5	43
Percentage franked	100	100
Net tangible assets per share ($)	0.82	0.43
Interest cover (times)	459.9	186.0
Return on equity (%)	36.1	34.3
Debt-to-equity ratio (%)	~	~
Current ratio	2.6	1.6

Lifestyle Communities Limited

ASX code: LIC

www.lifestylecommunities.com.au

Sector: Real estate management & development	
Share price ($)	17.44
12-month high ($)	20.32
12-month low ($)	14.01
Market capitalisation ($mn)	1823.3
Price/earnings ratio (times)	25.5
Dividend yield (%)	0.7
Price-to-NTA-per-share ratio	3.5
5-year share price return (% p.a.)	24.6
Dividend reinvestment plan	No

Melbourne company Lifestyle Communities, founded in 2003, develops and maintains residential and retirement communities throughout Victoria, in growth areas of Melbourne and in regional centres. These are aimed at over 50s and retirees. At June 2023 it had 21 communities in operation and was managing 3549 homes with more than 5000 residents.

Latest business results (June 2023, full year)

Revenues and underlying profits rose more modestly than in the previous year, when the company had been bouncing back from the depths of the COVID pandemic, which had necessitated the lockdown of many of its facilities and also led to a sharp slowing of business activity. The company settled 356 new homes, down from 401 in the previous year. A growing number of homes under management meant that annuity income rose 16 per cent to $47.2 million, comprising $34.3 million in site rental fees, up from $29.7 million a year earlier, and $12.9 million in deferred management fees from the resale of existing homes, up from $10.9 million. The launch of seven new projects during the year led to a substantial increase in debt. Note that on a statutory basis the company's profit figures also include non-cash property revaluations, which are not included in the figures in these pages. Thus, on a statutory basis the after-tax profit actually fell from $88.9 million in the June 2022 year to $81.9 million in June 2023.

Outlook

Lifestyle Communities operates on a model that differs from many retirement facilities, in that its residents own their homes but pay a site rental fee to the company for the land, on a 90-year lease. It thus has a growing annuity-style income as its business expands. It promotes its communities to active seniors, and the average age of new residents is around 67, which is about 10 years younger than the average age for new residents of retirement homes generally in Australia. Its goal has been to buy two or three new sites each year, focused on Melbourne's growth corridors and on key Victorian regional centres. It accelerated its activities during the June 2023 year with construction beginning on seven new projects. It is also ready to commence work on a further three communities. These, along with other projects already in development, are expected to generate 1400 to 1700 new home settlements by June 2026. As the company expands, its site rental income will increase. In addition, the number of resales — sales of established homes — will also grow, boosting its deferred management fee income.

Year to 30 June	2022	2023
Revenues ($mn)	224.2	232.1
EBIT ($mn)	101.2	109.4
EBIT margin (%)	45.1	47.1
Gross margin (%)	20.8	21.0
Profit before tax ($mn)	99.6	106.5
Profit after tax ($mn)	61.4	71.1
Earnings per share (c)	59.00	68.41
Cash flow per share (c)	61.21	71.59
Dividend (c)	10.5	11.5
Percentage franked	100	100
Net tangible assets per share ($)	4.33	4.99
Interest cover (times)	71.5	40.8
Return on equity (%)	14.8	14.5
Debt-to-equity ratio (%)	53.6	69.8
Current ratio	0.8	2.2

Lindsay Australia Limited

ASX code: LAU www.lindsayaustralia.com.au

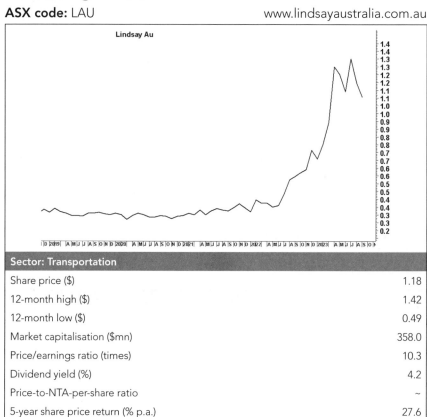

Sector: Transportation	
Share price ($)	1.18
12-month high ($)	1.42
12-month low ($)	0.49
Market capitalisation ($mn)	358.0
Price/earnings ratio (times)	10.3
Dividend yield (%)	4.2
Price-to-NTA-per-share ratio	~
5-year share price return (% p.a.)	27.6
Dividend reinvestment plan	Yes

Brisbane-based trucking company Lindsay Australia was established as Lindsay Brothers in 1953. It quickly developed a specialty in the transportation of fruit and vegetables and became a pioneer in the use of refrigerated trailers. It is today a fully integrated transport, logistics and rural supply company, servicing customers in the food-processing, food services, rural and horticultural sectors, mainly in the eastern states. It operates from 19 branches, with 16 terminals and a fleet of more than 1000 vehicles. Its Lindsay Rural business operates from 21 stores, supplying more than 1500 farmers with an extensive range of agricultural services and products. In August 2023 it acquired rural merchandise retailer W.B. Hunter.

Latest business results (June 2023, full year)

The company benefited from strongly growing demand for transportation and logistics services, and recorded double-digit rises in revenues and sales. Its transport business saw revenues up 29.5 per cent to $513 million, with profits surging 76.1 per cent as the company built up its fleet and expanded its activities. It benefited from what it described as unprecedented demand for road and rail services and was able to implement price increases to meet inflationary pressures, especially rising fuel costs.

By contrast, its rural activities saw revenue growth of just 4 per cent to $163 million as the company expanded its business activities, but with profits falling by 9.5 per cent, due especially to rising costs.

Outlook

Lindsay occupies a strong position in the transportation and rural supplies sectors within its regions of operation. It has benefited from consolidation within the industry, and during the June 2023 year was able to acquire a large parcel of assets as a result of the collapse of a major competitor, Scotts Refrigerated Logistics. During the June 2024 year it expects to invest in the growth of its road fleet, including the acquisition of larger new trailer combinations that will boost operational performance. Its rail business continues to grow in importance, and rail revenues now represent a quarter of total transport income. Lindsay Rural uses its branch network to supply its customer base with a wide diversity of agricultural products. It also provides specialty advisory services through a team of agronomists. Lindsay has particular strength in horticulture and through its association with Visy Board is a leading provider of cardboard packaging for the horticultural industry. The $35 million acquisition of W.B. Hunter boosts Lindsay's exposure to the Victorian and New South Wales rural economies, and the company is seeking further acquisition opportunities.

Year to 30 June	2022	2023
Revenues ($mn)	553.1	676.2
Horticulture (%)	63	59
Commercial (%)	37	41
EBIT ($mn)	34.2	59.2
EBIT margin (%)	6.2	8.8
Profit before tax ($mn)	27.5	49.4
Profit after tax ($mn)	19.2	34.5
Earnings per share (c)	6.39	11.40
Cash flow per share (c)	19.23	25.55
Dividend (c)	3.2	4.9
Percentage franked	0	61
Net tangible assets per share ($)	~	~
Interest cover (times)	5.4	6.8
Return on equity (%)	20.1	30.0
Debt-to-equity ratio (%)	2.9	~
Current ratio	1.1	1.4

Lovisa Holdings Limited

ASX code: LOV   www.lovisa.com.au

Sector: Consumer discretionary distribution & retail	
Share price ($)	21.99
12-month high ($)	27.21
12-month low ($)	17.88
Market capitalisation ($mn)	2371.5
Price/earnings ratio (times)	34.8
Dividend yield (%)	3.1
Price-to-NTA-per-share ratio	~
5-year share price return (% p.a.)	17.0
Dividend reinvestment plan	No

Melbourne-based jewellery and accessories retailer Lovisa Holdings was established in 2010. It specialises in lower-cost but up-to-date fashion pieces. It has grown significantly since its launch, and at July 2023 operated 168 stores in Australia and a further 633 in nearly 40 countries globally, including 190 stores in the US.

Latest business results (July 2023, full year)

Revenues and profits rose strongly in a good result. Much of the good performance came from an expansion of the store network, but the company also benefited from same-store sales growth of 6.3 per cent. Price increases introduced in the previous year, in response to inflationary pressures, helped the result. Tight cost control boosted margins. Higher borrowings, to finance store expansion, led to rising interest payments. The strongest growth came from abroad. Australian sales were up 12.9 per cent to $174.8 million, European sales rose 29.6 per cent to $181.6 million and for the Americas the growth was 78.1 per cent to $128.2 million. During the year the company opened 210 new stores, including 78 in the US and 60 in Europe, and closed 38. It entered 12 new markets—Hong Kong, Taiwan, Namibia, Botswana, Mexico, Colombia, Peru, Morocco, Italy, Spain, Hungary and Romania.

Outlook

Lovisa remains optimistic about the outlook, despite a slowdown in discretionary consumer spending in many countries, as it continues to build its store network. It aims to develop some 100 new fashion jewellery lines every week for a younger demographic and sees digital media, rather than traditional media, as an important part of its strategy. It operates dedicated e-commerce sites across all its key markets and also maintains a presence on popular online marketplaces. Product innovation is a key component of what Lovisa believes to be its competitive advantage, and the company employs large product development teams in Melbourne, London and Los Angeles to ensure the company meets market demand. It is working to streamline and optimise its supply base in Asia while also ensuring it can speedily deliver new products to its stores. It operates a warehouse in China to support its Asian, American and African stores, another in Australia and has opened a large new company-operated warehouse in Poland to replace the former third-party logistics warehouse, providing the company with enhanced flexibility and improved service levels. It is changing its Middle Eastern business from a franchise arrangement to a company-operated one. With its business largely transacted in US dollars, it is affected by currency rate trends.

Year to 2 July*	2022	2023
Revenues ($mn)	458.7	596.5
Australia/New Zealand (%)	38	33
Europe (%)	31	31
Americas (%)	16	21
Africa (%)	10	8
Asia (%)	5	6
EBIT ($mn)	83.0	106.0
EBIT margin (%)	18.1	17.8
Profit before tax ($mn)	76.7	92.9
Profit after tax ($mn)	58.4	68.2
Earnings per share (c)	54.33	63.25
Cash flow per share (c)	109.96	132.13
Dividend (c)	74	69
Percentage franked	30	87
Net tangible assets per share ($)	~	~
Interest cover (times)	13.8	8.3
Return on equity (%)	106.1	94.5
Debt-to-equity ratio (%)	~	41.7
Current ratio	0.8	1.0

*3 July 2022

Lycopodium Limited

ASX code: LYL

www.lycopodium.com

Sector: Capital goods	
Share price ($)	10.18
12-month high ($)	11.42
12-month low ($)	6.30
Market capitalisation ($mn)	400.3
Price/earnings ratio (times)	8.6
Dividend yield (%)	8.0
Price-to-NTA-per-share ratio	4.2
5-year share price return (% p.a.)	21.4
Dividend reinvestment plan	No

Founded in 1992, Perth-based Lycopodium is an engineering and project management company with activities around the world. Its particular specialty is the evaluation and development of projects related to minerals processing, materials handling and infrastructure, across a wide range of commodities, and for clients in many countries. Lycopodium has offices in Australia, South Africa, Canada, Ghana and the Philippines.

Latest business results (June 2023, full year)

Lycopodium reported an excellent result, with growth in revenues and profits and strength across its three core operating sectors of resources, infrastructure and industrial processes. Several major projects were completed during the year, including the Bomboré Gold Project in Burkina Faso, the Motheo Copper Project in Botswana and the Séguéla Gold Project in the Ivory Coast. Domestically, the company worked with the Australian Rail Track Corporation on boosting the efficiency of rail services between Sydney and Melbourne. It also continued to provide design consultancy services to biotechnology company CSL for the development of new production facilities and to Australia's Nuclear Science and Technology Organisation for its synchrotron facility. On a divisional basis, the Minerals Asia Pacific division achieved an excellent increase in revenues, but with profits lower. Minerals Africa had an excellent year, with growing revenues and profits more than doubling. The small, high-margin Process Industries division also recorded strong growth in profits.

Outlook

Despite slowing economies around the world, Lycopodium expects a significant level of investment to continue in the resources sector, related especially to the global energy transition, which is boosting demand for low-emission technologies. Thanks to many new development projects, especially for lithium, copper, cobalt and nickel, it forecasts solid demand for its services. Lycopodium claims to be a leader in the design and delivery of battery metals projects and has begun work on two major lithium projects, at Kathleen Valley in Western Australia and at the Goulamina project in Mali. It also sees continuing steady growth in demand for iron ore and for gold as supporting further growth in new and expansion projects, and it is involved with early work on Barrick Gold's Reko Diq project in Pakistan, one of the world's largest undeveloped copper–gold deposits. Domestically, it is optimistic that a number of large, publicly funded infrastructure projects will ramp up across the country, including rail developments, in which Lycopodium already has a significant involvement. In the industrial processes sector it believes it will benefit from a slow return to domestic manufacturing, together with the rise of new markets in recycling, wastewater and hydrogen.

Year to 30 June	2022	2023
Revenues ($mn)	228.7	323.9
Minerals Asia Pacific (%)	45	54
Minerals Africa (%)	19	19
Minerals North America (%)	21	13
Process industries (%)	5	4
Project services Africa (%)	3	3
EBIT ($mn)	39.8	64.1
EBIT margin (%)	17.4	19.8
Profit before tax ($mn)	38.9	63.3
Profit after tax ($mn)	27.2	46.8
Earnings per share (c)	68.39	117.71
Cash flow per share (c)	82.53	133.73
Dividend (c)	54	81
Percentage franked	100	100
Net tangible assets per share ($)	2.04	2.41
Interest cover (times)	123.3	~
Return on equity (%)	28.8	43.5
Debt-to-equity ratio (%)	~	~
Current ratio	1.6	1.9

Macquarie Group Limited

ASX code: MQG   www.macquarie.com

Sector: Financial services	
Share price ($)	177.65
12-month high ($)	195.74
12-month low ($)	149.51
Market capitalisation ($mn)	68 657.6
Price/earnings ratio (times)	12.7
Dividend yield (%)	4.2
Price-to-NTA-per-share ratio	2.3
5-year share price return (% p.a.)	9.9
Dividend reinvestment plan	Yes

Sydney-based Macquarie Group was established in 1969 as Hill Samuel Australia, a subsidiary of a British merchant bank. It is now Australia's leading locally owned investment bank, with a wide spread of activities and boasting special expertise in specific industries that include finance, resources and commodities, energy, infrastructure and real estate. It operates in 34 markets around the world, and international business accounts for around 70 per cent of total company revenue.

Latest business results (March 2023, full year)

Macquarie achieved another solid result, with rising revenues and profits, though not on the sparkling scale of the previous year. The largest of the bank's four broad operating segments, Commodities and Global Markets, posted its third straight gain in profits of more than 50 per cent, thanks especially once again to the volatility of global energy markets. There was also a strong contribution from financial markets, particularly in foreign exchange, interest rate and credit products. The Banking and Financial Services segment was also again strong, with growth in the loan portfolio and in deposits, along with improved margins, partially offset by credit impairment charges and rising costs. By contrast, the Macquarie Capital segment, which had seen profits in the previous year surge more than threefold, in the latest reporting period experienced a sharp earnings decline, with lower fee income for both capital markets and mergers and acquisitions. The fourth segment, Macquarie Asset Management, reversed its gains of the previous year, with reduced gains on asset realisations.

Outlook

At a time of global economic uncertainty, Macquarie is not prepared to make forecasts for the March 2024 year, although it is well positioned to profit from economic and market volatility. For future growth it is placing a strong emphasis on building a portfolio of decarbonisation assets, through its Green Investment Group, with green energy projects in hand across more than 25 countries and profits growing strongly. It has become a leader in the wind and solar industries, and is expanding its involvement in emerging technologies, including utility-scale energy storage, hydrogen fuel and zero-emission transport. Already it has some 14GW of clean energy projects in operation, and the planned capacity of new investments under development more than tripled during the March 2023 year to over 95GW. It is also helping European countries as they work to strengthen their energy security, including the development of Germany's first privately financed liquefied natural gas terminal. Domestically it has slowed its advance into the home loans market as intense competition slashes margins.

Year to 31 March	2022	2023
Operating income ($mn)	17 324.0	19 122.0
Net interest income ($mn)	2860.0	3028.0
Operating expenses ($mn)	10 785.0	12 130.0
Profit before tax ($mn)	6539.0	6992.0
Profit after tax ($mn)	4706.0	5182.0
Earnings per share (c)	1312.71	1398.75
Dividend (c)	622	750
Percentage franked	40	40
Non-interest income to total income (%)	83.5	84.2
Net tangible assets per share ($)	64.59	75.89
Cost-to-income ratio (%)	62.3	63.4
Return on equity (%)	18.6	16.8
Return on assets (%)	1.5	1.3

Magellan Financial Group Limited

ASX code: MFG   www.magellangroup.com.au

Sector: Financial services	
Share price ($)	9.28
12-month high ($)	13.30
12-month low ($)	7.52
Market capitalisation ($mn)	1683.7
Price/earnings ratio (times)	9.7
Dividend yield (%)	9.3
Price-to-NTA-per-share ratio	2.0
5-year share price return (% p.a.)	−8.2
Dividend reinvestment plan	No

Sydney-based Magellan is a specialist investment management company that evolved in 2006 from the ASX-listed Pengana Hedgefunds Limited. Its main business is Magellan Asset Management, which offers managed funds to retail and institutional investors, with particular specialties in global equities, global listed infrastructure, Australian equities—through Airlie Funds Management—and sustainable asset investments.

Latest business results (June 2023, full year)

Revenues and underlying profits crashed in a second bad year for Magellan as it continued to suffer from a series of client outflows from its funds. Consequently, funds under management plummeted from $113.9 billion at June 2021 to $61.3 billion in June 2022 and $39.7 billion at June 2023. Management and services fees were down 44 per cent to $330.2 million, with performance fees flat at just $11.5 million. With a reduced headcount the company managed a small reduction in its expenses during the year, but such was the fall in revenues that the cost-to-income ratio rose from 20.7 per cent to 35.2 per cent.

Outlook

Magellan has been through a torrid period, as the continuing underperformance of its main global funds sparked a chain of client withdrawals. It led to management upheavals, including the departure of its co-founder and chief investment officer Hamish Douglass. Now, under new management, it is seeking to rebuild, based on a five-year transformation program. The company recognises that its business is heavily dependent on the quality of its staff, in order to boost investment performance, and it has announced a staff engagement and retention program, including a bonus plan and the issue of share options to employees. In October 2022 it changed the organisational structure of its investment team, with a view to improving investment decisions, based especially on its well-established research capability. Seeking near-term growth opportunities, it has launched the Energy Transition Investment Strategy for its clients. This is a portfolio of global companies that will benefit from moves around the world towards a low-carbon future and takes advantage of Magellan's extensive infrastructure and sustainability research experience. In March 2023 it launched the new Airlie Small Companies Fund, a retail fund that leverages the Airlie team's strong track record in the Australian market. For the longer term the company is seeking to reduce the risk associated with concentration on a small number of strategies and individuals. It is also looking for opportunities in growth areas such as alternative investments and private markets. Magellan remains debt-free, with more than $373 million in cash holdings at June 2023.

Year to 30 June	2022	2023
Revenues ($mn)	605.6	343.0
EBIT ($mn)	518.7	254.1
EBIT margin (%)	85.6	74.1
Profit before tax ($mn)	516.5	252.6
Profit after tax ($mn)	401.0	174.3
Earnings per share (c)	216.61	95.43
Cash flow per share (c)	220.47	98.73
Dividend (c)	179	86.7
Percentage franked	77	85
Net tangible assets per share ($)	4.89	4.66
Interest cover (times)	441.8	~
Return on equity (%)	39.8	17.5
Debt-to-equity ratio (%)	~	~
Current ratio	2.4	2.0

Medibank Private Limited

ASX code: MPL   www.medibank.com.au

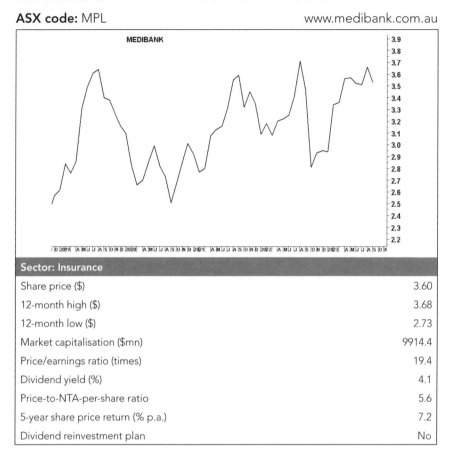

Sector: Insurance	
Share price ($)	3.60
12-month high ($)	3.68
12-month low ($)	2.73
Market capitalisation ($mn)	9914.4
Price/earnings ratio (times)	19.4
Dividend yield (%)	4.1
Price-to-NTA-per-share ratio	5.6
5-year share price return (% p.a.)	7.2
Dividend reinvestment plan	No

Melbourne-based Medibank Private was established by the Australian government in 1976 as a not-for-profit private health insurer under the Health Insurance Commission. It was privatised and listed on the ASX in 2014. Today it is Australia's largest private health insurer, with a market share of around 27 per cent, operating under the Medibank and ahm brands. It has also branched into other areas, including travel insurance, pet insurance, life insurance, income protection and funeral insurance. Its Medibank Health division specialises in the provision of healthcare services over the phone, online or face-to-face.

Latest business results (June 2023, full year)

Rising policyholder numbers helped generate a good result for Medibank, although a $163.4 million increase in net investment income also made a significant contribution. The company reported that underlying after-tax profit, which adjusts for the normalisation of investment returns, rose 14.8 per cent to $499.6 million. Policyholder numbers grew by a net 0.9 per cent during the year, with this increase again concentrated in the budget ahm health insurance brand, which is aimed at younger customers. Health insurance revenues rose 4.2 per cent, and net claims were up 3.4 per cent. The very small Medibank Health business saw revenues edge down on a reduction in telehealth business, but profits continued to grow. During the year Medibank was hit by a major cyberattack and consequently incurred substantial costs, which have been reported as significant items.

Outlook

Medibank occupies a central role in the national health sector. Nevertheless, its business is heavily regulated, and it is difficult to achieve significant growth. In addition, as the population ages, customer claim volumes have sometimes been growing faster than premium rises. Maintaining a tight control on expenses is important for the company, and it has a target of $30 million in productivity savings in the three years to June 2025. It also aims for annual organic profit growth of at least 15 per cent in the three years to June 2026, and with a rising market share. It is benefiting from an apparent new focus among Australians on their health and wellbeing, triggered by the COVID pandemic. Young people particularly—a lower-claiming customer demographic—are now more inclined than ever to seek out private health insurance. It is also realising substantial growth in travel insurance and in the provision of insurance for non-residents in Australia. It is expanding its no-gap network of health providers who offer members a range of selected medical procedures with no out-of-pocket costs.

Year to 30 June	2022	2023
Revenues ($mn)	7128.5	7355.3
EBIT ($mn)	562.4	728.9
EBIT margin (%)	7.9	9.9
Profit before tax ($mn)	560.0	727.1
Profit after tax ($mn)	393.9	511.1
Earnings per share (c)	14.30	18.56
Cash flow per share (c)	18.48	22.86
Dividend (c)	13.4	14.6
Percentage franked	100	100
Net tangible assets per share ($)	0.59	0.64
Interest cover (times)	~	~
Return on equity (%)	20.5	25.4
Debt-to-equity ratio (%)	~	~
Current ratio	1.5	1.8

Metcash Limited

ASX code: MTS   www.metcash.com

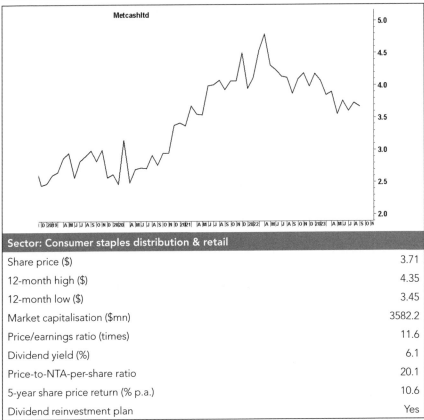

Sector: Consumer staples distribution & retail

Share price ($)	3.71
12-month high ($)	4.35
12-month low ($)	3.45
Market capitalisation ($mn)	3582.2
Price/earnings ratio (times)	11.6
Dividend yield (%)	6.1
Price-to-NTA-per-share ratio	20.1
5-year share price return (% p.a.)	10.6
Dividend reinvestment plan	Yes

Sydney-based Metcash, with a history dating back to the 1920s, is a leading food and liquor wholesaler. Its Food division supports a network of more than 1600 independently owned grocery stores and supermarkets, mainly under the IGA and Foodland brands. The Liquor division is Australia's largest supplier of liquor to independently owned liquor retailers, with more than 12 000 customers. These include the Independent Brands Australia network of Cellarbrations, The Bottle-O, Duncans, Thirsty Camel, IGA Liquor, Big Bargain and Porters. The Hardware division operates the Independent Hardware Group, which supplies more than 1500 stores, including the Mitre 10, Home Timber & Hardware and Total Tools chains.

Latest business results (April 2023, full year)

Metcash reported another positive result, with all divisions achieving growth. The core Food division saw EBIT up 1.8 per cent on a small increase in sales. Convenience stores were particularly strong, thanks especially to excellent food service sales and the normalisation of customer activity after the restrictions of COVID. Liquor division EBIT rose 6.9 per cent, with sales revenues up 6.2 per cent, as customers maintained their preference for local shopping, along with a continuation of the drink-at-home trend. Once again the best result came from the Hardware division. It recorded a 14.6 per cent increase in EBIT, with sales up 15.3 per cent, thanks to solid underlying demand, as well as a reflection of the success of the company's strategy of investing in its own stores, often together with independent partners. Though just 15 per cent of total revenues, the Hardware division now contributes more than 40 per cent of company EBIT.

Outlook

Metcash is reaping the rewards of its five-year MFuture restructuring process that has cut costs and enhanced the attractiveness of its offerings. It expects by 2026 to have upgraded around 90 per cent of its store network. It also believes that it is a beneficiary of a move by consumers to local neighbourhood shopping, and it has noted a change during 2023, with customers focusing more on value items. It has been working to improve the competitiveness of the IGA network, with a particular focus on price, range of products and quality. As Australia's leading supplier to independent liquor retailers, it has noted a slowdown in the rate of sales growth during 2023 as consumers are hit by cost-of-living pressures. Hardware sales continue to grow, and the company is expanding its hardware network, although business could be dented by a slowing of construction activity.

Year to 30 April	2022	2023
Revenues ($mn)	15 164.8	15 803.4
Food (%)	55	53
Liquor (%)	31	32
Hardware (%)	14	15
EBIT ($mn)	434.8	461.4
EBIT margin (%)	2.9	2.9
Gross margin (%)	11.1	11.7
Profit before tax ($mn)	423.8	436.1
Profit after tax ($mn)	299.6	307.5
Earnings per share (c)	30.48	31.85
Cash flow per share (c)	48.38	49.97
Dividend (c)	21.5	22.5
Percentage franked	100	100
Net tangible assets per share ($)	0.29	0.18
Interest cover (times)	60.4	20.0
Return on equity (%)	25.4	28.6
Debt-to-equity ratio (%)	17.3	32.2
Current ratio	1.1	1.1

Michael Hill International Limited

ASX code: MHJ · investor.michaelhill.com

Sector: Consumer discretionary distribution & retail	
Share price ($)	0.95
12-month high ($)	1.25
12-month low ($)	0.86
Market capitalisation ($mn)	360.7
Price/earnings ratio (times)	10.3
Dividend yield (%)	7.9
Price-to-NTA-per-share ratio	~
5-year share price return (% p.a.)	6.5
Dividend reinvestment plan	No

Jewellery retailer Michael Hill dates back to the opening of its first store in Whangarei, New Zealand, in 1979. It grew steadily, expanding to Australia and Canada, and it moved its headquarters to Brisbane. In June 2023 it acquired the jewellery and watch retailer Bevilles. In July 2023, thanks to this acquisition, it incorporated 304 stores, up from 280 a year earlier, with 172 in Australia, 86 in Canada and 46 in New Zealand.

Latest business results (July 2023, full year)

The company reported its third consecutive year of higher sales, but rising costs sent profits down. Sales grew by 5.8 per cent, or 8 per cent for the year on a same-store basis — with double-digit growth in the second half — as the company closed five underperforming stores. There was also a one-month contribution from Bevilles. The best growth came from Australia, with New Zealand also firm. Canada, which in the previous year achieved a 40 per cent jump in revenues, this time saw flat sales. Digital sales of $41.3 million were a touch down from June 2022. During the year the company opened two new stores in Australia and one in Canada.

Outlook

Michael Hill has a combination of strategies that it believes can deliver sustainable long-term growth. A key tactic is the elevation of the Michael Hill brand, driving its transition from a name associated with discount-led promotions into a brand for unique high-margin, high-quality jewellery. The $45 million acquisition of Bevilles is part of the growth strategy. Bevilles operates 26 stores in Australia, with an emphasis on the value end of the fine jewellery category, and Michael Hill believes it can expand the business to Canada and New Zealand, with the possibility of 80 to 100 Bevilles stores by 2028. It also plans a significant rollout of new Michael Hill stores. A new bespoke brand, TenSevenSeven, being introduced during the June 2024 year, focuses on serving the high end of the market, with unique personalised diamond rings. The Brilliance by Michael Hill loyalty program has grown to more than two million members, from 200 000 in June 2020, with members shopping more frequently and spending considerably more than other customers. It is seeking further international expansion, and has begun marketing to customers in Singapore and Malaysia through the online fashion store Zalora. New Zealand business has been hurt by heightened crime, with $5 million spent in the June 2023 year on security measures to protect staff, customers and stores.

Year to 2 July*	2022	2023
Revenues ($mn)	595.2	629.6
Australia (%)	51	53
Canada (%)	29	28
New Zealand (%)	20	19
EBIT ($mn)	73.3	59.7
EBIT margin (%)	12.3	9.5
Gross margin (%)	64.7	64.2
Profit before tax ($mn)	65.7	49.7
Profit after tax ($mn)	46.7	35.2
Earnings per share (c)	12.03	9.20
Cash flow per share (c)	25.41	24.30
Dividend (c)	7.5	7.5
Percentage franked	0	0
Net tangible assets per share ($)	0.20	~
Interest cover (times)	9.7	6.5
Return on equity (%)	25.3	18.3
Debt-to-equity ratio (%)	~	~
Current ratio	1.8	1.6

*26 June 2022

Mineral Resources Limited

ASX code: MIN　　　　　　　　　　www.mineralresources.com.au

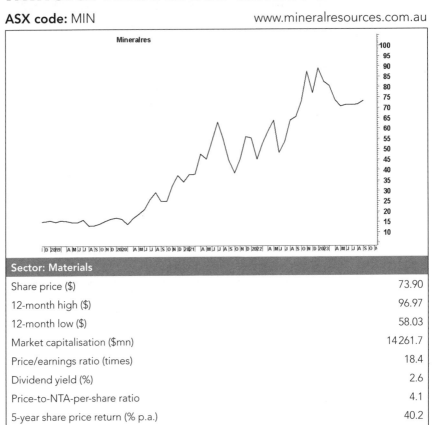

Sector: Materials	
Share price ($)	73.90
12-month high ($)	96.97
12-month low ($)	58.03
Market capitalisation ($mn)	14261.7
Price/earnings ratio (times)	18.4
Dividend yield (%)	2.6
Price-to-NTA-per-share ratio	4.1
5-year share price return (% p.a.)	40.2
Dividend reinvestment plan	Yes

Mineral Resources, based in Perth, was founded in 1993, and is a mining and mining services company. Its iron ore business incorporates two producing hubs in Western Australia, at Yilgarn and Pilbara, and it is developing a new project at Onslow. Its lithium business incorporates holdings in the Wodgina and the Mount Marion lithium mines. The mining services side incorporates several subsidiaries: CSI Mining Services provides contract crushing, screening and processing services; Process Minerals International is a minerals processor and exporter, with a specialty in bringing new mines into production; and Mining Wear Parts provides specialist parts to the mining, quarrying and recycling industries.

Latest business results (June 2023, full year)

The company's surging lithium business generated a big jump in revenues and profits, easily offsetting some relative weakness in other businesses. A near-doubling of spodumene concentrate prices saw the company's lithium revenues and underlying EBITDA more than double. Iron ore sales of 17.5 million tonnes were down from 19.2 million tonnes in the previous year. However, the average price received by the company of US$93 per tonne was 13 per cent higher, and total iron ore revenues and profits rose, although at the EBIT level this business remained in the red. The mining services business performed well, thanks especially to a high level of demand from the company's own mining activities, and revenues rose. However, mining services profits fell as the company was hit by price inflation and rising labour costs. The company also reported a $787 million impairment charge, related mainly to a write-down of iron ore assets, and on a statutory basis the after-tax profit was $243.3 million.

Outlook

As lithium demand grows Mineral Resources is moving towards investing in its own downstream processing plant, either in Western Australia, near its Wodgina mine, or in Asia. It has been in talks with automotive companies as possible partners for this development. It has rejected proposals by its Wodgina partner Albermarle to invest in processing facilities in China. The two companies are working to boost output at Wodgina. Mineral Resources is investigating moves into underground mining at its Mt Marion joint venture and is seeking further opportunities to strengthen its upstream lithium businesses. Its iron ore business is set to expand substantially with its $3 billion Onslow Iron Project, one of Western Australia's largest-ever iron ore developments. Initial shipments are expected by mid 2024, with a target of 35 million tonnes annually from the first stage and a mine life of at least 30 years.

Year to 30 June	2022	2023
Revenues ($mn)	3418.0	4779.1
Iron ore (%)	58	45
Lithium (%)	23	40
Mining services (%)	19	15
EBIT ($mn)	669.5	1343.2
EBIT margin (%)	19.6	28.1
Profit before tax ($mn)	559.0	1110.0
Profit after tax ($mn)	400.0	769.0
Earnings per share (c)	211.76	402.57
Cash flow per share (c)	398.22	638.35
Dividend (c)	100	190
Percentage franked	100	100
Net tangible assets per share ($)	17.02	17.89
Interest cover (times)	6.7	6.9
Return on equity (%)	12.4	22.9
Debt-to-equity ratio (%)	21.3	52.7
Current ratio	3.7	2.8

Monadelphous Group Limited

ASX code: MND   www.monadelphous.com.au

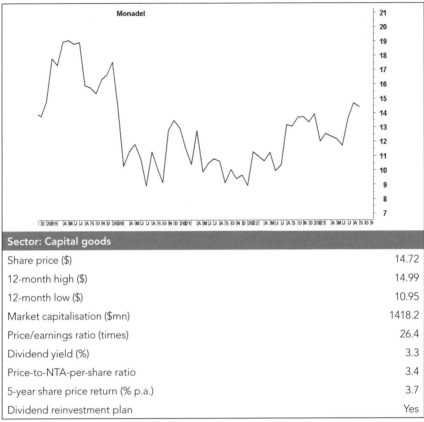

Sector: Capital goods	
Share price ($)	14.72
12-month high ($)	14.99
12-month low ($)	10.95
Market capitalisation ($mn)	1418.2
Price/earnings ratio (times)	26.4
Dividend yield (%)	3.3
Price-to-NTA-per-share ratio	3.4
5-year share price return (% p.a.)	3.7
Dividend reinvestment plan	Yes

Perth-based Monadelphous, established in 1972, is an engineering company that provides a wide range of construction, maintenance, project management and support services to the minerals, energy and infrastructure industries. It operates from branches throughout Australia, with a client base that includes most of the country's resource majors. It has also established a presence in overseas markets that include New Zealand, China, Mongolia, Papua New Guinea, Chile and the Philippines. Its Zenviron joint venture is involved in large-scale renewable energy projects and its Mondium joint venture is involved in minerals processing.

Latest business results (June 2023, full year)

Revenues fell back and profits were largely flat in a mixed year for the company. Monadelphous classifies its activities into two broad segments. The Maintenance and Industrial Services division enjoyed a second successful year, with 11 per cent growth in revenues to $1.3 billion and high levels of demand for maintenance services across all sectors, with oil and gas especially strong. By contrast, the Engineering Construction division, which in the previous year suffered a 21 per cent decline in sales, reported a further 30 per cent drop, following delays in the start of some major new projects.

Productivity improvements led to higher profit margins, despite inflationary pressures on its businesses. The Zenviron joint venture made a growing contribution, thanks to its exposure to the renewable energy sector.

Outlook

Monadelphous plays an important role in the Australian minerals, energy and infrastructure industries, and with an order backlog of some $2 billion at August 2023 it stands to benefit from growing demand for its services over coming years. More than 30 per cent of its income derives from the iron ore sector, where the outlook is positive. A growing relationship with Fortescue Metals Group has led to some significant new contracts. A further 30 per cent of revenues comes from the oil and gas sector, and it is experiencing a steady flow of work for new LNG projects and strong demand for maintenance services. In addition, it sees strongly growing investment in projects relating to lithium and other battery metals as providing more opportunities. It is also optimistic about the outlook for clean energy, with its Zenviron joint venture actively involved in the wind energy and battery storage sectors, and with hydrogen developments showing potential. But the company is concerned about skills shortages, which are driving labour costs higher and leading to delays in completing projects. At June 2023 Monadelphous had net cash holdings of more than $175 million.

Year to 30 June	2022	2023
Revenues ($mn)	1809.5	1721.0
Maintenance & industrial services (%)	60	71
Engineering construction (%)	40	29
EBIT ($mn)	76.9	76.9
EBIT margin (%)	4.2	4.5
Gross margin (%)	6.8	6.9
Profit before tax ($mn)	73.5	73.4
Profit after tax ($mn)	52.2	53.5
Earnings per share (c)	54.90	55.85
Cash flow per share (c)	89.70	90.43
Dividend (c)	49	49
Percentage franked	100	100
Net tangible assets per share ($)	4.28	4.37
Interest cover (times)	29.4	~
Return on equity (%)	12.9	12.6
Debt-to-equity ratio (%)	~	~
Current ratio	2.0	2.0

National Australia Bank Limited

ASX code: NAB   www.nab.com.au

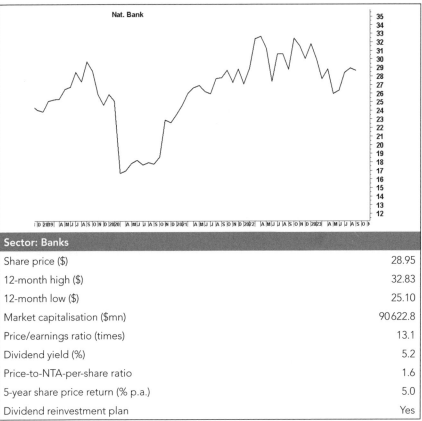

Sector: Banks	
Share price ($)	28.95
12-month high ($)	32.83
12-month low ($)	25.10
Market capitalisation ($mn)	90 622.8
Price/earnings ratio (times)	13.1
Dividend yield (%)	5.2
Price-to-NTA-per-share ratio	1.6
5-year share price return (% p.a.)	5.0
Dividend reinvestment plan	Yes

National Australia Bank, based in Melbourne, has a history dating back to the establishment of the National Bank of Australasia in 1858. It is one of Australia's largest banks, with a wide spread of financial activities and particular strength in business banking. It owns the Bank of New Zealand, and also operates offices in several countries in Asia. It is involved in financial planning and wealth management, including with its long-established JBWere advisory service. Other activities include the nabtrade online broking service and the ubank online bank.

Latest business results (March 2023, half year)

Rising interest rates and NAB's strength in business banking helped it post a solid increase in profits. The Business and Private Banking division represents some 40 per cent of bank income and earnings, and profits rose nearly 20 per cent from the March 2022 half, thanks to volume growth and increased margins, partially offset by rising costs. By contrast, the Personal Banking division saw profits slide again, although underlying profit was up, with a notable benefit from the June 2022 acquisition of Citibank's Australian consumer business. New Zealand was strong, with double-digit gains in revenues and profits, reflecting rising margins and volume growth.

The Corporate and Institutional Banking division also recorded higher income and profits, with increased market activity more than offsetting lower lending volumes.

Outlook

NAB expects a slowdown in economic growth, but believes Australia can avoid a pronounced economic correction. A key focus for the bank in recent years has been to simplify, automate and digitise its businesses, while also increasing its use of data and analytics. This has helped it manage costs, and consequently in the September 2023 year it was expecting productivity benefits of some $400 million, helping offset short-term inflationary pressures. It is working to boost its Business and Private Banking division, where it is already a market leader. It is realising excellent growth in new business transaction accounts for small and medium-sized enterprises, and has experienced an increase in its market share of small business lending. Its private wealth business has also been increasing its share of the home lending and deposits market. A further area of growth is the ubank online bank, which has been recording strong new customer acquisition in the target segment of under-35-year-olds. NAB continues its roll-out of a streamlined digital home loan system for mortgage brokers. However, due to intense levels of competition it sees little near-term growth potential for its mortgage business.

Year to 30 September	2021	2022
Operating income ($mn)	16931.0	18446.0
Net interest income ($mn)	13793.0	14840.0
Operating expenses ($mn)	7863.0	8702.0
Profit before tax ($mn)	9206.0	9897.0
Profit after tax ($mn)	6558.0	7104.0
Earnings per share (c)	199.33	220.69
Dividend (c)	127	151
Percentage franked	100	100
Non-interest income to total income (%)	18.5	19.5
Cost-to-income ratio (%)	46.4	47.2
Return on equity (%)	10.6	11.7
Return on assets (%)	0.7	0.7
Half year to 31 March	2022	2023
Operating income ($mn)	8828.0	10529.0
Profit before tax ($mn)	4863.0	5715.0
Profit after tax ($mn)	3480.0	4070.0
Earnings per share (c)	106.92	129.50
Dividend (c)	73	83
Percentage franked	100	100
Net tangible assets per share ($)	17.70	18.09

Netwealth Group Limited

ASX code: NWL   www.netwealth.com.au

Sector: Financial services	
Share price ($)	15.32
12-month high ($)	16.14
12-month low ($)	11.36
Market capitalisation ($mn)	3736.4
Price/earnings ratio (times)	55.6
Dividend yield (%)	1.6
Price-to-NTA-per-share ratio	36.0
5-year share price return (% p.a.)	14.1
Dividend reinvestment plan	No

Based in Melbourne, wealth management business Netwealth was founded in 1999. Through its wealth management platform it specialises in superannuation products, investor-directed portfolio services for self-managed superannuation, managed accounts and managed funds. The founding Heine family own more than half the company equity.

Latest business results (June 2023, full year)

In another uncertain period for financial markets, with a slight decline in the Australian wealth management market, Netwealth continued to grow. During the year it recorded inflows to its funds of $18.7 billion, in line with the previous year, but outflows of $8.8 billion, which was 55 per cent higher. Net inflows of $9.9 billion were down from $13 billion in the previous year. Total funds under administration at June 2023 of $70.3 billion were up 26 per cent from a year earlier and the number of client accounts was up 10 per cent to 127 507. Total operating expenses rose 24 per cent to $114 million, including a 65 per cent jump in investment in technology and communication infrastructure as the company continued its growth. An acceleration in marketing initiatives led to a sharp 82 per cent jump in advertising and marketing expenses.

Outlook

Netwealth runs a wealth management platform, which is a comprehensive software system that is designed to help financial advisers, clients and others to track their investment portfolios, perform research on new investments and execute trades. It is estimated that as much as $1 trillion in investor assets are currently being managed on such platforms in Australia and it is a highly competitive business. The leaders are major financial institutions such as Insignia Financial, BT Financial Group, AMP Group, Colonial First State and Macquarie Group. But catching up on them are several smaller and fast-growing firms like Netwealth, which have a particular strength in the development of user-friendly technology. Netwealth says that, based on industry analysis, it was again Australia's fastest-growing platform provider in the 12 months to March 2023, boosting its market share by 1 per cent to 6.7 per cent. It continues to invest heavily in its IT infrastructure in order to promote continuing growth, with a particular target of increased business from high net worth individuals. A major product relaunch in September 2023 is also expected to boost the company's presence in what it describes as the mass affluent and emerging affluent segments, generating new streams of revenue and boosting fund inflows. At June 2023 Netwealth had no debt and more than $109 million in cash holdings.

Year to 30 June	2022	2023
Revenues ($mn)	172.9	207.0
EBIT ($mn)	81.6	97.5
EBIT margin (%)	47.2	47.1
Profit before tax ($mn)	81.1	97.0
Profit after tax ($mn)	55.6	67.2
Earnings per share (c)	22.78	27.54
Cash flow per share (c)	24.01	28.88
Dividend (c)	20	24
Percentage franked	100	100
Net tangible assets per share ($)	0.36	0.43
Interest cover (times)	443.5	~
Return on equity (%)	56.3	59.1
Debt-to-equity ratio (%)	~	~
Current ratio	6.5	5.3

NIB Holdings Limited

ASX code: NHF www.nib.com.au

Sector: Insurance	
Share price ($)	8.04
12-month high ($)	8.95
12-month low ($)	6.52
Market capitalisation ($mn)	3886.8
Price/earnings ratio (times)	19.4
Dividend yield (%)	3.5
Price-to-NTA-per-share ratio	8.4
5-year share price return (% p.a.)	6.7
Dividend reinvestment plan	Yes

Newcastle private health insurer NIB Holdings was established as the Newcastle Industrial Benefits Hospital Fund in 1952 by workers at the BHP steelworks. It subsequently demutualised and became the first private health insurer to list on the ASX. It is also active in New Zealand. Other businesses are travel insurance and the provision of specialist insurance services to international students and workers in Australia. Through its new nib Thrive business it has entered the National Disability Insurance Scheme (NDIS) plan management sector.

Latest business results (June 2023, full year)

Revenues and profits rose, with a substantial contribution from gains in the investment portfolio. But underlying business was also strong, with profits up 11 per cent and strength across most lines of business. The company's flagship Australian Residents Health Insurance, representing 83 per cent of company income, saw premium revenues increase by 6.1 per cent. Policyholder numbers grew by 4.7 per cent, more than double the industry average. The total claims expense rose 6 per cent, having actually fallen in the previous year. New Zealand health insurance represents a further 11 per cent of company turnover. It enjoyed a solid year, with premium revenues up 13.2 per cent and policyholder numbers up 3.2 per cent. Claims inflation led to a 15.7 per cent jump in the claims expense. The company's health insurance program for international students and workers in Australia returned to profit as COVID-related border restrictions were lifted. The company's travel insurance business also returned to profit. The new nib Thrive business contributed a small underlying profit.

Outlook

NIB believes a growing and ageing population in Australia will help deliver continued growth in policyholder numbers for its health insurance business. It also benefits from its New Zealand exposure, where it is the country's second-largest health insurer. It is working to branch into new areas of business, and sees particularly strong potential for its moves into the NDIS plan management sector. During the June 2023 year it raised $158 million in capital to acquire four NDIS plan managers, and was managing the plans of more than 27000 NDIS participants. In July, August and September 2023 it acquired further NDIS-related businesses and it expects to be providing plan management services to around 50000 participants by 2025. Among other activities, it holds a 74 per cent stake in Midnight Health, which provides telehealth GP consultations and out-of-hours prescription delivery services, with a focus on remote regions. Its joint venture company Honeysuckle Health uses data analytics to deliver healthcare programs.

Year to 30 June	2022	2023
Premium revenues ($mn)	2703.4	2911.5
EBIT ($mn)	197.8	298.5
EBIT margin (%)	7.3	10.3
Profit before tax ($mn)	190.8	284.5
Profit after tax ($mn)	135.7	197.0
Earnings per share (c)	29.60	41.42
Cash flow per share (c)	36.52	49.22
Dividend (c)	22	28
Percentage franked	100	100
Net tangible assets per share ($)	0.78	0.96
Interest cover (times)	29.5	21.6
Return on equity (%)	19.2	23.4
Debt-to-equity ratio (%)	7.4	0.3
Current ratio	1.7	1.9

Nick Scali Limited

ASX code: NCK www.nickscali.com.au

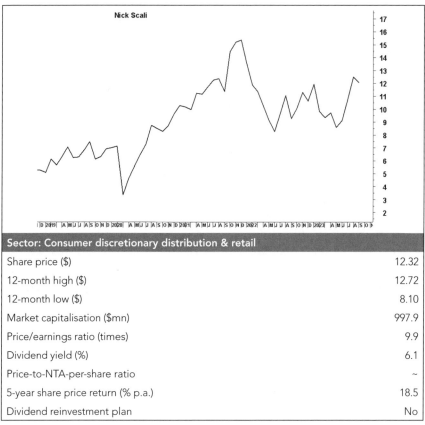

Sector: Consumer discretionary distribution & retail	
Share price ($)	12.32
12-month high ($)	12.72
12-month low ($)	8.10
Market capitalisation ($mn)	997.9
Price/earnings ratio (times)	9.9
Dividend yield (%)	6.1
Price-to-NTA-per-share ratio	~
5-year share price return (% p.a.)	18.5
Dividend reinvestment plan	No

Sydney-based Nick Scali is one of Australia's largest furniture importers and retailers, with a history dating back more than 50 years. It specialises in leather and fabric lounge suites along with dining room and bedroom furniture. In November 2021 it acquired Plush-Think Sofas. At June 2023 it operated 59 Nick Scali Furniture stores in Australia, and five in New Zealand, and 43 Plush stores.

Latest business results (June 2023, full year)

A combination of solid demand, the resolution of supply chain delays and a full-year's contribution from the Plush business generated a strong rise in sales and profits. During the previous year the company suffered from store closures affecting over 55 per cent of its network, along with COVID-related closures of manufacturing facilities in Vietnam and of port facilities in China. Total written sales orders for the year of $437 million actually represented an 8 per cent decline from the previous year, with first-half strength—driven in part by a large order backlog—more than offset by second-half weakness. The Nick Scali online business received written sales orders of $26.5 million, down from the previous year. During the year the company opened

Nick Scali showrooms at Helensvale, Queensland, and Shepparton, Victoria, and one Plush store at Capalaba, Queensland. It also closed three Plush stores.

Outlook

Nick Scali is directly affected by trends in consumer spending, interest rates, currency movements, housing sales, renovation activity and the general economy. After experiencing growing volatility in its sales it is now concerned about continuing inflationary pressures, as well as the possibility of a housing slowdown and a dampening of consumer spending. It has achieved success in boosting profit margins with its $102.5 million Plush acquisition. This has been successfully integrated into its own operations, and the company has initiated a program of refurbishing the Plush network stores, as well as changing the furniture mix. The result has been that the Plush gross margin for the June 2023 year climbed to 62.7 per cent, from 54.8 per cent in the previous year, while also contributing to higher margins for the company as a whole. The steady repayment of loans taken out to fund the Plush acquisition will lead to lower interest rate charges. The company's long-term target is for at least 86 Nick Scali stores and up to 100 Plush stores, across Australia and New Zealand. During the July to December 2023 half it expects to open three new Plush stores and one new Nick Scali store.

Year to 30 June	2022	2023
Revenues ($mn)	441.0	507.7
EBIT ($mn)	124.6	156.8
EBIT margin (%)	28.2	30.9
Gross margin (%)	61.0	63.5
Profit before tax ($mn)	115.3	143.5
Profit after tax ($mn)	80.2	101.1
Earnings per share (c)	99.01	124.79
Cash flow per share (c)	150.31	177.59
Dividend (c)	70	75
Percentage franked	100	100
Net tangible assets per share ($)	~	~
Interest cover (times)	13.6	14.5
Return on equity (%)	62.9	63.0
Debt-to-equity ratio (%)	12.1	1.4
Current ratio	0.8	1.1

Nine Entertainment Company Holdings Limited

ASX code: NEC www.nineforbrands.com.au

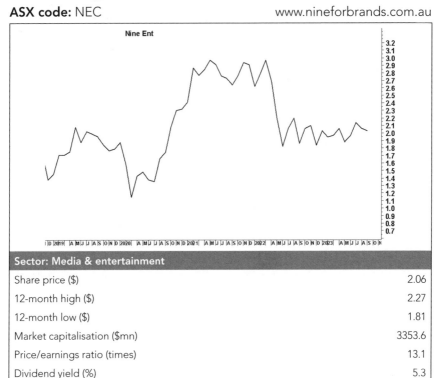

Sector: Media & entertainment	
Share price ($)	2.06
12-month high ($)	2.27
12-month low ($)	1.81
Market capitalisation ($mn)	3353.6
Price/earnings ratio (times)	13.1
Dividend yield (%)	5.3
Price-to-NTA-per-share ratio	~
5-year share price return (% p.a.)	2.0
Dividend reinvestment plan	No

With roots that stretch back to the first edition of the *Sydney Herald* in 1831 and the launch of channel TCN-9 in 1956, Sydney-based Nine Entertainment is today one of Australia's media giants. It divides its activities into four broad segments. The Broadcasting division incorporates its free-to-air television activities, its 9Now streaming video service and eight radio stations. Digital and Publishing comprises a portfolio of newspapers, including the *Sydney Morning Herald*, *The Age* and the *Australian Financial Review*, as well as magazines and online publications. The Stan division represents the Stan subscription video-on-demand service. The fourth segment, Domain Group, is a real estate media and services business.

Latest business results (June 2023, full year)

Revenues were flat but profits fell, in a reversal of the previous year's strong surge. The stand-out result came from the Stan division, with revenues up 12 per cent and profits jumping 30 per cent, reflecting price increases and reduced customer churn. Nevertheless, profit margins at Stan remained substantially below those at Nine's other divisions. The Broadcasting division reported a 20 per cent drop in profits on a small dip in revenues, with a weaker economy leading to a fall in advertising while programming costs rose. The Digital and Publishing division recorded single-digit declines in revenues and profits, with newspaper subscription growth more than offset by falling advertising. The Domain Group division saw profits down 15 per cent on a small decline in revenues as property listings fell.

Outlook

Nine Entertainment occupies a central position in Australia's media landscape. In the past it benefited from a robust economy and from its own restructuring efforts, which quite significantly reduced costs. The challenge now is to maintain this momentum as the economy slows and cost pressures grow. A key strategy is an acceleration of the shift to digital platforms for its content, and digital revenues now comprise 46 per cent of total group income. Its 9Now business continues to grow strongly and an increasing share of the company's radio audience is listening online or via apps. Nine targets a doubling of the number of digital subscribers to its newspapers within five years. Price rises are helping offset cost inflation. It believes that Stan is on a strong growth trajectory, thanks to investment in original programming, solid demand for Stan Sport and extensions to key strategic licensing deals. The company expects its $305 million contract for the next 10 years of Olympic broadcasting rights will provide a strong growth opportunity.

Year to 30 June	2022	2023
Revenues ($mn)	2691.4	2704.4
Broadcasting (%)	51	50
Digital & publishing (%)	22	21
Stan (%)	14	16
Domain Group (%)	13	13
EBIT ($mn)	552.7	442.8
EBIT margin (%)	20.5	16.4
Profit before tax ($mn)	526.4	394.1
Profit after tax ($mn)	348.5	262.1
Earnings per share (c)	20.46	15.68
Cash flow per share (c)	29.21	24.99
Dividend (c)	14	11
Percentage franked	100	100
Net tangible assets per share ($)	~	~
Interest cover (times)	22.0	10.5
Return on equity (%)	18.9	14.7
Debt-to-equity ratio (%)	15.7	27.9
Current ratio	1.0	1.0

NRW Holdings Limited

ASX code: NWH

www.nrw.com.au

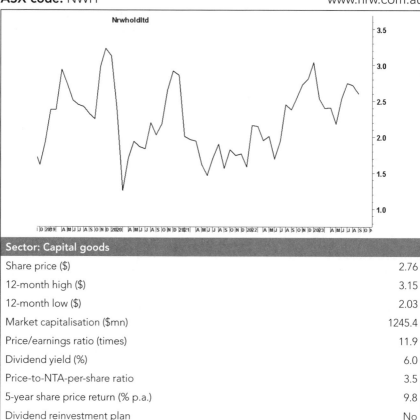

Sector: Capital goods	
Share price ($)	2.76
12-month high ($)	3.15
12-month low ($)	2.03
Market capitalisation ($mn)	1245.4
Price/earnings ratio (times)	11.9
Dividend yield (%)	6.0
Price-to-NTA-per-share ratio	3.5
5-year share price return (% p.a.)	9.8
Dividend reinvestment plan	No

Perth company NRW Holdings, a specialist provider of services to the mining and resources industries, was founded in 1994. It segments its operations into three divisions. The Mining division specialises in mine management, contract mining, drill and blast operations, and maintenance services. The Civil division is involved in the delivery of a wide range of private and public civil infrastructure projects, including roads, bridges and renewable energy facilities. The Minerals, Energy and Technologies division includes mining equipment manufacturer RCR Mining Technologies, specialist metals and mining engineer DIAB Engineering, resources and energy construction specialist Primero, and industrial electrical engineer OFI Group Holdings.

Latest business results (June 2023, full year)

In a good result, NRW achieved double-digit growth in revenues and profits. The Mining division enjoyed another excellent year, with revenues up 13 per cent and a 26 per cent jump in profits as margins expanded. The Minerals, Energy and Technologies division reported higher revenues, thanks especially to DIAB Engineering's filter building contract with Lynas Rare Earths. However, profits fell, with RCR

Mining Technologies suffering from delays in the award of new contracts and Primero experiencing cost overruns on fixed-price contracts. OFI, acquired in March 2023, made a small contribution. Rising levels of activity on major projects generated higher revenues for the Civil division, but profits only edged up as costs rose.

Outlook

NRW held an order book of $5.9 billion at June 2023, up from $5.2 billion a year earlier, with around $2.7 billion of this expected to be earned during the June 2024 year and a further $2.5 billion in the June 2025 year. It also sees ahead of it some $17.1 billion of potential projects coming up for tender, and it is optimistic about the long-term outlook. Its Mining division is showing particular strength, with a full order book, which allows it to be selective in targeting specific projects. Its particular focus is projects related to gold and key battery-critical minerals. The Civil division is benefiting from growth in public infrastructure projects, with notably robust markets expected in Western Australia and Queensland, particularly ahead of the 2032 Brisbane Olympic Games. NRW's Primero business has been involved in most of Australia's lithium concentration and refinery projects and is now working from offices in Montreal and Houston with a view to gaining contracts at similar projects in North America. For June 2024 NRW forecasts revenues of at least $2.8 billion and EBITA of $175 million to $185 million, compared to $166.3 million in June 2023.

Year to 30 June	2022	2023
Revenues ($mn)	2367.4	2667.1
Mining (%)	52	53
Minerals, energy & technologies (%)	28	27
Civil (%)	20	20
EBIT ($mn)	142.7	162.2
EBIT margin (%)	6.0	6.1
Profit before tax ($mn)	129.4	143.7
Profit after tax ($mn)	93.7	104.4
Earnings per share (c)	20.86	23.18
Cash flow per share (c)	48.31	51.69
Dividend (c)	12.5	16.5
Percentage franked	100	48
Net tangible assets per share ($)	0.77	0.78
Interest cover (times)	11.1	9.4
Return on equity (%)	16.4	17.4
Debt-to-equity ratio (%)	2.3	5.4
Current ratio	1.3	1.3

Objective Corporation Limited

ASX code: OCL   www.objective.com.au

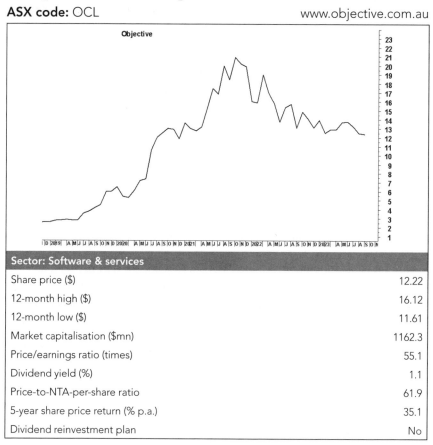

Sector: Software & services	
Share price ($)	12.22
12-month high ($)	16.12
12-month low ($)	11.61
Market capitalisation ($mn)	1162.3
Price/earnings ratio (times)	55.1
Dividend yield (%)	1.1
Price-to-NTA-per-share ratio	61.9
5-year share price return (% p.a.)	35.1
Dividend reinvestment plan	No

Sydney-based Objective, founded in 1987, provides information technology software and services. Its particular specialty is working with federal, state and local governments, as well as government agencies and regulated industries, and it has operations in Australia, New Zealand and the United Kingdom. It has grown substantially, organically and through acquisition, and now operates under numerous product categories.

Latest business results (June 2023, full year)

Revenues rose modestly, but profits were generally down, although a reduced tax bill meant the after-tax profit rose. For reporting purposes the company divides its businesses into three broad segments. The largest of these, Content and Process, representing around 70 per cent of total turnover, comprises the company's core products, which allow customers to manage, process and publish information and collaborate with external organisations. It saw revenue growth of 3 per cent, which would have been higher but for the company's decision to end its Perpetual Right to Use licences. A second segment, RegTech, comprising products that manage governmental safety and compliance regulatory processes, also achieved 3 per cent sales growth. The third segment, Planning and Building, digitally manages the development and construction planning consent process and recorded a small dip in revenues, after exiting from some low-margin contracts. Total company recurring revenue rose to represent 80 per cent of total income, up from 73 per cent. Overseas sales, primarily in New Zealand and the UK, comprised 27 per cent of total company income.

Outlook

Objective is a small company working in niche businesses but with a solid reputation and a high level of profitability. The company's particular goal is to help customers digitalise and streamline the processes of compliance, accountability and governance. It is working to move its businesses, as much as possible, to a subscription model, which will make revenues and earnings more predictable each year. It spends heavily on research and development, and this reached $27.2 million in the June 2023 year, up from $25 million a year earlier. It is steadily moving customers to its Objective Nexus next-generation software-as-a-service platform, introduced in mid 2023, presenting significant new marketing opportunities. Objective Build, launched in 2022, is achieving great success among local government authorities in New Zealand. Following the 2022 acquisition of the American software developer Simflofy it has introduced the Objective 3Sixty content management product and has initiated sales in the US, including with the California Department of Motor Vehicles. At June 2023 Objective had no debt and more than $72 million in cash holdings.

Year to 30 June	2022	2023
Revenues ($mn)	106.5	110.4
EBIT ($mn)	23.9	22.5
EBIT margin (%)	22.4	20.4
Profit before tax ($mn)	23.4	22.0
Profit after tax ($mn)	19.6	21.1
Earnings per share (c)	20.72	22.20
Cash flow per share (c)	26.57	27.39
Dividend (c)	11	13.5
Percentage franked	45	0
Net tangible assets per share ($)	0.15	0.20
Interest cover (times)	~	~
Return on equity (%)	35.9	31.1
Debt-to-equity ratio (%)	~	~
Current ratio	1.2	1.4

PeopleIn Limited

ASX code: PPE www.peoplein.com.au

Sector: Commercial & professional services	
Share price ($)	1.94
12-month high ($)	3.56
12-month low ($)	1.93
Market capitalisation ($mn)	197.0
Price/earnings ratio (times)	6.9
Dividend yield (%)	7.2
Price-to-NTA-per-share ratio	~
5-year share price return (% p.a.)	3.7
Dividend reinvestment plan	Yes

Brisbane-based labour hire company PeopleIn, formerly called People Infrastructure Group, was founded in 1996. It has grown substantially—organically and through acquisition—and today comprises 25 brands across three broad divisions: Health and Community, Professional Services, and Industrial and Specialist Services. It has also expanded to New Zealand.

Latest business results (June 2023, full year)

A tight labour market and a full year's contribution from two 2022 acquisitions generated strong revenue growth. However, rising costs—in particular a combined total of nearly $10 million in higher depreciation charges and interest payments—meant that the growth in underlying profits was more subdued. The company's largest division, Industrial and Specialist Services, enjoyed another good year, with strong double-digit growth in revenues and profits. A notable contribution came from the June 2022 acquisition of Food Industry People Group. This division also benefited from growing numbers of international backpackers and students arriving in Australia and seeking work. There was a record result from the division's Expect A Star childcare recruitment business. The Professional Services division achieved higher revenues, including a contribution from the 2022 acquisition of Perigon Group, but a decline in the technology recruitment sector helped send profits down. The Health and Community segment also experienced an increase in revenues but a decline in profits.

Outlook

PeopleIn is a beneficiary of low unemployment levels in Australia and the inability of many companies to find sufficient numbers of qualified staff. It also benefits from wage inflation, which boosts its margins. It has a strong pipeline of potential acquisitions, with a focus on expanding its services within health, federal and state government, and professional services. In addition, it has other strategies for growth. As it expands it sees many cross-selling opportunities between its various brands, and it believes this, together with moves to diversify its client base, will continue to generate strong organic growth. It is also working to boost its international recruitment services. It is seeing improvements in visa processing and qualification accreditation times for its international nursing recruitment program. In February 2023 it launched a new nurse recruiting campaign in the UK and Ireland, You+AUS, and has attracted strong candidate interest. It also expects a strong recovery during the June 2024 year in technological permanent recruitment, as companies upgrade their digital infrastructures to meet new challenges that include cyber-security and artificial intelligence. A new agreement with TAFE Queensland, announced in February 2023, will enable PeopleIn to provide employment placement services to TAFE Queensland graduates.

Year to 30 June	2022	2023
Revenues ($mn)	682.3	1186.4
Industrial & specialist services (%)	61	74
Professional services (%)	19	14
Health & community (%)	20	12
EBIT ($mn)	36.1	44.1
EBIT margin (%)	5.3	3.7
Profit before tax ($mn)	33.9	37.9
Profit after tax ($mn)	25.5	28.4
Earnings per share (c)	26.81	28.19
Cash flow per share (c)	38.49	45.04
Dividend (c)	13	14
Percentage franked	100	100
Net tangible assets per share ($)	~	~
Interest cover (times)	16.8	7.2
Return on equity (%)	20.2	19.2
Debt-to-equity ratio (%)	32.2	16.2
Current ratio	1.2	1.2

Pinnacle Investment Management Group Limited

ASX code: PNI   www.pinnacleinvestment.com

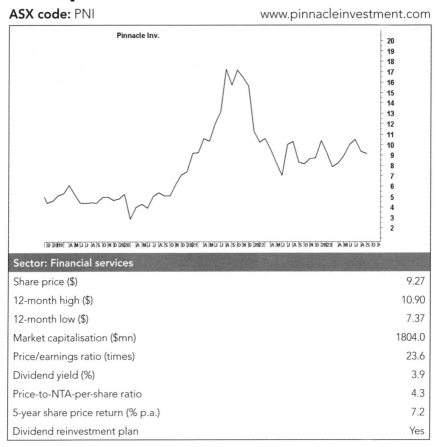

Sector: Financial services	
Share price ($)	9.27
12-month high ($)	10.90
12-month low ($)	7.37
Market capitalisation ($mn)	1804.0
Price/earnings ratio (times)	23.6
Dividend yield (%)	3.9
Price-to-NTA-per-share ratio	4.3
5-year share price return (% p.a.)	7.2
Dividend reinvestment plan	Yes

Sydney-based Pinnacle Investment Management started life in 2006 as a boutique funds management company that was majority-owned by Wilson HTM Investment Group. In 2016 it was fully acquired by Wilson Group, with Wilson Group changing its own name to Pinnacle. Today it is a prominent adviser to small funds management groups, providing them with distribution services, business support and responsible entity services, while also holding an equity stake in these companies.

Latest business results (June 2023, full year)

Profits marked time, despite a strong second-half rebound, as Pinnacle was hit by market volatility, rising interest rates and net inflows that were lower than expected. Funds that invested in real estate investment trusts were hit especially hard. At June 2023 the company comprised 15 fund management affiliates, collectively managing investments across a diverse range of asset classes. Pinnacle held shareholdings in these affiliates that ranged from 23.5 per cent to 49.9 per cent. Total revenues during the year for the 15 fund managers of $511.6 million were up from $505.5 million in the previous year, and this included $58.2 million in performance fees, up slightly from $57.8 million in the previous year, but well down from the $86.2 million figure of the June 2021 year. Total funds under management rose to $91.9 billion at June 2023, up from $83.7 billion a year before, thanks mainly to a solid investment performance, although there were also net inflows during the year to the 15 fund manager affiliates of $1.5 billion.

Outlook

Pinnacle's initial role is to provide its fund manager affiliates with equity, seed capital and working capital. It then allows its managers to focus on investment performance by providing them with marketing and other support services. Pinnacle's own revenues and profits derive from the revenues it receives from its affiliates for its services, together with its share of their profits, and performance is important. It has achieved success with the fund management companies it has chosen to join its group, reporting that 81 per cent of funds with a five-year track record had by June 2023 outperformed their benchmarks during this period. The company is confident about its long-term evolution, and has a variety of strategies for growth, including overseas expansion, investment in high-margin retail channels and moves into new asset classes. Nevertheless, it recognises that, at least in the short term, global economic conditions remain uncertain, with shifts in monetary policy and continuing geopolitical tensions exerting a significant impact on financial markets.

Year to 30 June	2022	2023
Revenues ($mn)	121.7	112.9
EBIT ($mn)	78.7	82.5
EBIT margin (%)	64.7	73.1
Profit before tax ($mn)	76.4	76.5
Profit after tax ($mn)	76.4	76.5
Earnings per share (c)	40.21	39.35
Cash flow per share (c)	40.73	39.51
Dividend (c)	35	36
Percentage franked	100	100
Net tangible assets per share ($)	2.06	2.16
Interest cover (times)	34.9	15.5
Return on equity (%)	23.6	18.5
Debt-to-equity ratio (%)	20.3	21.9
Current ratio	14.5	7.2

Platinum Asset Management Limited

ASX code: PTM www.platinum.com.au

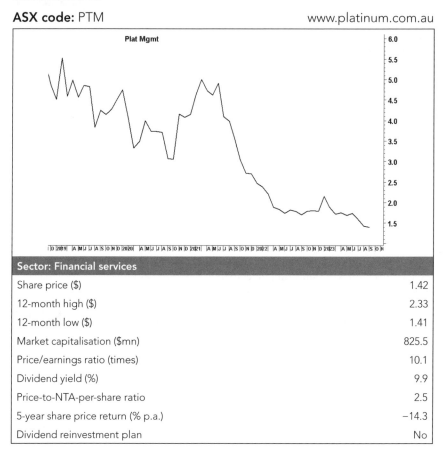

Sector: Financial services	
Share price ($)	1.42
12-month high ($)	2.33
12-month low ($)	1.41
Market capitalisation ($mn)	825.5
Price/earnings ratio (times)	10.1
Dividend yield (%)	9.9
Price-to-NTA-per-share ratio	2.5
5-year share price return (% p.a.)	−14.3
Dividend reinvestment plan	No

Sydney funds management company Platinum Asset Management was established in 1994. It has developed a specialty in managing portfolios of international equities. Its flagship product is the $6.6 billion Platinum International Fund. Other funds specialise in Europe, Asia, Japan, healthcare, technology, international brands and energy transition.

Latest business results (June 2023, full year)

Revenues and profits fell again, despite the good performance of some of the company's funds. Management fees of $201.4 million were down 18 per cent from June 2022 as average funds under management during the year fell from $21.4 billion to $18.1 billion. Performance fees fell from $6.7 million to $1.2 million. Platinum said that on an underlying basis, excluding investment gains and losses, its after-tax profit fell 35.3 per cent to $76.5 million. Staffing costs, which had edged down in the previous year, jumped 31.3 per cent, due to the fact that much staff compensation is linked to fund investment performance. At June 2023 Platinum held funds under management of

$17.3 billion, down from $18.2 billion in June 2022, driven by a positive investment performance of $2 billion, net fund outflows of $2.4 billion and $0.4 billion in net distributions to investors.

Outlook

Platinum gained a degree of renown among Australian investors for an impressive long-term period of outperformance for its international equity funds, thanks to its stock-picking skills, and this sparked some solid growth in funds under management. However, in recent years the performance has been mixed. The company has attributed this to its preference for value stocks, at a time when growth stocks were leading global markets higher. It launched two new products during the June 2023 year. The first of these, the Platinum World Portfolios – Health Sciences Fund, provides foreign investors with access to Platinum's existing healthcare investment products. The second, the Platinum Global Transition Fund, is the company's first new investment strategy in 19 years, and provides Australian and New Zealand investors with an opportunity to invest in global companies that will benefit financially from trends in energy transition. The company views this transition as a structural area of change that will span many decades and provide significant investment opportunities across a variety of industries. In 2023 Platinum hired a new Head of Stewardship to work closely with the investment team on environmental, social and corporate governance issues. Though it views investment performance as the key to turning around fund flows, it is also working to boost its marketing efforts.

Year to 30 June	2022	2023
Revenues ($mn)	252.7	202.7
EBIT ($mn)	146.7	116.8
EBIT margin (%)	58.1	57.6
Profit before tax ($mn)	146.7	116.8
Profit after tax ($mn)	101.5	80.9
Earnings per share (c)	17.54	14.10
Cash flow per share (c)	18.03	14.57
Dividend (c)	17	14
Percentage franked	100	100
Net tangible assets per share ($)	0.56	0.57
Interest cover (times)	~	~
Return on equity (%)	30.5	24.8
Debt-to-equity ratio (%)	~	~
Current ratio	12.8	12.9

Premier Investments Limited

ASX code: PMV www.premierinvestments.com.au

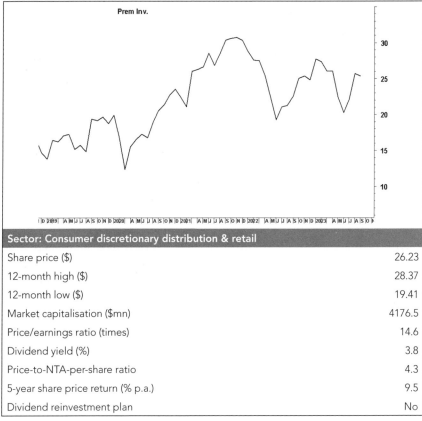

Sector: Consumer discretionary distribution & retail	
Share price ($)	26.23
12-month high ($)	28.37
12-month low ($)	19.41
Market capitalisation ($mn)	4176.5
Price/earnings ratio (times)	14.6
Dividend yield (%)	3.8
Price-to-NTA-per-share ratio	4.3
5-year share price return (% p.a.)	9.5
Dividend reinvestment plan	No

Melbourne-based Premier was founded in 1987 and operates as an investment company. Its main holding is a 100 per cent stake in the retailer Just Group, which was founded in 1970. The Just Group incorporates the brands Just Jeans, Smiggle, Peter Alexander, Jay Jays, Portmans, Jacqui E and Dotti, with more than 1100 stores in six countries. Premier also holds 26 per cent of the equity in both home appliance specialist Breville Group and department store chain Myer Holdings. Premier's chairman, Solomon Lew, owns more than 40 per cent of the company's equity.

Latest business results (January 2023, half year)

Sales and profits rose in a good result for the company. The Peter Alexander sleepwear chain was again an excellent performer, with sales of $262 million, up 15.1 per cent from the January 2022 half, and with strength across all product categories. The company's other main driver of growth is Smiggle, which specialises in colourful school stationery and other products for children, with stores around the world. It continued its recovery from the COVID period, which forced the closure of many stores, with sales growth of 30.3 per cent to $191 million. The other five apparel brands delivered sales growth of 14.3 per cent, with particular strength from Just

Jeans, Portmans and Dotti. Online sales, which had soared during the period of COVID, fell 12.5 per cent to $171 million.

Outlook

Premier operates seven strong brands and continues to expand. Nevertheless, as much retail activity moves online it is rationalising its activities, including the closure of some stores. It is also vulnerable to a slowing of discretionary spending by consumers, and with most of its product lines sourced from overseas manufacturers, the company can be affected by currency rate trends. It is working to boost online sales, which generate significantly higher profit margins than the retail store network. In March 2023 it launched a new website that allows customers to shop across all the company's brands, with one checkout and one delivery. It sees particular potential for its Peter Alexander brand, which has seen sales more than double over four years. It plans a series of new Peter Alexander stores and is working to develop an offshore business. It is also seeing growing demand for Smiggle products, and plans further global expansion. In August 2023 the company initiated a strategic review that could lead to the eventual demerger of some of its retail assets.

Year to 30 July*	2021	2022
Revenues ($mn)	1443.2	1497.5
EBIT ($mn)	391.2	401.5
EBIT margin (%)	27.1	26.8
Profit before tax ($mn)	379.6	392.7
Profit after tax ($mn)	271.8	285.2
Earnings per share (c)	171.15	179.40
Cash flow per share (c)	283.39	283.94
Dividend (c)	80	100
Percentage franked	100	100
Interest cover (times)	37.5	53.2
Return on equity (%)	18.9	17.8
Half year to 28 January**	2022	2023
Revenues ($mn)	769.9	905.2
Profit before tax ($mn)	229.3	242.9
Profit after tax ($mn)	163.6	174.3
Earnings per share (c)	102.97	109.58
Dividend (c)	46	54
Percentage franked	100	100
Net tangible assets per share ($)	4.99	6.08
Debt-to-equity ratio (%)	~	~
Current ratio	1.7	1.9

*31 July 2021
**29 January 2022

Pro Medicus Limited

ASX code: PME

www.promed.com.au

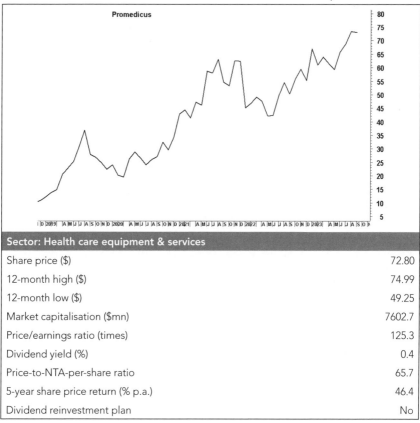

Sector: Health care equipment & services	
Share price ($)	72.80
12-month high ($)	74.99
12-month low ($)	49.25
Market capitalisation ($mn)	7602.7
Price/earnings ratio (times)	125.3
Dividend yield (%)	0.4
Price-to-NTA-per-share ratio	65.7
5-year share price return (% p.a.)	46.4
Dividend reinvestment plan	No

Melbourne-based Pro Medicus, established in 1983, provides software and internet products and services to the medical profession. Its Visage 7.0 medical imaging software provides radiologists and clinicians with advanced visualisation capability for the rapid viewing of medical images. Its Radiology Information Systems (RIS) product provides proprietary medical software for practice management. In Australia it operates the Promedicus.net online network for doctors. It has extensive business operations throughout Australia, the US and Germany, and overseas sales represent more than 85 per cent of total turnover.

Latest business results (June 2023, full year)

Pro Medicus enjoyed another successful year of strong double-digit revenue and profit growth. America is by far the company's largest market, accounting for more than 80 per cent of sales, and revenues there soared 42 per cent, with the signing of seven new contracts and the renewal of one more. The relatively small German operation saw sales down 12 per cent, with a German government hospital contract extension in the previous year not replicated in the June 2023 year. Australian sales rose 9 per cent, again due especially to RIS contracts with Healius and I-MED Radiology Network. The result also benefited from dollar weakness.

Outlook

Pro Medicus continues to enjoy some outstanding success in America for its Visage 7 software, which has the speed, functionality and versatility to meet the requirements of many different kinds of users. The company is now one of the market leaders in this business, and says that nine of the 22 leading American hospitals are using its products. A global shortage of radiologists is helping boost demand. It is making a substantial investment in research and development activities aimed at new products and enhancements to existing products, including artificial intelligence–based products. It is benefiting from moves to cloud-based systems. It has established an R&D centre in New York in order to collaborate with customer research projects. It is working on the addition of a cardiology application to its existing imaging platform, and together with Yale New Haven Health has developed a promising breast density algorithm based on artificial intelligence. With no debt and cash holdings of more than $91 million in June 2023 it is also seeking out acquisition opportunities offering access to new technologies. Most of the company's revenue is recurring in nature, and, with seven new contract signings and one contract renewal in the June 2023 year, and a further signing in July 2023, the outlook for June 2024 is very positive.

Year to 30 June	2022	2023
Revenues ($mn)	93.5	124.9
EBIT ($mn)	63.1	86.1
EBIT margin (%)	67.5	69.0
Profit before tax ($mn)	63.1	86.1
Profit after tax ($mn)	44.4	60.6
Earnings per share (c)	42.60	58.09
Cash flow per share (c)	49.62	65.68
Dividend (c)	22	30
Percentage franked	100	100
Net tangible assets per share ($)	0.74	1.11
Interest cover (times)	~	~
Return on equity (%)	48.5	50.4
Debt-to-equity ratio (%)	~	~
Current ratio	4.5	5.3

PWR Holdings Limited

ASX code: PWH   www.pwr.com.au

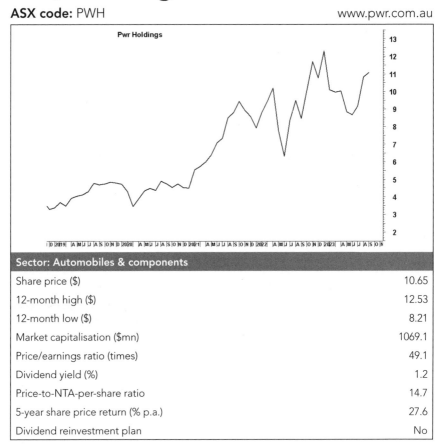

Sector: Automobiles & components

Share price ($)	10.65
12-month high ($)	12.53
12-month low ($)	8.21
Market capitalisation ($mn)	1069.1
Price/earnings ratio (times)	49.1
Dividend yield (%)	1.2
Price-to-NTA-per-share ratio	14.7
5-year share price return (% p.a.)	27.6
Dividend reinvestment plan	No

Based on the Gold Coast, automotive products company PWR got its start in 1987. It specialises in cooling systems, including aluminium radiators, intercoolers and oil coolers. It has a particular specialty in the supply of cooling systems to racing car teams. Other customers include the automotive original equipment manufacturing (OEM) sector and the automotive after-market sector, along with the aerospace, defence and renewable energy industries. It operates from manufacturing and distribution facilities in Australia, the United States and the United Kingdom. It owns the American cooling products manufacturer C&R Racing. Some 90 per cent of company sales are to customers overseas, mainly in Europe and North America.

Latest business results (June 2023, full year)

Revenues and profits continued to rise, although not at the pace of the previous two years, but with strength in all key markets. The company also benefited from favourable currency exchange rate movements. The motorsports business remains responsible for more than half the company's sales, and revenues grew 13 per cent to $62 million. However, the best growth again came from other sectors. The aerospace and defence sector achieved 48 per cent growth, building on the 56 per cent growth of the previous year, although this business represents just 9 per cent of total sales. Automotive OEM sales comprise 22 per cent of company income, and revenues grew by 19 per cent. Automotive aftermarket revenues rose 12 per cent. The company also classifies its sales into its mainstream advanced cooling activities and its emerging technologies, with the latter representing 19 per cent of total revenues.

Outlook

PWR supplies its cooling systems to most Formula One racing teams, as well as to teams in other motor sports around the world, including Nascar and Indycar. It also supplies bespoke cooling systems to a range of high-performance automobile companies such as Aston Martin. It spends heavily on research and development in order to maintain its market-leading position, and it is working to move into other market areas with high growth potential. It opened its new North American aerospace and defence machining centre in October 2022 and a European manufacturing base in the UK in December 2022. It plans a large new Australian factory capable of supporting growth for the next 10 to 20 years. It sees particular potential in the advance of electric vehicles, and it is working with several electric car manufacturers for the supply of sophisticated cooling technology. Other applications include helicopters, drones and storage batteries for alternative energy systems.

Year to 30 June	2022	2023
Revenues ($mn)	101.1	118.3
PWR performance products (%)	72	72
PWR North America (%)	28	28
EBIT ($mn)	28.7	30.8
EBIT margin (%)	28.4	26.0
Profit before tax ($mn)	28.5	30.2
Profit after tax ($mn)	20.8	21.8
Earnings per share (c)	20.79	21.67
Cash flow per share (c)	28.00	30.12
Dividend (c)	12	12.5
Percentage franked	100	100
Net tangible assets per share ($)	0.61	0.72
Interest cover (times)	956.5	92.4
Return on equity (%)	29.7	26.4
Debt-to-equity ratio (%)	~	~
Current ratio	3.5	3.3

REA Group Limited

ASX code: REA

www.rea-group.com

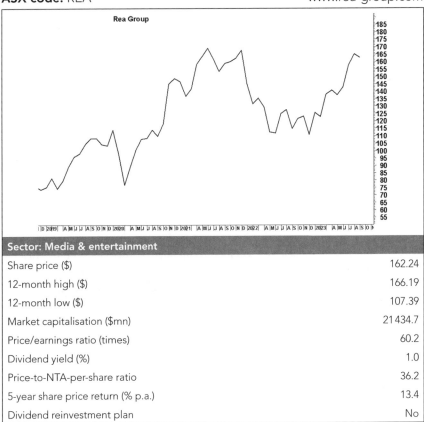

Rea Group

Sector: Media & entertainment	
Share price ($)	162.24
12-month high ($)	166.19
12-month low ($)	107.39
Market capitalisation ($mn)	21 434.7
Price/earnings ratio (times)	60.2
Dividend yield (%)	1.0
Price-to-NTA-per-share ratio	36.2
5-year share price return (% p.a.)	13.4
Dividend reinvestment plan	No

Melbourne-based REA was founded in 1995. Through its websites realestate.com.au and realcommercial.com.au it is the leader in the provision of online real estate advertising services in Australia. It also operates the share property website flatmates.com.au and the property research website property.com.au. In addition, it owns the mortgage broking franchise groups Smartline Home Loans and Mortgage Choice, the property data company PropTrack and the advertising and home preparation finance platform Campaign Agent. It has interests in property websites throughout Asia, and holds a 20 per cent shareholding in the Move online property marketing company in the US. News Corp owns more than 60 per cent of REA's equity.

Latest business results (June 2023, full year)

Revenues edged up but profits fell, as the company was hit by a 12 per cent decline in residential listings, driven by weakness in the Sydney and Melbourne markets. Australian revenues actually fell slightly, but a strong performance from the small REA India business—with income up 46 per cent to $79 million—pushed overall revenues higher. Commercial and developer revenues rose 4 per cent to $142 million, with strength in commercial business again offsetting a decline in developer income. The company's media, data and other segment saw revenues flat at $97 million, with reduced developer and media display revenues offset by continuing strength from the PropTrack market intelligence operation. The financial services businesses saw revenues down 8 per cent to $61 million. American business, represented by the company's 20 per cent shareholding in Move, was hit by lower transaction volumes, and moved from profit to loss.

Outlook

REA is heavily geared to trends in the domestic housing market, and it expects continuing growth, thanks to healthy auction clearance rates and property prices returning to growth during 2023. Underlying fundamentals are also positive, with low unemployment, wages growth, increasing migration and the possible peaking of interest rates. The company will also benefit from price increases and planned new product launches. It holds more than 5 per cent of the Australian mortgage market and its long-term target is to double this share. It has expressed a desire for further acquisitions and has flagged property insurance as a sector it could enter. It expects further growth from its Indian operation, and also holds a 17.5 per cent equity stake in PropertyGuru, which operates throughout South-East Asia. REA's shareholding in Move, one of the largest real estate websites in the US, has given the company a foothold in the vast American property market.

Year to 30 June	2022	2023
Revenues ($mn)	1160.2	1183.2
EBIT ($mn)	556.0	530.4
EBIT margin (%)	47.9	44.8
Profit before tax ($mn)	547.9	512.9
Profit after tax ($mn)	384.8	356.1
Earnings per share (c)	291.37	269.67
Cash flow per share (c)	361.87	339.19
Dividend (c)	164	158
Percentage franked	100	100
Net tangible assets per share ($)	3.48	4.48
Interest cover (times)	81.8	51.5
Return on equity (%)	32.5	25.7
Debt-to-equity ratio (%)	17.5	9.5
Current ratio	1.6	1.7

Reece Limited

ASX code: REH

group.reece.com

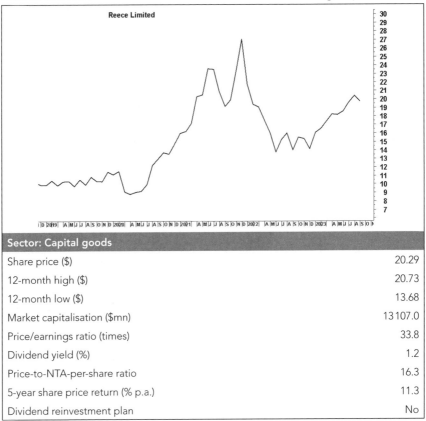

Sector: Capital goods	
Share price ($)	20.29
12-month high ($)	20.73
12-month low ($)	13.68
Market capitalisation ($mn)	13 107.0
Price/earnings ratio (times)	33.8
Dividend yield (%)	1.2
Price-to-NTA-per-share ratio	16.3
5-year share price return (% p.a.)	11.3
Dividend reinvestment plan	No

Melbourne-based plumbing supplies company Reece traces its origins back to 1919, when Harold Reece started selling his products from the back of a truck. It is today one of the country's leading suppliers of plumbing products, with operations also in the US and New Zealand, and it has expanded into related fields. These include a network of businesses in the heating, ventilation, air conditioning and refrigeration sectors and specialist stores for the landscape and agricultural industries. At June 2023 it operated 655 branches in Australia and New Zealand, up from 645 a year earlier, and 231 in the US, up from 204.

Latest business results (June 2023, full year)

Sales and profits generally rose, although a sharply higher tax bill meant the after-tax profit fell. The result was also affected by an impairment charge, and the company said that adjusted after-tax profit actually rose from $363 million in June 2022 to $405 million. Australian and New Zealand sales rose by 10 per cent, driven to a large extent by higher pricing for products, in order to meet inflationary pressures. EBITDA rose 9 per cent. During the year the company opened a net 10 new domestic branches. American revenues grew by 21 per cent, although in US dollar terms the increase was

12 per cent, with price increases again a leading contributor to the rise. EBITDA rose a pleasing 29 per cent, although American profit margins remain below those prevailing in Australia.

Outlook

Reece's operations are quite heavily geared to housing and renovation markets in Australia, New Zealand and the US, and the company expects demand to weaken in the near term. It also believes that inflation will continue to moderate. It plans to continue strengthening its networks, with the aim of long-term growth. In Australia it is investing heavily in digital innovation, to make business as smooth as possible for customers, and it also expects to continue opening new branches. It also hopes to add further non-plumbing businesses to its domestic network. However, it is in the US that Reece sees its best growth prospects, and its restructuring efforts there are steadily raising margins. It operates in 16 states and is carrying our trials of new branch formats and service concepts in order to expand business and lower costs. It is also seeking further US acquisitions. During the June 2023 year it opened 15 new American stores. It also acquired a small refrigeration and air conditioning wholesaler in Texas with a network of 12 branches.

Year to 30 June	2022	2023
Revenues ($mn)	7654.0	8839.6
EBIT ($mn)	577.2	648.1
EBIT margin (%)	7.5	7.3
Gross margin (%)	27.9	28.4
Profit before tax ($mn)	509.4	567.8
Profit after tax ($mn)	392.5	387.6
Earnings per share (c)	60.76	60.03
Cash flow per share (c)	100.73	104.92
Dividend (c)	22.5	25
Percentage franked	100	100
Net tangible assets per share ($)	1.01	1.25
Interest cover (times)	8.6	8.7
Return on equity (%)	12.6	11.2
Debt-to-equity ratio (%)	26.2	20.0
Current ratio	2.1	2.3

Reliance Worldwide Corporation Limited

ASX code: RWC   www.rwc.com

Sector: Capital goods	
Share price ($)	4.12
12-month high ($)	4.38
12-month low ($)	2.80
Market capitalisation ($mn)	3255.2
Price/earnings ratio (times)	14.0
Dividend yield (%)	3.5
Price-to-NTA-per-share ratio	76.4
5-year share price return (% p.a.)	−1.9
Dividend reinvestment plan	No

Melbourne-based engineering firm Reliance dates back to 1949 and the establishment of a small tool shop in Brisbane. It is today a major global manufacturer and distributor of a range of products, particularly for the plumbing and heating industries. Its businesses and brands include SharkBite, Speedfit, HoldRite, MultiSafe, Reliance Valves and John Guest.

Latest business results (June 2023, full year)

In another mixed year for the company, revenues rose but profits fell. However, Reliance reports its results in American dollars and its profits actually rose when converted to Australian dollars. The company benefited from an easing of supply chain pressures, but it was hurt by subdued consumer spending in most of the markets in which it operates. American sales and profits rose by double-digit amounts, but much of this reflected a full year's contribution from the recently acquired plumbing products manufacturer EZ-Flo. Price increases and new product revenues also helped the result. Strong plumbing and heating demand pushed British sales higher, but continental Europe was weak, hurt by reduced sales for water filtration products. Asia-Pacific sales and profits fell, due especially to the company's exposure to the Australian new residential construction market. As noted, Reliance reports its results in US dollars. The June 2023 figures have been converted at prevailing exchange rates and are for guidance only.

Outlook

Reliance has a significant exposure to housing markets in many countries, including both new house construction and renovation activity. Consequently it is wary about the outlook for its businesses, with economic conditions expected to remain challenging across most of its markets. In particular, rising inflation and higher interest rates have hit consumer confidence, with discretionary spending falling, and the company expects reduced demand for its products during the June 2024 year. In response, it is working to lower its cost base. It also plans price increases. It expects some significant new products, introduced during the June 2023 year, to generate rising sales. The first is a new generation of brass push-to-connect plumbing fittings. This product range comes after several years of development work and is the first major update of Reliance's SharkBite product line in 20 years. The second new product is an innovative new pipe and fitting system, PEX-a. The company has also introduced changes to its manufacturing operations, freeing up capacity at its Australian plants and enabling the pursuit of new growth opportunities. It sees great potential in its US$332 million EZ-Flo acquisition, which enjoys particular strength in the US$1.2 billion large appliance connector market.

Year to 30 June	2022	2023
Revenues ($mn)	1605.7	1856.4
Americas (%)	67	71
Europe/Middle East/Africa (%)	22	19
Asia Pacific (%)	11	10
EBIT ($mn)	298.7	331.9
EBIT margin (%)	18.6	17.9
Gross margin (%)	39.3	38.4
Profit before tax ($mn)	281.5	283.1
Profit after tax ($mn)	221.1	232.4
Earnings per share (c)	27.98	29.41
Cash flow per share (c)	36.22	39.36
Dividend (c)	13.42	14.24
Percentage franked	15	5
Net tangible assets per share ($)	~	0.05
Interest cover (times)	17.5	6.9
Return on equity (%)	13.7	13.0
Debt-to-equity ratio (%)	48.7	35.2
Current ratio	3.2	3.0

Ridley Corporation Limited

ASX code: RIC

www.ridley.com.au

Sector: Food, beverage & tobacco	
Share price ($)	2.22
12-month high ($)	2.38
12-month low ($)	1.80
Market capitalisation ($mn)	701.1
Price/earnings ratio (times)	16.8
Dividend yield (%)	3.7
Price-to-NTA-per-share ratio	2.9
5-year share price return (% p.a.)	12.2
Dividend reinvestment plan	No

Melbourne-based Ridley, founded in 1987, is a leading producer of animal feed. It operates from some 20 sites in Victoria, New South Wales, Queensland and South Australia, producing around two million tonnes annually of finished feeds and feed ingredients, based on locally grown cereal grains. It also owns an aquafeed manufacturing facility in Thailand. It classifies its production into two broad segments. Bulk stockfeeds comprises the company's animal nutrition feed that is delivered in bulk. Packaged feeds and ingredients represents animal nutrition feed and ingredients that are delivered in packaged form, ranging from three-kilogram bags to one-tonne containers.

Latest business results (June 2023, full year)

Ridley enjoyed another good year, with rises in revenues and underlying profits, and success in passing through inflationary costs. The packaged feeds and ingredients operation was once again notably strong, with benefits from the continuing premiumisation of products and higher market prices for rendered tallows, oils and protein meals. Packaged products saw revenues up by 6 per cent as the company expanded its sales of pet products to urban retail chains and boosted market share. The bulk stockfeeds segment benefited from 11 per cent growth in ruminant sales. The company reported that continuing improvements in operating efficiency at its Thai facility are delivering reductions to the company's cost base.

Outlook

Ridley occupies a prominent place in the Australian agricultural sector as one of the leading producers of stockfeeds, nutritional blocks, mineral concentrates, supplements and other products for a wide range of animal species that include dairy cows, poultry, pigs, beef cattle, horses, sheep, working dogs, pets and fish. It has an extensive research and development program and strong partnerships with industry bodies, universities and key research organisations. It benefits as the Australian agricultural sector expands and has adopted an ambitious three-year growth plan. The streamlining of its bulk stockfeeds facilities is expected to lead to increased production and the company is hoping to move into new markets. It also wishes to boost exports for the packaged feeds and ingredients segment. Thanks to the addition of new premium products to its petfood lines it continues to boost sales. It benefits from a flourishing prawn and barramundi industry in Northern Australia and has announced that it is making its first profits from the innovative NovaqPro prawn feed that was developed by the CSIRO. It is also working to develop an export market for this product. Prawns fed with NovaqPro grow 20 per cent to 40 per cent faster.

Year to 30 June	2022	2023
Revenues ($mn)	1049.1	1260.1
Bulk stockfeeds (%)	66	69
Packaged feeds & ingredients (%)	34	31
EBIT ($mn)	54.4	64.1
EBIT margin (%)	5.2	5.1
Gross margin (%)	9.5	8.8
Profit before tax ($mn)	51.6	58.6
Profit after tax ($mn)	36.2	41.8
Earnings per share (c)	11.33	13.24
Cash flow per share (c)	19.40	21.09
Dividend (c)	7.4	8.25
Percentage franked	100	100
Net tangible assets per share ($)	0.75	0.76
Interest cover (times)	19.1	12.6
Return on equity (%)	12.0	13.2
Debt-to-equity ratio (%)	7.3	9.3
Current ratio	1.2	1.2

Rio Tinto Limited

ASX code: RIO

www.riotinto.com

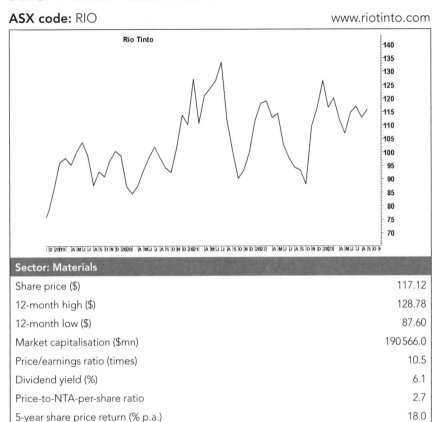

Sector: Materials	
Share price ($)	117.12
12-month high ($)	128.78
12-month low ($)	87.60
Market capitalisation ($mn)	190 566.0
Price/earnings ratio (times)	10.5
Dividend yield (%)	6.1
Price-to-NTA-per-share ratio	2.7
5-year share price return (% p.a.)	18.0
Dividend reinvestment plan	Yes

British-based Rio Tinto, one of the world's largest mining companies, was founded by European investors in 1873 in order to reopen some ancient copper mines at the Tinto River in Spain. It maintains an ASX presence in a dual-listing structure and continues to pay franked dividends to Australian shareholders. Its products include iron ore, copper, gold, industrial minerals, diamonds and aluminium. Subsidiaries include the 86 per cent–owned uranium miner Energy Resources of Australia.

Latest business results (June 2023, half year)

Falling commodities prices caused a decline in revenues and profits. The average iron ore price for the period was down 14 per cent, although this was partially offset by higher sales volumes and an improved product mix. Average production costs actually edged down, despite inflationary pressures, thanks to a weaker Australian dollar and the higher volumes. Iron ore represented 55 per cent of total company revenues but accounted for more than 80 per cent of underlying profit during the period. The Aluminium division, representing 22 per cent of revenues, reversed its strong gains of the June 2022 half, with a lower average sales price and rising costs combining to deliver a sharp fall in profits. Copper profits were also well down, despite the first sustainable production from the Oyu Tolgoi mine in Mongolia. Average sales prices were lower and costs were up. The company's Minerals division, incorporating iron ore pellets and concentrates, titanium dioxide, borates and diamonds, also posted an earnings decline, with lower prices for iron ore pellets and concentrates. Altogether, 58 per cent of total company sales were to China and a further 14 per cent to the rest of Asia. Note that Rio Tinto reports its results in US dollars. The tables in this book are based on Australian dollar figures and exchange rates supplied by the company.

Outlook

Rio Tinto maintains a substantial portfolio of well-run assets across many countries, and with generally low operating costs. It forecasts capital expenditure of up to US$10 billion in each of 2024 and 2025. It continues to boost production at Oyu Tolgoi, which is set to become the world's fourth-largest copper mine by 2030. It is also working to bring the giant Simandou iron ore project in Guinea into production. In Argentina it has acquired the Rincon lithium project and sees this as a further engine of growth. It has also announced plans to spend US$700 million for a 50 per cent holding in the Canadian metals recycling company Matalco.

Year to 31 December	2021	2022
Revenues ($mn)	84 488.0	80 513.0
EBIT ($mn)	41 351.0	27 531.9
EBIT margin (%)	48.9	34.2
Profit before tax ($mn)	41 027.0	27 046.4
Profit after tax ($mn)	28 449.0	18 000.0
Earnings per share (c)	1757.85	1111.25
Cash flow per share (c)	2144.81	1559.51
Dividend (c)	1086.46	710.19
Percentage franked	100	100
Interest cover (times)	173.3	121.8
Return on equity (%)	43.2	25.0
Half year to 30 June	2022	2023
Revenues ($mn)	41 374.0	39 216.2
Profit before tax ($mn)	17 112.0	12 142.6
Profit after tax ($mn)	11 988.0	8382.4
Earnings per share (c)	740.30	518.97
Dividend (c)	383.7	260.89
Percentage franked	100	100
Net tangible assets per share ($)	41.23	43.91
Debt-to-equity ratio (%)	4.1	6.9
Current ratio	1.8	2.0

Santos Limited

ASX code: STO www.santos.com

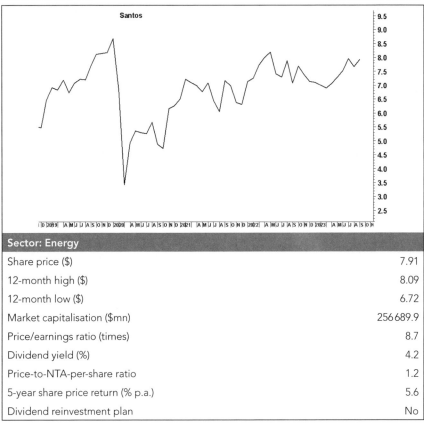

Sector: Energy	
Share price ($)	7.91
12-month high ($)	8.09
12-month low ($)	6.72
Market capitalisation ($mn)	256 689.9
Price/earnings ratio (times)	8.7
Dividend yield (%)	4.2
Price-to-NTA-per-share ratio	1.2
5-year share price return (% p.a.)	5.6
Dividend reinvestment plan	No

Adelaide-based Santos, established in 1954, is one of Australia's leading producers of oil and gas. Following a new organisational structure, announced in May 2023, it arranges its operations into three regional business units: the Eastern Australia and Papua New Guinea (PNG) unit produces natural gas, gas liquids and crude oil at the Cooper Basin and liquefied natural gas (LNG) in Queensland and PNG; the Western Australia, Northern Australia and Timor-Leste unit produces natural gas at the Bayu-Undan field in Timor-Leste and LNG at Darwin, along with natural gas, gas liquids and crude oil in Western Australia; the Alaskan unit incorporates the Pikka oil and gas development. In addition to the three regional business units, Santos also manages Santos Energy Solutions, which provides mid-stream processing of gas and liquids along with decarbonisation and carbon management services and long-term portfolio strategy services.

Latest business results (June 2023, half year)

Lower production and falling prices sent revenues and profits down. Production of 45 million barrels of oil equivalent (boe) was 13 per cent lower than in the June 2022 half, with reduced gas output in Western Australia, lower volumes from

Bayu-Undan as the field approaches the end of its life and falling production in PNG due to natural field decline. The average realised oil price fell 26 per cent, with the average realised LNG price down 7 per cent. Note that Santos reports its results in US dollars. The Australian dollar figures in this book—converted at prevailing exchange rates—are for guidance only.

Outlook

Santos is involved in some large development projects aimed at securing long-term supplies of oil and gas, and with the potential to transform the company's business. One of the biggest is the $5.8 billion Barossa gas project in the Timor Sea, which is aimed at supplying gas for the Darwin LNG plant to replace supplies from the Bayu-Undan field. However, environmental protests have forced a suspension of operations, although Santos remains hopeful of delivering the first gas in 2025. At the Pikka project in Alaska the company believes it can be delivering oil from 2026. In PNG it is involved in planning for a major new LNG project. It has deferred a final investment decision on the proposed Dorado oil and gas project in Western Australia. It is waiting for an appeals court decision on whether it can proceed with its Narrabri domestic gas project in New South Wales. Santos expects to produce between 89 million boe and 93 million boe during 2023.

Year to 31 December	2021	2022
Revenues ($mn)	6284.0	11289.9
EBIT ($mn)	1902.7	4718.8
EBIT margin (%)	30.3	41.8
Gross margin (%)	36.7	49.9
Profit before tax ($mn)	1606.7	4272.5
Profit after tax ($mn)	877.3	3060.9
Earnings per share (c)	41.13	91.35
Cash flow per share (c)	118.82	166.92
Dividend (c)	19.5	33.29
Percentage franked	82	0
Interest cover (times)	6.6	12.8
Return on equity (%)	6.3	15.1
Half year to 30 June	2022	2023
Revenues ($mn)	5230.6	4363.2
Profit before tax ($mn)	2263.9	1435.3
Profit after tax ($mn)	1620.8	1161.8
Earnings per share (c)	48.06	35.44
Dividend (c)	10.93	13.4
Percentage franked	0	0
Net tangible assets per share ($)	5.60	6.35
Debt-to-equity ratio (%)	20.9	20.9
Current ratio	1.6	1.6

Seek Limited

ASX code: SEK

seek.com.au

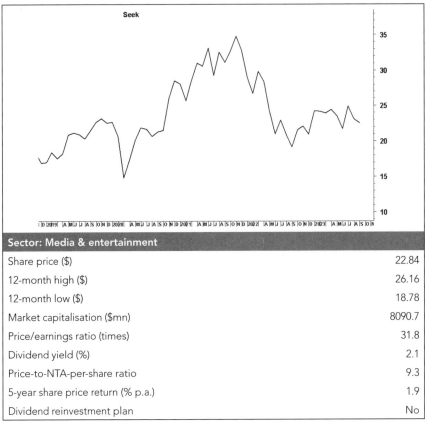

Sector: Media & entertainment	
Share price ($)	22.84
12-month high ($)	26.16
12-month low ($)	18.78
Market capitalisation ($mn)	8090.7
Price/earnings ratio (times)	31.8
Dividend yield (%)	2.1
Price-to-NTA-per-share ratio	9.3
5-year share price return (% p.a.)	1.9
Dividend reinvestment plan	No

Melbourne-based Seek, founded in 1997, operates Australia's largest website for job-seekers. It has expanded to New Zealand, and also has equity stakes in leading online employment businesses in Asia and Latin America, with more than a quarter of company revenues deriving from outside Australia. In Asia it operates employment platforms in Hong Kong, the Philippines, Thailand, Malaysia, Singapore and Indonesia under the brands JobStreet and JobsDB. In Brazil it runs the Brasil Online business and in Mexico it operates Online Career Centre.

Latest business results (June 2023, full year)

Price increases helped boost revenues, but underlying profits edged down as the company experienced a decline domestically in online jobs advertising. The core Australia/New Zealand segment achieved a 5 per cent increase in revenues, a sharp fall from the 53 per cent growth of the previous year, when a tight employment market led to a surge in jobs advertising. Seek Asia enjoyed a good year, with double-digit gains in revenues and profits, despite a decline in advertising volumes. The Mexican operation also performed well, but Brazilian business continued to decline on a constant currency basis and remained in the red. During the year the company deconsolidated its Seek Growth Fund — which comprises a portfolio of start-up companies in which Seek has invested — and recognised a one-off gain of $840 million, which is treated in the accounts as a significant item.

Outlook

The company maintains its dominance of the online job advertising market in Australia, with a high degree of brand awareness and solid profit margins. It attributes its strength to an ongoing reinvestment strategy, with continuing new products and enhanced services that lead to higher revenues, even when advertising volumes fall. It is experiencing an increase in advertising for government-related jobs, even while corporate advertising declines. In Asia it is benefiting from price increases and moves to higher-margin premium advertising. It sees great potential for its Asian activities, and is working to build a unified online marketplace platform across Australia, New Zealand and Asia. It believes that when this work is completed, by the end of the June 2024 year, it will allow new products to be deployed at scale across all markets, as well as enabling rapid innovation and enhanced reliability and security. However, for the near term it predicts rising unemployment and reduced demand for labour in Australia, and its early forecast is for June 2024 revenues of $1.18 billion to $1.26 billion and an after-tax profit of $220 million to $260 million.

Year to 30 June	2022	2023
Revenues ($mn)	1116.5	1225.3
Australia/New Zealand (%)	74	71
Seek Asia (%)	18	20
OCC (%)	3	3
Brasil Online (%)	3	2
EBIT ($mn)	415.3	434.7
EBIT margin (%)	37.2	35.5
Profit before tax ($mn)	360.8	356.1
Profit after tax ($mn)	256.8	255.0
Earnings per share (c)	72.57	71.84
Cash flow per share (c)	97.92	102.02
Dividend (c)	44	47
Percentage franked	100	100
Net tangible assets per share ($)	0.41	2.45
Interest cover (times)	8.0	6.0
Return on equity (%)	14.1	11.4
Debt-to-equity ratio (%)	55.2	39.5
Current ratio	2.0	0.9

Servcorp Limited

ASX code: SRV

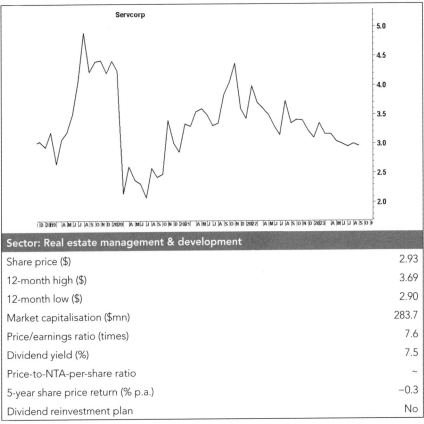

Sector: Real estate management & development	
Share price ($)	2.93
12-month high ($)	3.69
12-month low ($)	2.90
Market capitalisation ($mn)	283.7
Price/earnings ratio (times)	7.6
Dividend yield (%)	7.5
Price-to-NTA-per-share ratio	~
5-year share price return (% p.a.)	−0.3
Dividend reinvestment plan	No

Sydney-based Servcorp was founded in 1978 to provide serviced office space to small businesses. It has expanded to provide advanced corporate infrastructure, including IT and telecommunications services, and office support services. It also offers what it terms virtual offices, providing a prestigious address and a range of services—such as message forwarding and access to meeting rooms—for people or businesses not needing a physical office. More than a third of the company's business is in Europe and the Middle East and a further third in North Asia. In June 2023 it was operating 129 floors of offices in 40 cities across 20 countries.

Latest business results (June 2023, full year)

Underlying revenues and profits grew well in a good result as Servcorp continued to recover from the COVID pandemic, which badly hit its operations. For a second consecutive year the Europe/Middle East segment showed strong growth, with double-digit rises in sales and profits, and it edged ahead of North Asia as the company's largest region. The Australia/New Zealand/South-East Asia segment also grew strongly as demand continued to build. The smaller US operation continued its recovery, although profit margins remained low. By contrast, North Asia once again underperformed, with revenues and profits falling as China only slowly recovered from severe COVID restrictions, combined with Servcorp's decision to cease operations in Hong Kong. During the year the company opened five new floors and closed five. The total occupancy rate at June 2023 of 71 per cent was down from 72 per cent in the previous year.

Outlook

Servcorp is a world leader in its business, with good market shares and a reputation for quality. However, it was badly hurt by the COVID pandemic, which led many workers to abandon their offices and work from home. Now, as conditions recover, and with high levels of client retention, the company has made the decision to invest heavily in further expansion. In February 2023 it announced plans to spend up to $60 million over 18 months on the development of 15 further floors of offices. By June 2023 it had spent $20 million and opened five floors, with an additional eight scheduled to open during the June 2024 year. A restructuring of US operations is expected to boost profitability there. At June 2023 Servcorp had no debt and more than $105 million in cash holdings. Its early forecast is for underlying profits to rise by at least 9 per cent in the June 2024 year.

Year to 30 June	2022	2023
Revenues ($mn)	274.5	293.8
EBIT ($mn)	41.1	53.5
EBIT margin (%)	15.0	18.2
Profit before tax ($mn)	31.0	42.3
Profit after tax ($mn)	25.3	37.1
Earnings per share (c)	26.13	38.32
Cash flow per share (c)	150.24	164.22
Dividend (c)	20	22
Percentage franked	0	11
Net tangible assets per share ($)	~	~
Interest cover (times)	~	6.4
Return on equity (%)	12.9	19.2
Debt-to-equity ratio (%)	~	~
Current ratio	0.9	0.8

Smartgroup Corporation Limited

ASX code: SIQ

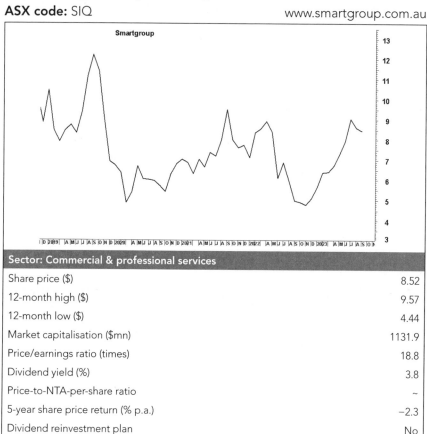

Sector: Commercial & professional services	
Share price ($)	8.52
12-month high ($)	9.57
12-month low ($)	4.44
Market capitalisation ($mn)	1131.9
Price/earnings ratio (times)	18.8
Dividend yield (%)	3.8
Price-to-NTA-per-share ratio	~
5-year share price return (% p.a.)	−2.3
Dividend reinvestment plan	No

Sydney-based specialist employee management services provider Smartgroup got its start in 1999 as Smartsalary, a salary packaging specialist. It later branched into other businesses, and has grown significantly, both organically and through acquisition. It is now engaged in salary packaging services, as well as vehicle novated leasing, fleet management, payroll administration, share plan administration and workforce optimisation consulting services.

Latest business results (June 2023, half year)

Revenues rose from the June 2022 half, but higher staffing costs sent profits down. Salary packaging customer numbers of 385 000 were up from 383 000 a year earlier, thanks to new clients and organic growth from existing clients. The company noted that vehicle supply disruptions were steadily easing. Nevertheless, delivery times remained well above historic levels, hurting its vehicle-related businesses. Novated leases under management fell 7 per cent to 58 300, primarily due to the exit of a large client. By contrast, the high-margin managed fleet vehicle business saw numbers rise 5 per cent to 26 200. At June 2023 the company had a pipeline of unfulfilled vehicle orders worth approximately $20 million.

Outlook

Smartgroup is one of Australia's largest companies involved in the salary packaging and novated leasing businesses. Essentially this latter business involves taking advantage of complex legislation to provide tax deductions for employees, mainly those working in charities or in the public sector. Smartgroup has grown considerably through a series of acquisitions, with around 3700 employer clients. As it grows it achieves economies of scale, and profit margins increase. It has been achieving success in renewing or extending the contracts of its leading clients. It has announced a strategic plan, named Smart Future, aimed at boosting annual EBITDA by $15 million to $20 million from 2024 through the introduction of new and upgraded technology software and infrastructure. It sees great potential in its new online car leasing portal—introduced on a trial basis in February 2023—which allows customers to obtain quotes and to process applications. The trials have shown that it leads to a significant increase in client activity, and the company plans to roll it out progressively during 2023 to the bulk of its clients. The abolition of fringe benefits tax on many electric vehicles has led to a sharp rise in demand for these, with electric vehicles representing 30 per cent of all new car novated lease quotes in the June 2023 half. The company believes that as new, cheaper electric vehicle models are released this demand will continue to grow.

Year to 31 December	2021	2022
Revenues ($mn)	221.8	224.7
EBIT ($mn)	86.8	86.0
EBIT margin (%)	39.2	38.3
Profit before tax ($mn)	85.2	83.6
Profit after tax ($mn)	58.8	58.8
Earnings per share (c)	45.40	45.33
Cash flow per share (c)	55.18	51.47
Dividend (c)	36.5	32
Percentage franked	100	100
Interest cover (times)	52.2	41.3
Return on equity (%)	21.9	23.2
Half year to 30 June	2022	2023
Revenues ($mn)	113.6	116.6
Profit before tax ($mn)	44.7	41.6
Profit after tax ($mn)	30.9	28.9
Earnings per share (c)	23.80	22.30
Dividend (c)	17	15.5
Percentage franked	100	100
Net tangible assets per share ($)	~	~
Debt-to-equity ratio (%)	11.0	17.2
Current ratio	0.9	0.9

Steadfast Group Limited

ASX code: SDF

investor.steadfast.com.au

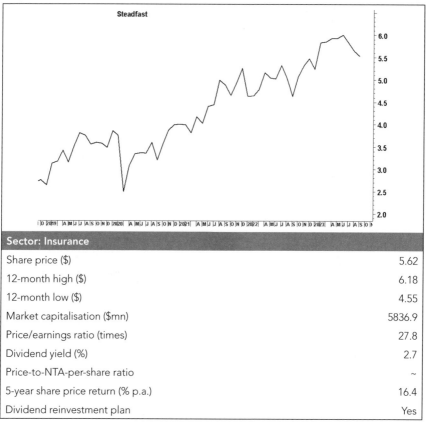

Sector: Insurance	
Share price ($)	5.62
12-month high ($)	6.18
12-month low ($)	4.55
Market capitalisation ($mn)	5836.9
Price/earnings ratio (times)	27.8
Dividend yield (%)	2.7
Price-to-NTA-per-share ratio	~
5-year share price return (% p.a.)	16.4
Dividend reinvestment plan	Yes

Melbourne-based insurance broking firm Steadfast launched in 1996 with the aim of boosting the buying power of small independent general insurance brokers in their dealings with insurers. It has since grown to become the largest insurance broker network and underwriting group in Australasia, with further operations in Asia and Europe. It also manages a range of complementary businesses that include back-office services, risk services guidance, work health consultancy, reinsurance and legal advice. It has taken a 60 per cent stake in Hamburg-based UnisonSteadfast, one of the world's largest networks of general insurance brokers.

Latest business results (June 2023, full year)

Steadfast reported another excellent result, with double-digit rises in revenues and profits. Its core Steadfast Broking business recorded gross written premium of $11.6 billion, up 12.8 per cent from the previous year after adjusting for the exit from the company of PSC Insurance Group. The benefits of $574 million of acquisitions during the year, along with solid organic growth, offset rising costs. At June 2023 Steadfast incorporated a network of 337 brokerages in Australia, 63 in New Zealand and 26 in Singapore. It had equity holdings in 68 of the brokerages.

The 60 per cent–owned UnisonSteadfast incorporated a further 271 brokerages across 115 countries. The Steadfast Underwriting Agencies business, comprising 29 specialist agencies offering over 100 niche products, generated gross written premium of $2.1 billion, up 16.7 per cent, with premium price increases also boosting this business.

Outlook

Steadfast operates nine complementary businesses supporting its broker network and underwriting agencies and is involved in an assortment of initiatives aimed at delivering long-term growth. The company claims that through its Steadfast Technologies business it is a global leader in broker insurance technology that supports interactions with broker partners and clients and underpins its strong market position. Its fast-growing Steadfast Client Trading Platform provides brokers with automated access to its network and the ability to make comparisons of policies and prices on a single screen. It is delivering efficiency gains and the company continues to add more product lines, new insurers and other capabilities. The company is also investing heavily in its cloud-based Insight insurance broking platform, with members of its broker network steadily migrating to this system. Thanks to a pipeline of some $280 million of additional acquisitions, along with further planned premium price rises, Steadfast is forecasting a June 2024 after-tax profit of $230 million to $240 million, with EPS growth of 10 per cent to 15 per cent.

Year to 30 June	2022	2023
Revenues ($mn)	1135.9	1409.5
EBIT ($mn)	299.7	378.8
EBIT margin (%)	26.4	26.9
Profit before tax ($mn)	281.7	347.8
Profit after tax ($mn)	169.0	207.0
Earnings per share (c)	17.62	20.19
Cash flow per share (c)	25.26	28.81
Dividend (c)	13	15
Percentage franked	100	100
Net tangible assets per share ($)	~	~
Interest cover (times)	20.5	49.8
Return on equity (%)	11.9	11.1
Debt-to-equity ratio (%)	33.4	31.7
Current ratio	1.6	1.4

Super Retail Group Limited

ASX code: SUL
www.superretailgroup.com.au

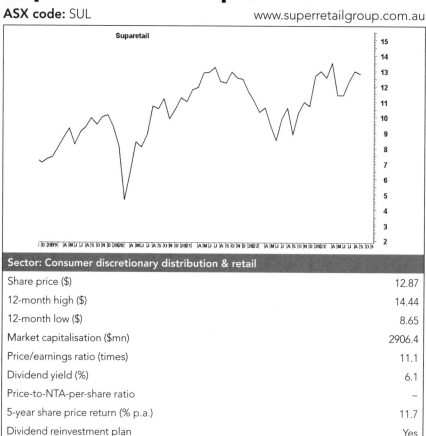

Suparetail

Sector: Consumer discretionary distribution & retail	
Share price ($)	12.87
12-month high ($)	14.44
12-month low ($)	8.65
Market capitalisation ($mn)	2906.4
Price/earnings ratio (times)	11.1
Dividend yield (%)	6.1
Price-to-NTA-per-share ratio	~
5-year share price return (% p.a.)	11.7
Dividend reinvestment plan	Yes

Specialist retail chain Super Retail Group was established as a mail-order business in 1972 and has its headquarters in Strathpine, Queensland. It now comprises a number of key retail brands, with more than 730 stores throughout Australia and New Zealand. Supercheap Auto is a retailer of automotive spare parts and related products. Rebel is a prominent sporting goods chain. BCF is a retailer of boating, camping and fishing products. Macpac is an outdoor adventure and activity specialist retailer.

Latest business results (July 2023, full year)

Super Retail overcame a weak consumer spending environment to post a solid result, though with a pronounced slowdown in the second half. On a like-for-like basis total group sales rose by 8 per cent. The best result came from the small Macpac division, with sales up 22 per cent, thanks to an increase in travel and outdoor adventure activity after the removal of COVID-related restrictions. The big Supercheap Auto business also achieved success, with sales up 8 per cent. Auto maintenance was the strongest category, which the company attributed to a growing do-it-yourself trend. Rebel sales were also up 8 per cent, reflecting a rebound in participation in sporting activities. The weakest performance came from BCF, with sales up 1 per cent. Total group online sales of $445 million were down 17 per cent. During the year the company opened 24 new stores. Note that the July 2023 result represented 52 weeks, compared to 53 weeks for the July 2022 result.

Outlook

Super Retail controls four prominent brands with strong positions in their respective markets. Nevertheless, it operates in a challenging and competitive retail environment at a time when rising interest rates and inflationary pressures have been dampening consumer spending. With much of its product range imported, it is also vulnerable to currency fluctuations and supply chain disruptions. In response, it plans a rollout of 24 new stores during the June 2024 year. It will continue to upgrade Rebel stores to the attractive rCX (Rebel Customer Experience) format, aimed at giving shoppers a more interactive and immersive experience. It sees scope for leveraging its loyalty program, with some 10.3 million active club members, one of the largest such schemes in Australia. Already nearly three-quarters of group sales come from club members. It has signed an agreement with the Goodman Group to develop a major new $80 million, 65 000 square metre automated distribution centre in Melbourne. At June 2023 Super Retail had no debt and cash holdings of $192 million.

Year to 1 July*	2022	2023
Revenues ($mn)	3550.9	3802.6
Supercheap Auto (%)	38	38
Rebel (%)	34	34
BCF (%)	23	22
Macpac (%)	5	5
EBIT ($mn)	392.7	426.8
EBIT margin (%)	11.1	11.2
Gross margin (%)	46.8	46.2
Profit before tax ($mn)	345.7	379.4
Profit after tax ($mn)	241.2	263.0
Earnings per share (c)	106.81	116.46
Cash flow per share (c)	241.96	262.41
Dividend (c)	70	78
Percentage franked	100	100
Net tangible assets per share ($)	~	~
Interest cover (times)	8.4	9.9
Return on equity (%)	19.2	19.8
Debt-to-equity ratio (%)	~	~
Current ratio	1.2	1.3

*2 July 2022

Supply Network Limited

ASX code: SNL   www.supplynetwork.com.au

Sector: Consumer discretionary distribution & retail	
Share price ($)	15.35
12-month high ($)	15.62
12-month low ($)	9.91
Market capitalisation ($mn)	637.9
Price/earnings ratio (times)	23.1
Dividend yield (%)	3.1
Price-to-NTA-per-share ratio	15.9
5-year share price return (% p.a.)	32.4
Dividend reinvestment plan	Yes

Sydney-based Supply Network is a supplier of bus and truck parts in the commercial vehicle aftermarket, operating under the brand name Multispares, which was established in 1976. It manages offices, distribution centres and workshops at 20 locations throughout Australia and five in New Zealand.

Latest business results (June 2023, full year)

Continuing strong demand for its products and services generated another excellent result for Supply Network. Further efficiency gains helped to boost margins. Sales in Australia were up 30 per cent, with EBIT jumping 50 per cent. New Zealand, representing 16 per cent of total income, saw revenues up 17 per cent in local dollars, but profits were down as costs rose. In addition, the company said that new network stocking strategies that had brought down costs in Australia were yet to be introduced to New Zealand. The company reported that COVID-related global supply chain problems had largely dissipated. In February 2023 Supply Network commenced operations at its new Melbourne distribution centre in Truganina.

Outlook

Supply Network is one of the leaders in the Australian market for the supply of truck and bus parts. With a great diversity of vehicle makes and models, and with a considerable difference in requirements between various regions of the country, the company has established a decentralised management structure with a strong regional focus. Its core activity in recent years has become the supply of truck components, and this now represents more than 80 per cent of total income. Company fleets are the largest customer group, and these are sophisticated buyers of parts with a focus on costs, making this business highly competitive. Independent repair workshops are the next-largest customer group. The company is a beneficiary of the increasing complexity of trucks, which require an ever-growing range of expensive components. It has a range of projects designed to lay the foundations for future growth, with a view to reaching annual revenues of $350 million. In particular, it plans a major upgrade of its technology systems, targeting transaction efficiency and the speed and accuracy of customer service, as well as standardising its internal catalogue and rolling out new scanning technologies. The company opened a new Gold Coast branch at Yatala in August 2023 and it plans two additional branches by 2025. Thanks to product range expansion initiatives it is also working to increase the size of several other branches. Its early June 2024 forecast is for revenue growth close to its 10-year average of 14 per cent.

Year to 30 June	2022	2023
Revenues ($mn)	198.4	252.3
EBIT ($mn)	29.9	40.9
EBIT margin (%)	15.1	16.2
Profit before tax ($mn)	28.5	39.0
Profit after tax ($mn)	20.0	27.4
Earnings per share (c)	49.02	66.51
Cash flow per share (c)	65.31	84.71
Dividend (c)	32	48
Percentage franked	100	100
Net tangible assets per share ($)	0.63	0.96
Interest cover (times)	20.5	23.4
Return on equity (%)	36.9	40.0
Debt-to-equity ratio (%)	4.1	2.8
Current ratio	2.4	2.5

Technology One Limited

ASX code: TNE www.technologyonecorp.com

Sector: Software & services	
Share price ($)	15.94
12-month high ($)	17.12
12-month low ($)	10.39
Market capitalisation ($mn)	5175.5
Price/earnings ratio (times)	57.9
Dividend yield (%)	0.9
Price-to-NTA-per-share ratio	132.8
5-year share price return (% p.a.)	23.7
Dividend reinvestment plan	No

Brisbane-based Technology One, founded in 1987, designs, develops, implements and supports a wide range of financial management, accounting and business software. It enjoys particular strength in local government. Its software is also used by educational institutions, including many Australian universities. Other key markets are financial services, central government, and health and community services. It derives revenues not only from the supply of its products but also from annual licence fees. It operates from offices in Australia, New Zealand, Malaysia and the UK.

Latest business results (March 2023, half year)

Technology One posted another strong result, with profits up for the 14th straight March half year. With earnings growing at a faster pace than sales, the company continued to expand its profit margins. Once again it enjoyed success in moving its customers onto its Software as a Service (SaaS) cloud platforms, and this now represents 98 per cent of total income. The number of large-scale enterprise SaaS customers rose to 903, up from 714 a year earlier. SaaS annual recurring revenue was a 40 per cent jump from a year before. Consulting services—essentially the business of implementing the company's software, and representing about 15 per cent of company turnover — saw sales and profits down. The pre-tax profit for UK operations rose 29 per cent to $3 million. The company maintained its high level of research and development spending, up 19 per cent to $49.4 million.

Outlook

Technology One has become a star among Australian high-tech companies, with growing profits and regular dividend increases. In large part this reflects a strong product line, a solid flow of recurring income, and a heavy investment in new products and services, which it believes will enable it to double in size every five years. It has achieved great success with its SaaS offerings, which put software in the cloud, rather than on the customers' own computers, meaning that the customers always have the latest software versions, and giving them greater flexibility than previously. It currently receives annual recurring revenues of $350 million from its SaaS business, and believes it is on track to boost this to more than $500 million by 2026, with growing profit margins. It believes it can enhance its competitive position in the UK through its new Scientia business, which provides academic timetabling and resource scheduling software to educational institutions. It is also considering expansion to other markets. At March 2023 Technology One had no debt and cash holdings of $139 million.

Year to 30 September	2021	2022
Revenues ($mn)	311.3	368.2
EBIT ($mn)	99.3	114.2
EBIT margin (%)	31.9	31.0
Profit before tax ($mn)	97.8	112.3
Profit after tax ($mn)	72.7	88.8
Earnings per share (c)	22.64	27.51
Cash flow per share (c)	30.69	39.31
Dividend (c)	13.91	15.02
Percentage franked	60	60
Interest cover (times)	78.3	80.3
Return on equity (%)	43.7	41.4
Half year to 31 March	2022	2023
Revenues ($mn)	172.0	201.0
Profit before tax ($mn)	42.6	52.7
Profit after tax ($mn)	33.2	41.3
Earnings per share (c)	10.29	12.73
Dividend (c)	4.2	4.62
Percentage franked	60	60
Net tangible assets per share ($)	0.02	0.12
Debt-to-equity ratio (%)	~	~
Current ratio	1.0	1.1

Telstra Group Limited

ASX code: TLS www.telstra.com.au

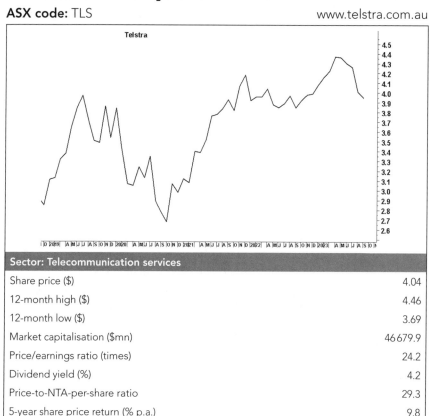

Sector: Telecommunication services	
Share price ($)	4.04
12-month high ($)	4.46
12-month low ($)	3.69
Market capitalisation ($mn)	46 679.9
Price/earnings ratio (times)	24.2
Dividend yield (%)	4.2
Price-to-NTA-per-share ratio	29.3
5-year share price return (% p.a.)	9.8
Dividend reinvestment plan	Yes

Melbourne-based Telstra traces its origins back to the construction of Australia's first telegraph line in 1854. It later became part of the Postmaster-General's department. Subsequently, a privatisation process began in 1997. It is today Australia's premier provider of telecommunication services, with 22.5 million retail mobile services, 2 million wholesale mobile services and 3.4 million consumer and small business bundle and data services. It also has substantial business interests throughout the Asia-Pacific, including operation of the region's largest sub-sea cable network. In July 2022, working with the Australian government, it completed the $2.4 billion acquisition of Digicel Pacific, a major Pacific-region telecommunication services provider with some 2.8 million customers.

Latest business results (June 2023, full year)

Revenues and profits bounced back from the decline of the previous year. Once again the company's mobile activities drove much of the good result, with revenues up 8.3 per cent and margins improving as competitive pressures eased. By contrast, the low-margin fixed-line businesses saw sales down. International activities grew substantially, thanks to the Digicel Pacific acquisition. Telstra's InfraCo Fixed operation, responsible for much of the company's infrastructure work, recorded a 4.1 per cent rise in revenues, thanks especially to recurring National Broadband Network contracts.

Outlook

Telstra has embarked on its three-year T25 strategy. This involves a significant reorganisation of its corporate structure and an ambitious range of performance targets. It plans to expand its mobile network, particularly in regional areas, and has a target that 80 per cent of its traffic will be on the advanced 5G standard by June 2025, up from around 40 per cent at present. It is also working to expand its international business, with its Digicel Pacific acquisition providing an important foothold in some Pacific-region countries. Thanks to the emergence of artificial intelligence and demand for cloud storage Telstra is optimistic about the long-term growth potential for its InfraCo Fixed division, which owns a substantial portfolio of digital assets, including fibre optic cable, data centres and subsea cables. Consequently, it has reversed an earlier plan to sell this business. It is benefiting from an easing of intense competition in the mobile phone market, allowing it to raise prices while retaining market share. Nevertheless, it is vulnerable to any economic downturn. The company's early forecast is for June 2024 revenues of $22.8 billion to $24.8 billion, underlying EBITDA of $8.2 billion to $8.4 billion—compared to $7.9 billion in June 2023—with expected capital spending of $3.6 billion to $3.7 billion.

Year to 30 June	2022	2023
Revenues ($mn)	21 277.0	22 702.0
Mobility (%)	43	44
Fixed—consumer & small business (%)	20	19
Fixed—enterprise (%)	17	16
International (%)	7	10
InfraCo Fixed (%)	7	6
EBIT ($mn)	3008.0	3493.0
EBIT margin (%)	14.1	15.4
Profit before tax ($mn)	2481.0	2863.0
Profit after tax ($mn)	1688.0	1928.0
Earnings per share (c)	14.36	16.70
Cash flow per share (c)	51.43	55.43
Dividend (c)	13.5	17
Percentage franked	100	100
Net tangible assets per share ($)	0.37	0.14
Interest cover (times)	7.2	6.6
Return on equity (%)	11.3	12.5
Debt-to-equity ratio (%)	59.0	65.9
Current ratio	0.6	0.7

Wesfarmers Limited

ASX code: WES   www.wesfarmers.com.au

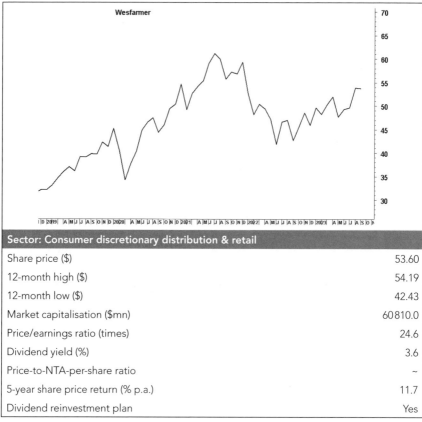

Sector: Consumer discretionary distribution & retail

Share price ($)	53.60
12-month high ($)	54.19
12-month low ($)	42.43
Market capitalisation ($mn)	60810.0
Price/earnings ratio (times)	24.6
Dividend yield (%)	3.6
Price-to-NTA-per-share ratio	~
5-year share price return (% p.a.)	11.7
Dividend reinvestment plan	Yes

Perth-based Wesfarmers, founded in 1914 as a farmers' cooperative, is now a conglomerate with many areas of operation. Its primary business is the Bunnings network of hardware stores. Other retail businesses include the Officeworks, Kmart, Priceline and Target chains and the Catch online marketplace. In addition, it produces fertilisers, chemicals and industrial safety products. It holds 50 per cent of the Flybuys loyalty card business, owns a 25 per cent interest in the ASX-listed BWP property trust—which owns many Bunnings warehouses—and holds half the equity in the financial services business Gresham Partners, the timber business Wespine Industries and the lithium producer Covalent Lithium. At June 2023 Wesfarmers operated 1782 stores in Australia and New Zealand.

Latest business results (June 2023, full year)

Sales and profits rose, with a full year's contribution from the 2022 acquisition of Australian Pharmaceutical Industries (API), but also with good results from most of the company's businesses. One of the best performances came from the Kmart Group, which had suffered from COVID-related lockdowns in the previous year, with sales up 16.5 per cent and profits rebounding by more than 50 per cent. The core Bunnings business reported increased sales and a small rise in profits. The new Health division, based on the API acquisition, benefited from strong wholesale demand and growing customer numbers, and moved from loss to profit. Officeworks achieved higher sales and profits. The WesCEF Chemicals, Energy and Fertilisers division enjoyed another strong rise in profits, underpinned by favourable global ammonia prices.

Outlook

Wesfarmers has a variety of strategies for growth, although it is concerned about the impact that elevated inflation and higher interest rates will have on certain of its businesses. However, it views low levels of unemployment and a rising population as positives. A transformation program is driving profitable growth for the new Health division. It sees particular potential in the health, beauty and wellbeing sector and its $180 million acquisition in 2023 of aesthetics clinic operator SILK Laser Australia is intended to complement its existing Clear Skincare clinic network. The company's Covalent Lithium joint venture is constructing a $1.9 billion mine and refinery in Western Australia with the goal of producing up to 50 000 tonnes annually of lithium hydroxide, for use in lithium batteries, with initial output expected in early 2024. The Bunnings business continues to expand its network, and has moved into pet supplies. The creation of the OneDigital division promotes operational efficiencies and digital growth across the company's diverse range of businesses.

Year to 30 June	2022	2023
Revenues ($mn)	36 838.0	43 550.0
Bunnings (%)	48	43
Kmart Group (%)	25	24
Health (%)	3	12
Officeworks (%)	9	8
WesCEF (%)	8	8
EBIT ($mn)	3416.0	3644.0
EBIT margin (%)	9.3	8.4
Profit before tax ($mn)	3320.0	3509.0
Profit after tax ($mn)	2352.0	2465.0
Earnings per share (c)	207.77	217.76
Cash flow per share (c)	346.91	368.02
Dividend (c)	180	191
Percentage franked	100	100
Net tangible assets per share ($)	~	~
Interest cover (times)	37.5	30.6
Return on equity (%)	26.6	30.3
Debt-to-equity ratio (%)	53.3	45.4
Current ratio	1.1	1.2

WiseTech Global Limited

ASX code: WTC www.wisetechglobal.com

Sector: Software & services

Share price ($)	70.00
12-month high ($)	88.69
12-month low ($)	48.78
Market capitalisation ($mn)	23233.0
Price/earnings ratio (times)	92.6
Dividend yield (%)	0.2
Price-to-NTA-per-share ratio	~
5-year share price return (% p.a.)	26.9
Dividend reinvestment plan	Yes

Sydney-based logistics software specialist WiseTech was founded in 1994 to supply code for local freight forwarders. Today it is a global leader in international logistics software, with customers that include most of the world's largest freight forwarders and logistics providers. It has more that 50 offices worldwide and 39 product development centres. Its flagship product CargoWise is available in 30 languages and is sold in 174 countries, with more than 17000 customers.

Latest business results (June 2023, full year)

Revenues and profits rose strongly in another good result for WiseTech, although this time revenues rose at a faster pace than profits as expenses increased, placing margins under pressure. There was solid organic growth, with increasing usage of CargoWise products by the company's large existing customer base, and it also won new customers during the year. It benefited from price increases, implemented in part to offset the impact of rising costs, and also from favourable foreign exchange movements. Acquisitions during the year contributed revenues of $43 million. Recurring revenues rose from 89 per cent to 96 per cent of total income. The customer attrition rate remained below 1 per cent. The research and development expense jumped 45 per cent to $262 million, with the product design and development budget up 30 per cent to $186 million.

Outlook

WiseTech's strategy is to target the 25 leading global freight forwarders and the 200 leading global logistics providers, and it benefits as these companies consolidate and increasingly dominate their industries. It says its focus is on growth through six key development priorities—landside container haulage logistics, warehousing, Neo (the company's global integrated platform for consumers of logistics services), digital documents, customs and compliance, and international eCommerce. Having completed 45 acquisitions in seven years, the company has a highly experienced mergers and acquisitions division. It is now seeking further acquisitions to help introduce new technology to its operations. However, with its high levels of R&D spending it also expects further strong organic growth. Its 2023 acquisition for US$414 million of the prominent American intermodal rail network specialist Blume Global extends WiseTech's presence in landside logistics. During the June 2023 year it signed its first global customs contract with the world's largest freight forwarder, Kuehne+Nagel, and regards this as a watershed development that could open up a significant new market. Its early forecast is for June 2024 revenues of $1.04 billion to $1.095 billion, with EBITDA of $455 million to $490 million, compared to $385.7 million in June 2023.

Year to 30 June	2022	2023
Revenues ($mn)	632.2	816.8
EBIT ($mn)	266.6	349.5
EBIT margin (%)	42.2	42.8
Profit before tax ($mn)	262.5	342.4
Profit after tax ($mn)	189.8	247.6
Earnings per share (c)	58.22	75.60
Cash flow per share (c)	77.85	101.74
Dividend (c)	11.15	15
Percentage franked	100	100
Net tangible assets per share ($)	1.08	~
Interest cover (times)	98.7	~
Return on equity (%)	15.7	15.4
Debt-to-equity ratio (%)	~	4.3
Current ratio	2.9	0.6

Woodside Energy Group Limited

ASX code: WDS   www.woodside.com

Sector: Energy	
Share price ($)	38.24
12-month high ($)	39.58
12-month low ($)	29.55
Market capitalisation ($mn)	72608.2
Price/earnings ratio (times)	6.1
Dividend yield (%)	9.8
Price-to-NTA-per-share ratio	1.5
5-year share price return (% p.a.)	5.5
Dividend reinvestment plan	No

Perth-based Woodside, founded in 1954, is a leading specialist energy company. It is one of Australia's largest producers of oil and gas and one of the world's largest producers of liquefied natural gas (LNG). It is part owner and operator of the giant North West Shelf natural gas project in Western Australia. It also produces at the Pluto LNG project in Western Australia. It has a portfolio of other Australian interests. In addition, it produces oil and gas at the Shenzi field in the Gulf of Mexico and at the Greater Angostura field in Trinidad.

Latest business results (June 2023, half year)

Revenues and profits rose, largely reflecting an additional five-month contribution from the assets of BHP Petroleum, which merged with Woodside in June 2022. This offset a general decline in energy prices during the period. Gas production of 63.5 million barrels of oil equivalent (boe) was 52 per cent higher than in the June 2022 half. Liquids production of 27.8 million boe was 114 per cent higher. The average realised price for its output of US$74 per boe was down 23 per cent. As a result of the merger with BHP Petroleum, Woodside's share of North West Shelf production jumped 73 per cent to 22.7 million boe. Pluto production of 23.5 million boe was down 3 per cent. Other notable contributors to the result were the Gulf of Mexico, with production for Woodside of 14.8 million boe, and Bass Strait, with 10.9 million boe.

Outlook

Thanks to the merger with BHP Petroleum, Woodside has doubled in size and is now a world-scale energy producer with a significant portfolio of producing and developing assets. Its Sangomar oil and gas project in Senegal is 88 per cent complete, with the first oil expected in mid 2024. The Scarborough natural gas project in Western Australia is 38 per cent complete, with the first LNG expected in 2026. Two Japanese corporations have taken a 10 per cent stake in this development. In mid 2023 Woodside announced that it will proceed with the US$7.2 billion Trion oil project in Mexico, with the first oil in 2028. The company also maintains an active exploration program and it is moving actively into new energy schemes. Nevertheless, oil and gas exploration is expensive and inherently risky, with few guarantees of success. Developing a new project is a lengthy process. Protests by environmental groups can delay or even halt some developments. Profits are heavily influenced by energy price trends and currency rate movements.

Year to 31 December	2021	2022
Revenues ($mn)	9282.7	24372.5
EBIT ($mn)	4693.3	13537.7
EBIT margin (%)	50.6	55.5
Gross margin (%)	44.8	61.1
Profit before tax ($mn)	4386.7	13295.7
Profit after tax ($mn)	2644.0	9417.4
Earnings per share (c)	274.67	623.15
Cash flow per share (c)	508.76	905.86
Dividend (c)	187.19	375.39
Percentage franked	100	100
Interest cover (times)	17.3	778.4
Return on equity (%)	15.5	26.2
Half year to 30 June	2022	2023
Revenues ($mn)	8069.4	10882.4
Profit before tax ($mn)	4065.3	4158.8
Profit after tax ($mn)	2277.8	2558.8
Earnings per share (c)	202.08	134.85
Dividend (c)	159.95	124.3
Percentage franked	100	100
Net tangible assets per share ($)	21.87	24.93
Debt-to-equity ratio (%)	2.3	4.5
Current ratio	1.3	1.2

Woolworths Group Limited

ASX code: WOW   www.woolworthsgroup.com.au

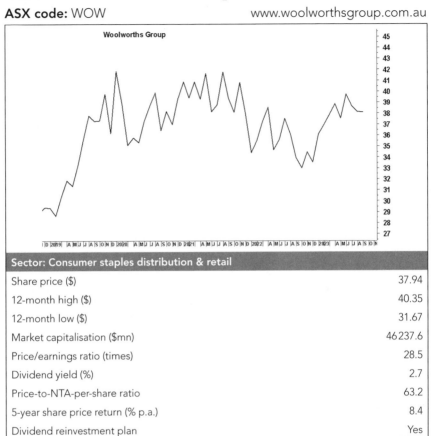

Sector: Consumer staples distribution & retail	
Share price ($)	37.94
12-month high ($)	40.35
12-month low ($)	31.67
Market capitalisation ($mn)	46237.6
Price/earnings ratio (times)	28.5
Dividend yield (%)	2.7
Price-to-NTA-per-share ratio	63.2
5-year share price return (% p.a.)	8.4
Dividend reinvestment plan	Yes

Woolworths, founded in Sydney in 1924, is one of Australia's retail giants. Its 1460 outlets across Australia and New Zealand are centred on Woolworths and Countdown supermarkets and Big W mixed goods stores. It has created a new wholesale food and drinks business, called Australian B2B. Other brands include PFD Food Services, Australian Grocery Wholesalers, Everyday Rewards, Everyday Insurance, Pet Culture, Healthylife Pharmacy, Primary Connect, Cartology, Quantium and WPay.

Latest business results (June 2023, full year)

In an environment of reduced consumer spending, Woolworths reported higher sales and profits. The core Australian Food division saw rising supermarket revenues, in part reflecting inflationary pressures that pushed up prices. Online sales edged higher, while five new stores helped Metro convenience stores achieve 22 per cent sales growth. Category mix benefits, including reduced low-margin tobacco sales, helped boost profits, partially offset by higher rates of theft. New Zealand supermarkets achieved higher sales but with profits well down, as the company faced increased costs from rising freight and online delivery charges and an increase in distribution centre expenses. Big W recovered from the previous year, when lockdowns forced the closure of many stores, with sales and profits up. The Australian B2B division recorded double-digit gains in sales and profits.

Outlook

The Woolworths chain of Australian supermarkets, relying to a large degree on non-discretionary spending, can expect to continue to do well, especially if inflation eases. The company is finding that many customers are trading down to own-brand items, and it is boosting the range of these products. However, rising costs, particularly wage increases and inflation in energy and transport, are a concern. An increase in shoplifting is another problem, and the company is working to boost security at its stores. It expects sales to continue to expand at its New Zealand supermarkets, though costs remain high. In addition, New Zealand stores are struggling with a significant shoplifting trend as well as growing aggression towards staff. Big W has been experiencing some weakness and the company is uncertain about the outlook for this business as customers spend less than previously. It has announced plans to spend $586 million for a 55 per cent holding in Petspiration Group, which runs the PETstock chain of stores. Woolworths believes the pet industry has great potential, though it is still awaiting regulatory approval for the acquisition. It has also bought SuperPharmacy, an online pharmacy specialist with six stores, and is thought to be eyeing further moves into the pharmacy sector

Year to 25 June*	2022	2023
Revenues ($mn)	60849.0	64294.0
Australian food (%)	75	75
New Zealand food (%)	11	11
Big W (%)	7	7
Australian B2B (%)	7	7
EBIT ($mn)	2723.0	3048.0
EBIT margin (%)	4.5	4.7
Gross margin (%)	29.7	26.7
Profit before tax ($mn)	2091.0	2322.0
Profit after tax ($mn)	1547.0	1618.0
Earnings per share (c)	126.65	133.25
Cash flow per share (c)	319.93	345.55
Dividend (c)	92	104
Percentage franked	100	100
Net tangible assets per share ($)	0.58	0.60
Interest cover (times)	4.4	4.3
Return on equity (%)	42.0	26.1
Debt-to-equity ratio (%)	53.4	39.9
Current ratio	0.6	0.5

*26 June 2022

PART II
THE TABLES

Table A

Market capitalisation

A company's market capitalisation is determined by multiplying the share price by the number of shares. To be included in this book, a company must be in the All Ordinaries Index, which comprises the 500 largest companies by market capitalisation.

	$mn
BHP Group	232 608.3
Rio Tinto	190 566.0
Commonwealth Bank Australia	170 817.7
CSL	129 482.4
National Australia Bank	90 622.8
ANZ Group	75 551.6
Woodside Energy Group	72 608.2
Macquarie Group	68 657.6
Fortescue Metals Group	62 195.1
Wesfarmers	60 810.0
Telstra Group	46 679.9
Woolworths Group	46 237.6
Aristocrat Leisure	27 142.0
Santos	25 689.9
WiseTech Global	23 233.0
REA Group	21 434.7
Coles Group	21 147.7
Cochlear	17 593.4
Computershare	15 178.3
Mineral Resources	14 261.7
Insurance Australia Group	14 127.6
Reece	13 107.0
ASX	10 942.0
IGO	10 806.2
Carsales.com	10 804.7
BlueScope Steel	9 943.2
Medibank Private	9 914.4
Seek	8 090.7
Pro Medicus	7 602.7
IDP Education	7 055.8
Altium	6 319.1
Steadfast Group	5 836.9
Technology One	5 175.5
Harvey Norman Holdings	5 033.9
JB Hi-Fi	5 007.5
Brickworks	4 240.0
Premier Investments	4 176.5
NIB Holdings	3 886.8
Netwealth Group	3 736.4
Beach Energy	3 695.8
Iluka Resources	3 663.7
Metcash	3 582.2
Breville Group	3 466.7
Nine Entertainment Co. Holdings	3 353.6
Reliance Worldwide Corporation	3 255.2

Super Retail Group	2 906.4
CSR	2 902.5
ARB Corporation	2 782.3
Lovisa Holdings	2 371.5
Bapcor	2 263.9
Lifestyle Communities	1 823.3
IPH	1 820.1
Pinnacle Investment Management	1 804.0
GUD Holdings	1 714.9
Magellan Financial Group	1 683.7
Johns Lyng Group	1 660.3
Credit Corp Group	1 445.7
Codan	1 433.0
Monadelphous Group	1 418.2
NRW Holdings	1 245.4
Collins Foods	1 169.7
Objective Corporation	1 162.3
Smartgroup Corporation	1 131.9
Accent Group	1 127.0
Data#3	1 125.5
Hansen Technologies	1 090.5
PWR Holdings	1 069.1
Elders	998.6
Nick Scali	997.9
Jumbo Interactive	974.9
Clinuvel Pharmaceuticals	896.8
Platinum Asset Management	825.5
Ridley Corporation	701.1
Supply Network	637.9
Grange Resources	532.4
GWA Group	511.8
Australian Ethical Investment	497.4
Beacon Lighting Group	408.8
Lycopodium	400.3
Michael Hill International	360.7
Lindsay Australia	358.0
Baby Bunting Group	290.0
Servcorp	283.7
Adairs	245.7
PeopleIn	197.0
Fiducian Group	187.3
Clover Corporation	170.3
Enero Group	148.1

Table B

Revenues

This list ranks the companies in the book according to their most recent full-year revenues figures (operating income for the banks). The figures include revenues from sales and services, but other revenues—such as interest receipts and investment income—are not generally included.

	$mn
Rio Tinto	80 513.0
BHP Group	80 323.9
Woolworths Group	64 294.0
Wesfarmers	43 550.0
Coles Group	40 483.0
Commonwealth Bank Australia	27 530.0
Fortescue Metals Group	25 180.6
Woodside Energy Group	24 372.5
Telstra Group	22 702.0
CSL	19 865.7
Insurance Australia Group	19 851.0
ANZ Group	19 426.0
Macquarie Group	19 122.0
National Australia Bank	18 446.0
BlueScope Steel	18 242.5
Metcash	15 803.4
Santos	11 289.9
JB Hi-Fi	9 626.4
Reece	8 839.6
Medibank Private	7 355.3
Aristocrat Leisure	5 573.7
Mineral Resources	4 779.1
Computershare	4 726.5
Harvey Norman Holdings	4 275.2
Super Retail Group	3 802.6
Elders	3 445.3
NIB Holdings	2 911.5
Nine Entertainment Co. Holdings	2 704.4
NRW Holdings	2 667.1
CSR	2 613.3
Data#3	2 560.7
Bapcor	2 021.1
Cochlear	1 936.1
Reliance Worldwide Corporation	1 856.4
Monadelphous Group	1 721.0
Beach Energy	1 646.4
Iluka Resources	1 611.3
Premier Investments	1 497.5
Breville Group	1 478.6
Steadfast Group	1 409.5
Accent Group	1 409.0
Collins Foods	1 348.6
Johns Lyng Group	1 281.3

Ridley Corporation	1 260.1
Seek	1 225.3
PeopleIn	1 186.4
REA Group	1 183.2
Brickworks	1 093.2
GUD Holdings	1 036.9
IGO	1 014.7
ASX	1 010.2
IDP Education	981.9
WiseTech Global	816.8
Carsales.com	781.2
Enero Group	740.2
Lindsay Australia	676.2
ARB Corporation	671.2
Michael Hill International	629.6
Adairs	621.3
Lovisa Holdings	596.5
Grange Resources	594.6
Baby Bunting Group	524.3
Nick Scali	507.7
IPH	490.1
Credit Corp Group	473.4
Codan	456.5
GWA Group	411.8
Altium	393.0
Technology One	368.2
Magellan Financial Group	343.0
Lycopodium	323.9
Beacon Lighting Group	312.0
Hansen Technologies	311.8
Servcorp	293.8
Supply Network	252.3
Lifestyle Communities	232.1
Smartgroup Corporation	224.7
Netwealth Group	207.0
Platinum Asset Management	202.7
Pro Medicus	124.9
Jumbo Interactive	118.7
PWR Holdings	118.3
Pinnacle Investment Management	112.9
Objective Corporation	110.4
Australian Ethical Investment	81.1
Clinuvel Pharmaceuticals	78.3
Fiducian Group	72.4
Clover Corporation	70.7

Table C
Year-on-year revenues growth

Companies generally strive for growth, though profit growth is usually of far more significance than a boost in revenues. In fact, it is possible for a company to increase its revenues by all kinds of means—including cutting profit margins or acquiring other companies—and year-on-year revenues growth is of little relevance if other ratios are not also improving. The figures used for this calculation are the latest full-year figures.

	%
Woodside Energy Group	162.6
Santos	79.7
PeopleIn	73.9
Carsales.com	53.5
Johns Lyng Group	43.2
Enero Group	41.8
Lycopodium	41.6
Mineral Resources	39.8
CSL	37.3
Elders	35.2
Computershare	34.7
Pro Medicus	33.6
Lovisa Holdings	30.0
Altium	29.9
WiseTech Global	29.2
Brickworks	28.5
IPH	27.3
Supply Network	27.1
Accent Group	26.1
GUD Holdings	25.4
Steadfast Group	24.1
IDP Education	23.8
Iluka Resources	22.4
Lindsay Australia	22.3
Ridley Corporation	20.1
Netwealth Group	19.8
Clinuvel Pharmaceuticals	19.2
Technology One	18.3
Wesfarmers	18.2
Aristocrat Leisure	17.7
Cochlear	17.5
PWR Holdings	17.1
Data#3	16.8
Clover Corporation	16.8
Reliance Worldwide Corporation	15.6
Reece	15.5
Nick Scali	15.1
Credit Corp Group	15.1
Australian Ethical Investment	14.6
Jumbo Interactive	13.9
Collins Foods	13.5
CSR	13.1
IGO	12.7

NRW Holdings	12.7
ANZ Group	11.5
Commonwealth Bank Australia	10.4
Macquarie Group	10.4
Adairs	10.1
Seek	9.7
Bapcor	9.7
National Australia Bank	8.9
Insurance Australia Group	8.2
NIB Holdings	7.7
Super Retail Group	7.1
Servcorp	7.0
Telstra Group	6.7
Coles Group	5.9
Michael Hill International	5.8
Fortescue Metals Group	5.7
Woolworths Group	5.7
Hansen Technologies	5.1
Fiducian Group	4.4
JB Hi-Fi	4.3
Breville Group	4.2
Metcash	4.2
Premier Investments	3.8
Objective Corporation	3.6
Lifestyle Communities	3.5
Baby Bunting Group	3.4
Medibank Private	3.2
Beacon Lighting Group	2.4
REA Group	2.0
Smartgroup Corporation	1.3
Nine Entertainment Co. Holdings	0.5
ASX	−1.2
GWA Group	−1.7
ARB Corporation	−3.4
BlueScope Steel	−4.1
Rio Tinto	−4.7
Monadelphous Group	−4.9
Harvey Norman Holdings	−5.1
Beach Energy	−7.1
Pinnacle Investment Management	−7.2
Codan	−9.8
BHP Group	−9.9
Platinum Asset Management	−19.8
Grange Resources	−23.9
Magellan Financial Group	−43.4

Table D
EBIT margin

A company's earnings before interest and taxation (EBIT) is sometimes regarded as a better measure of its profitability than the straight pre-tax or post-tax profit figure. EBIT is derived by adding interest payments to the pre-tax profit. Different companies choose different methods of financing their operations; by adding back interest payments to their profits we can help minimise these differences and make comparisons between companies more valid.

The EBIT margin is the EBIT figure as a percentage of annual sales. Clearly a high figure is to be desired, though of course this can be achieved artificially by inflating borrowings (and hence interest payments). And it is noteworthy that efficient companies with strong cashflow like some of the retailers can operate most satisfactorily on low margins.

The EBIT margin figure has little relevance for banks, and they have been excluded.

	%
IGO	168.4
ASX	102.7
Brickworks	90.9
Magellan Financial Group	74.1
Pinnacle Investment Management	73.1
Pro Medicus	69.0
Clinuvel Pharmaceuticals	58.2
Platinum Asset Management	57.6
Woodside Energy Group	55.5
Carsales.com	53.3
Lifestyle Communities	47.1
Netwealth Group	47.1
Iluka Resources	45.7
REA Group	44.8
BHP Group	43.6
WiseTech Global	42.8
Fortescue Metals Group	42.4
Grange Resources	42.4
Santos	41.8
Jumbo Interactive	40.6
Smartgroup Corporation	38.3
Beach Energy	35.9
Seek	35.5
Rio Tinto	34.2
Altium	33.6
IPH	31.7
Technology One	31.0
Nick Scali	30.9
Credit Corp Group	30.7
Aristocrat Leisure	28.4
Mineral Resources	28.1
CSL	27.8
Steadfast Group	26.9
Premier Investments	26.8
PWR Holdings	26.0
Fiducian Group	24.4
Computershare	23.7
IDP Education	22.8
Cochlear	21.3
Objective Corporation	20.4
Harvey Norman Holdings	20.3
Lycopodium	19.8
Australian Ethical Investment	19.6
Codan	19.3
Hansen Technologies	18.6
ARB Corporation	18.4
Servcorp	18.2
Reliance Worldwide Corporation	17.9
Lovisa Holdings	17.8
GUD Holdings	17.7
Beacon Lighting Group	17.6
GWA Group	17.1
Nine Entertainment Co. Holdings	16.4
Supply Network	16.2
Telstra Group	15.4
Clover Corporation	14.6
CSR	12.9
Breville Group	11.7
Adairs	11.5
Super Retail Group	11.2
NIB Holdings	10.3
Bapcor	10.1
Accent Group	10.0
Medibank Private	9.9
Michael Hill International	9.5
Enero Group	9.3
Lindsay Australia	8.8
Wesfarmers	8.4
BlueScope Steel	8.3
Collins Foods	8.2
JB Hi-Fi	8.0
Johns Lyng Group	7.6
Reece	7.3
Elders	7.1
NRW Holdings	6.1
Baby Bunting Group	5.6
Ridley Corporation	5.1
Woolworths Group	4.7
Coles Group	4.6
Monadelphous Group	4.5
PeopleIn	3.7
Metcash	2.9
Data#3	2.1

Table E
Year-on-year EBIT margin growth

The EBIT (earnings before interest and taxation) margin is one of the measures of a company's efficiency. So a rising margin is much to be desired, as it suggests that a company is achieving success in cutting its costs. This table does not include banks.

	%
IGO	179.5
Brickworks	120.6
Accent Group	76.4
Computershare	64.6
Mineral Resources	43.5
Lindsay Australia	41.8
ASX	41.1
NIB Holdings	40.1
Santos	38.0
Medibank Private	25.6
Iluka Resources	21.7
Servcorp	21.6
Aristocrat Leisure	16.5
Johns Lyng Group	14.8
Lycopodium	13.7
IDP Education	13.1
Pinnacle Investment Management	13.0
Clinuvel Pharmaceuticals	11.4
Elders	10.2
Woodside Energy Group	9.9
Nick Scali	9.3
Altium	9.1
Telstra Group	8.8
Supply Network	7.5
Woolworths Group	5.9
Breville Group	5.7
IPH	5.5
Monadelphous Group	5.2
Lifestyle Communities	4.5
Clover Corporation	2.8
Data#3	2.6
Pro Medicus	2.2
Steadfast Group	1.9
Metcash	1.8
Super Retail Group	1.5
WiseTech Global	1.5
NRW Holdings	0.9
CSR	0.6
Netwealth Group	–0.3
Platinum Asset Management	–0.8
GUD Holdings	–0.9
Hansen Technologies	–0.9

Premier Investments	–1.1
Lovisa Holdings	–1.8
Ridley Corporation	–1.9
Smartgroup Corporation	–2.3
Reece	–2.8
Technology One	–2.8
Reliance Worldwide Corporation	–3.9
Coles Group	–3.9
GWA Group	–4.4
Seek	–4.6
Australian Ethical Investment	–5.0
CSL	–5.4
REA Group	–6.5
JB Hi-Fi	–6.7
PWR Holdings	–8.4
Cochlear	–8.8
Jumbo Interactive	–8.9
Objective Corporation	–9.2
Bapcor	–9.5
Wesfarmers	–9.8
Fiducian Group	–11.2
Collins Foods	–11.9
Beach Energy	–13.0
Magellan Financial Group	–13.5
Carsales.com	–14.5
Credit Corp Group	–14.8
Beacon Lighting Group	–16.0
BHP Group	–17.0
Enero Group	–17.9
Fortescue Metals Group	–17.9
Nine Entertainment Co. Holdings	–20.3
Adairs	–20.3
Michael Hill International	–23.0
Harvey Norman Holdings	–23.3
ARB Corporation	–23.7
Grange Resources	–28.2
Codan	–29.0
PeopleIn	–29.7
Rio Tinto	–30.1
Baby Bunting Group	–42.6
BlueScope Steel	–58.4

Table F
After-tax profit
This table ranks all the companies according to their most recent full-year after-tax profit.

	$mn
BHP Group	19 285.1
Rio Tinto	18 000.0
Commonwealth Bank Australia	10 164.0
Woodside Energy Group	9 417.4
Fortescue Metals Group	7 161.2
National Australia Bank	7 104.0
ANZ Group	6 515.0
Macquarie Group	5 182.0
CSL	3 895.5
Santos	3 060.9
Wesfarmers	2 465.0
Telstra Group	1 928.0
Woolworths Group	1 618.0
IGO	1 528.0
Coles Group	1 098.0
BlueScope Steel	1 009.2
Aristocrat Leisure	1 000.9
Insurance Australia Group	832.0
Mineral Resources	769.0
Brickworks	746.1
Computershare	663.8
Harvey Norman Holdings	539.5
JB Hi-Fi	524.6
Iluka Resources	517.3
Medibank Private	511.1
ASX	491.1
Reece	387.6
Beach Energy	384.8
REA Group	356.1
Metcash	307.5
Cochlear	305.2
Premier Investments	285.2
Carsales.com	278.2
Super Retail Group	263.0
Nine Entertainment Co. Holdings	262.1
Seek	255.0
WiseTech Global	247.6
Reliance Worldwide Corporation	232.4
CSR	225.0
Steadfast Group	207.0
NIB Holdings	197.0
Magellan Financial Group	174.3
Grange Resources	171.7
Elders	170.0
IDP Education	148.5
Bapcor	125.3
GUD Holdings	118.7
Breville Group	110.2
NRW Holdings	104.4
Nick Scali	101.1
Altium	99.0
IPH	99.0
Credit Corp Group	91.3
Technology One	88.8
Accent Group	88.7
ARB Corporation	88.5
Platinum Asset Management	80.9
Pinnacle Investment Management	76.5
Lifestyle Communities	71.1
Lovisa Holdings	68.2
Codan	67.8
Netwealth Group	67.2
Pro Medicus	60.6
Smartgroup Corporation	58.8
Monadelphous Group	53.5
Collins Foods	51.9
Johns Lyng Group	46.8
Lycopodium	46.8
GWA Group	44.1
Hansen Technologies	42.8
Ridley Corporation	41.8
Adairs	40.2
Servcorp	37.1
Data#3	37.0
Michael Hill International	35.2
Lindsay Australia	34.5
Beacon Lighting Group	33.6
Jumbo Interactive	33.1
Clinuvel Pharmaceuticals	30.6
PeopleIn	28.4
Supply Network	27.4
Enero Group	24.4
PWR Holdings	21.8
Objective Corporation	21.1
Baby Bunting Group	14.5
Fiducian Group	12.3
Australian Ethical Investment	11.8
Clover Corporation	7.1

Table G

Year-on-year earnings per share growth

The earnings per share (EPS) figure is a crucial one. It tells you — the shareholder — what your part is of the company's profits, for each of your shares. So investors invariably look for EPS growth in a stock. The year-on-year EPS growth figure is often one of the first ratios that investors look to when evaluating a stock. The figures used for this calculation are the latest full-year figures.

	%
IGO	278.2
Brickworks	206.0
Accent Group	178.2
Insurance Australia Group	140.6
Woodside Energy Group	126.9
Santos	122.1
Computershare	112.8
Mineral Resources	90.1
Lindsay Australia	78.4
Johns Lyng Group	73.6
Lycopodium	72.1
Servcorp	46.6
Clinuvel Pharmaceuticals	46.6
Iluka Resources	46.0
IDP Education	44.8
NIB Holdings	39.9
Pro Medicus	36.3
Supply Network	35.7
Altium	30.1
WiseTech Global	29.9
Medibank Private	29.8
Nick Scali	26.0
Aristocrat Leisure	25.5
Data#3	22.1
Technology One	21.5
Netwealth Group	20.9
Clover Corporation	18.8
CSR	18.0
Ridley Corporation	16.9
Lovisa Holdings	16.4
Telstra Group	16.3
IPH	16.2
CSL	16.1
Lifestyle Communities	15.9
Steadfast Group	14.6
Australian Ethical Investment	14.1
Carsales.com	13.3
GUD Holdings	12.7
Elders	12.4
NRW Holdings	11.1
National Australia Bank	10.7
Cochlear	10.2
Super Retail Group	9.0
Commonwealth Bank Australia	7.9

	%
Objective Corporation	7.1
Macquarie Group	6.6
ANZ Group	5.7
Woolworths Group	5.2
PeopleIn	5.1
Reliance Worldwide Corporation	5.1
Premier Investments	4.8
Wesfarmers	4.8
Metcash	4.5
Coles Group	4.5
PWR Holdings	4.3
Jumbo Interactive	2.1
Breville Group	1.8
Monadelphous Group	1.7
Hansen Technologies	1.1
JB Hi-Fi	0.2
Smartgroup Corporation	−0.2
Seek	−1.0
Reece	−1.2
Pinnacle Investment Management	−2.1
ASX	−3.4
Bapcor	−4.8
Collins Foods	−5.7
GWA Group	−6.8
REA Group	−7.4
Fiducian Group	−7.5
Credit Corp Group	−9.9
Enero Group	−14.6
Fortescue Metals Group	−15.6
Beacon Lighting Group	−17.5
Platinum Asset Management	−19.6
Adairs	−23.0
Nine Entertainment Co. Holdings	−23.4
Michael Hill International	−23.5
Beach Energy	−23.7
ARB Corporation	−27.8
Codan	−32.8
Harvey Norman Holdings	−33.5
Rio Tinto	−36.8
BHP Group	−37.2
Grange Resources	−46.7
Baby Bunting Group	−51.9
Magellan Financial Group	−55.9
BlueScope Steel	−60.4

Table H
Return on equity

Shareholders' equity is the company's assets minus its liabilities. It is, in theory, the amount owned by the shareholders of the company. Return on equity is the after-tax profit expressed as a percentage of that equity. Thus, it is the amount of profit that the company managers made for you—the shareholder—from your assets. For many investors it is one of the most important gauges of how well a company is doing. It is one of the requirements for inclusion in this book that all companies have a return on equity of at least 10 per cent in their latest financial year.

	%
Lovisa Holdings	94.5
Nick Scali	63.0
Netwealth Group	59.1
Data#3	57.0
Pro Medicus	50.4
Australian Ethical Investment	45.9
Lycopodium	43.5
IGO	42.3
Technology One	41.4
Supply Network	40.0
JB Hi-Fi	38.9
Jumbo Interactive	34.3
Coles Group	33.9
Objective Corporation	31.1
IDP Education	30.5
Wesfarmers	30.3
Lindsay Australia	30.0
Iluka Resources	29.7
BHP Group	29.1
Metcash	28.6
Fortescue Metals Group	27.3
PWR Holdings	26.4
Woodside Energy Group	26.2
Woolworths Group	26.1
Brickworks	26.0
REA Group	25.7
Medibank Private	25.4
Fiducian Group	25.1
Rio Tinto	25.0
Platinum Asset Management	24.8
Beacon Lighting Group	23.8
NIB Holdings	23.4
Smartgroup Corporation	23.2
Altium	23.0
Mineral Resources	22.9
Clinuvel Pharmaceuticals	21.1
Elders	20.9
Computershare	20.8
CSR	20.7
Aristocrat Leisure	20.2
Accent Group	20.1
Adairs	20.1
Super Retail Group	19.8

IPH	19.7
Grange Resources	19.3
Servcorp	19.2
PeopleIn	19.2
Pinnacle Investment Management	18.5
Michael Hill International	18.3
Cochlear	17.8
Premier Investments	17.8
Magellan Financial Group	17.5
Codan	17.5
NRW Holdings	17.4
CSL	17.3
Macquarie Group	16.8
Breville Group	15.9
WiseTech Global	15.4
ARB Corporation	15.2
Santos	15.1
Nine Entertainment Co. Holdings	14.7
Lifestyle Communities	14.5
GWA Group	14.5
Commonwealth Bank Australia	14.0
Johns Lyng Group	13.8
GUD Holdings	13.7
Carsales.com	13.6
Enero Group	13.6
Collins Foods	13.3
Ridley Corporation	13.2
ASX	13.2
Hansen Technologies	13.1
Baby Bunting Group	13.0
Reliance Worldwide Corporation	13.0
Insurance Australia Group	13.0
Monadelphous Group	12.6
Telstra Group	12.5
Harvey Norman Holdings	12.4
Clover Corporation	11.7
Credit Corp Group	11.7
National Australia Bank	11.7
Seek	11.4
Bapcor	11.3
Reece	11.2
Steadfast Group	11.1
Beach Energy	10.4
ANZ Group	10.1
BlueScope Steel	10.0

Table I
Year-on-year return on equity growth

Company managers have a variety of strategies they can use to boost profits. It is much harder to lift the return on equity (ROE). Find a company with a high ROE figure, and one that is growing year by year, and it is possible that you have found a real growth stock. This figure is simply the percentage change in the ROE figure from the previous year to the latest year.

	%
IGO	247.3
Accent Group	177.9
Brickworks	161.5
Santos	141.6
Insurance Australia Group	132.2
Computershare	106.0
Mineral Resources	84.5
Woodside Energy Group	69.0
Lycopodium	51.1
Lindsay Australia	49.5
Servcorp	49.2
IDP Education	25.6
Medibank Private	24.0
NIB Holdings	21.3
Iluka Resources	20.8
CSR	14.4
Wesfarmers	14.0
Clover Corporation	13.5
Clinuvel Pharmaceuticals	13.3
Metcash	12.5
Altium	12.1
Data#3	11.0
Commonwealth Bank Australia	10.8
Telstra Group	10.7
Ridley Corporation	10.4
National Australia Bank	10.3
Australian Ethical Investment	8.9
Supply Network	8.5
Cochlear	8.3
NRW Holdings	6.1
Johns Lyng Group	6.0
Smartgroup Corporation	6.0
Netwealth Group	5.0
Pro Medicus	4.1
Super Retail Group	3.2
IPH	2.2
ANZ Group	0.6
Nick Scali	0.2
Elders	−0.2
Lifestyle Communities	−1.5
WiseTech Global	−1.6
ASX	−2.2
Monadelphous Group	−2.6

Coles Group	−4.0
Jumbo Interactive	−5.0
Reliance Worldwide Corporation	−5.1
Peopleln	−5.2
Technology One	−5.4
GUD Holdings	−5.4
Hansen Technologies	−5.8
Premier Investments	−5.9
Steadfast Group	−6.5
Aristocrat Leisure	−7.1
JB Hi-Fi	−7.7
Collins Foods	−8.0
GWA Group	−8.1
Bapcor	−8.3
Macquarie Group	−9.7
Lovisa Holdings	−11.0
PWR Holdings	−11.2
Reece	−11.7
Objective Corporation	−13.4
Fiducian Group	−14.1
CSL	−14.4
Breville Group	−15.6
Credit Corp Group	−18.1
Platinum Asset Management	−18.6
Seek	−19.3
REA Group	−20.8
Fortescue Metals Group	−21.5
Pinnacle Investment Management	−21.6
Nine Entertainment Co. Holdings	−22.0
Michael Hill International	−27.5
Beacon Lighting Group	−28.2
Adairs	−29.4
Enero Group	−30.9
Carsales.com	−31.7
Beach Energy	−31.8
ARB Corporation	−35.1
BHP Group	−36.7
Harvey Norman Holdings	−37.9
Woolworths Group	−38.0
Codan	−41.7
Rio Tinto	−42.3
Baby Bunting Group	−51.4
Grange Resources	−52.4
Magellan Financial Group	−55.9
BlueScope Steel	−67.9

Table J
Debt-to-equity ratio

A company's borrowings as a percentage of its shareholders' equity is one of the most common measures of corporate debt. Many investors will be wary of a company with a ratio that is too high. However, a company with a steady business and a regular income flow—such as an electric power company or a large supermarket chain—is generally considered relatively safe with a high level of debt, whereas a small company in a new business field might be thought at risk with even moderate debt levels. Much depends on surrounding circumstances, including the prevailing interest rates. Of course, it is often from borrowing that a company grows, and some investors are not happy buying shares in a company with little or no debt.

There are various ways to calculate the ratio, but for this book the net debt position is used. That is, a company's cash has been deducted from its borrowings. For inclusion in this book no company was allowed a debt-to-equity ratio of more than 70 per cent. Some of the companies had no net debt—their cash position was greater than the amount of their borrowings, or they had no borrowings at all—and so have been assigned a zero figure in this table. The ratio has no relevance for banks, and they have been excluded.

	%
Altium	0.0
ARB Corporation	0.0
Aristocrat Leisure	0.0
ASX	0.0
Australian Ethical Investment	0.0
BlueScope Steel	0.0
Clinuvel Pharmaceuticals	0.0
Cochlear	0.0
CSR	0.0
Data#3	0.0
Enero Group	0.0
Fiducian Group	0.0
Grange Resources	0.0
Hansen Technologies	0.0
IGO	0.0
Iluka Resources	0.0
JB Hi-Fi	0.0
Johns Lyng Group	0.0
Jumbo Interactive	0.0
Lindsay Australia	0.0
Lycopodium	0.0
Magellan Financial Group	0.0
Medibank Private	0.0
Michael Hill International	0.0
Monadelphous Group	0.0
Netwealth Group	0.0
Objective Corporation	0.0
Platinum Asset Management	0.0
Premier Investments	0.0
Pro Medicus	0.0
PWR Holdings	0.0
Servcorp	0.0
Super Retail Group	0.0
Technology One	0.0
NIB Holdings	0.3
Beacon Lighting Group	1.2
Nick Scali	1.4
Supply Network	2.8
Beach Energy	4.2
WiseTech Global	4.3
Woodside Energy Group	4.5
NRW Holdings	5.4
Clover Corporation	5.7
Fortescue Metals Group	5.7
Baby Bunting Group	5.8
Rio Tinto	6.9
IDP Education	8.2
Ridley Corporation	9.3
REA Group	9.5
Codan	12.7
Harvey Norman Holdings	14.1
Coles Group	15.5
Breville Group	15.8
PeopleIn	16.2
Brickworks	16.7
Smartgroup Corporation	17.2
Reece	20.0
BHP Group	20.4
Santos	20.9
Pinnacle Investment Management	21.9
Bapcor	22.4
Insurance Australia Group	23.6
Accent Group	27.1
Nine Entertainment Co. Holdings	27.9
Credit Corp Group	30.4
Carsales.com	31.2
Steadfast Group	31.7
Metcash	32.2
Reliance Worldwide Corporation	35.2
Adairs	36.4
GWA Group	37.9
Seek	39.5
Woolworths Group	39.9
Lovisa Holdings	41.7
GUD Holdings	45.2
Wesfarmers	45.4
Elders	49.6
IPH	51.0
Mineral Resources	52.7
Collins Foods	55.0
Computershare	56.8
CSL	59.9
Telstra Group	65.9
Lifestyle Communities	69.8

Table K
Current ratio

The current ratio is simply the company's current assets divided by its current liabilities. Current assets are cash or assets that can, in theory, be converted quickly into cash. Current liabilities are normally those payable within a year. The current ratio helps measure the ability of a company to repay in a hurry its short-term debt, should the need arise. Banks are not included.

Company	Ratio	Company	Ratio
Platinum Asset Management	12.9	REA Group	1.7
Grange Resources	7.8	Codan	1.7
Clinuvel Pharmaceuticals	7.4	Beacon Lighting Group	1.7
Pinnacle Investment Management	7.2	Computershare	1.7
Credit Corp Group	5.7	Jumbo Interactive	1.6
Pro Medicus	5.3	Michael Hill International	1.6
Netwealth Group	5.3	Santos	1.6
Iluka Resources	5.0	Beach Energy	1.5
Clover Corporation	4.5	Steadfast Group	1.4
ARB Corporation	4.2	Objective Corporation	1.4
PWR Holdings	3.3	Lindsay Australia	1.4
Aristocrat Leisure	3.3	IDP Education	1.3
IPH	3.2	Super Retail Group	1.3
Reliance Worldwide Corporation	3.0	NRW Holdings	1.3
Altium	2.8	Johns Lyng Group	1.3
IGO	2.8	BHP Group	1.2
Mineral Resources	2.8	Enero Group	1.2
Breville Group	2.6	Woodside Energy Group	1.2
Supply Network	2.5	Baby Bunting Group	1.2
Harvey Norman Holdings	2.5	Elders	1.2
Fiducian Group	2.5	JB Hi-Fi	1.2
Fortescue Metals Group	2.5	PeopleIn	1.2
Cochlear	2.4	Wesfarmers	1.2
GUD Holdings	2.3	Ridley Corporation	1.2
Reece	2.3	Technology One	1.1
Bapcor	2.3	Nick Scali	1.1
Lifestyle Communities	2.2	Accent Group	1.1
Australian Ethical Investment	2.0	ASX	1.1
CSL	2.0	Metcash	1.1
Monadelphous Group	2.0	Data#3	1.1
Rio Tinto	2.0	Nine Entertainment Co. Holdings	1.0
Brickworks	2.0	Lovisa Holdings	1.0
Magellan Financial Group	2.0	Adairs	1.0
Lycopodium	1.9	Seek	0.9
BlueScope Steel	1.9	Smartgroup Corporation	0.9
Premier Investments	1.9	Servcorp	0.8
Hansen Technologies	1.9	Collins Foods	0.7
NIB Holdings	1.9	Telstra Group	0.7
GWA Group	1.8	WiseTech Global	0.6
Carsales.com	1.8	Coles Group	0.6
Medibank Private	1.8	Woolworths Group	0.5
CSR	1.7		

Table L
Price/earnings ratio

The price/earnings ratio (PER) — the current share price divided by the earnings per share figure — is one of the best known of all sharemarket ratios. Essentially it expresses the amount of money investors are ready to pay for each cent or dollar of a company's profits, and it allows you to compare the share prices of different companies of varying sizes and with widely different profits. A high PER suggests the market has a high regard for the company and its growth prospects; a low one may mean that investors are disdainful of the stock. The figures in this table are based on share prices as of 4 September 2023.

Company	PER	Company	PER
Grange Resources	3.1	Bapcor	18.1
Brickworks	5.7	Mineral Resources	18.4
Elders	5.9	Smartgroup Corporation	18.8
Enero Group	6.1	Coles Group	19.3
Adairs	6.1	Medibank Private	19.4
Woodside Energy Group	6.1	NIB Holdings	19.4
PeopleIn	6.9	Baby Bunting Group	19.9
Iluka Resources	7.0	Codan	21.1
IGO	7.1	ASX	22.3
Servcorp	7.6	Collins Foods	22.5
Lycopodium	8.6	Computershare	22.9
Santos	8.7	Supply Network	23.1
Fortescue Metals Group	8.7	Pinnacle Investment Management	23.6
Harvey Norman Holdings	9.3	Clover Corporation	23.8
JB Hi-Fi	9.5	Telstra Group	24.2
Beach Energy	9.6	Wesfarmers	24.6
Magellan Financial Group	9.7	Lifestyle Communities	25.5
Nick Scali	9.9	Hansen Technologies	25.5
Platinum Asset Management	10.1	Monadelphous Group	26.4
BlueScope Steel	10.1	Aristocrat Leisure	27.5
Michael Hill International	10.3	Steadfast Group	27.8
Lindsay Australia	10.3	Woolworths Group	28.5
Rio Tinto	10.5	Clinuvel Pharmaceuticals	29.3
ANZ Group	11.0	Jumbo Interactive	29.5
Super Retail Group	11.1	Data#3	30.4
GWA Group	11.6	ARB Corporation	31.4
Metcash	11.6	Breville Group	31.4
NRW Holdings	11.9	Seek	31.8
BHP Group	12.1	CSL	33.2
Beacon Lighting Group	12.1	Reece	33.8
Accent Group	12.6	Lovisa Holdings	34.8
Macquarie Group	12.7	Johns Lyng Group	35.3
CSR	13.0	Carsales.com	36.7
National Australia Bank	13.1	Australian Ethical Investment	41.7
Nine Entertainment Co. Holdings	13.1	IDP Education	47.5
Reliance Worldwide Corporation	14.0	PWR Holdings	49.1
GUD Holdings	14.4	Objective Corporation	55.1
Premier Investments	14.6	Netwealth Group	55.6
Fiducian Group	15.2	Cochlear	57.7
Credit Corp Group	15.8	Technology One	57.9
Ridley Corporation	16.8	REA Group	60.2
Commonwealth Bank Australia	17.0	Altium	63.8
Insurance Australia Group	17.1	WiseTech Global	92.6
IPH	17.7	Pro Medicus	125.3

Table M
Price-to-NTA-per-share ratio

The NTA-per-share figure expresses the worth of a company's net tangible assets—that is, its assets minus its liabilities and intangible assets—for each share of the company. Intangible assets, such as goodwill or the value of newspaper mastheads, are excluded because it is deemed difficult to place a value on them (though this proposition is debatable), and also because they might not have much worth if separated from the company. The price-to-NTA-per-share ratio relates this figure to the share price.

A ratio of one means that the company is valued exactly according to the value of its assets. A ratio below one suggests that the shares are a bargain, though usually there is a good reason for this. Profits are more important than assets.

In some respects, this is an 'old economy' ratio. For many high-tech companies in the 'new economy' the most important assets are human ones whose worth does not appear on the balance sheet.

Companies with a negative NTA-per-share figure, as a result of having intangible assets valued at more than their net assets, have been omitted from this table.

Company	Ratio	Company	Ratio
Grange Resources	0.6	Insurance Australia Group	5.3
Beach Energy	1.0	Clinuvel Pharmaceuticals	5.5
ANZ Group	1.2	Medibank Private	5.6
Santos	1.2	NIB Holdings	8.4
Brickworks	1.3	Seek	9.3
BlueScope Steel	1.3	ASX	9.7
Harvey Norman Holdings	1.4	Fiducian Group	9.9
Woodside Energy Group	1.5	Breville Group	11.5
National Australia Bank	1.6	Aristocrat Leisure	12.0
Iluka Resources	1.8	PWR Holdings	14.7
Credit Corp Group	1.9	Beacon Lighting Group	15.0
Magellan Financial Group	2.0	Codan	15.2
Fortescue Metals Group	2.3	Cochlear	15.5
Macquarie Group	2.3	Supply Network	15.9
Elders	2.3	Reece	16.3
Platinum Asset Management	2.5	Altium	16.5
CSR	2.6	Metcash	20.1
Commonwealth Bank Australia	2.6	Australian Ethical Investment	20.3
Rio Tinto	2.7	Telstra Group	29.3
Clover Corporation	2.7	Johns Lyng Group	32.4
IGO	2.9	Data#3	35.1
Ridley Corporation	2.9	Netwealth Group	36.0
Monadelphous Group	3.4	REA Group	36.2
Lifestyle Communities	3.5	Jumbo Interactive	36.3
NRW Holdings	3.5	Bapcor	54.4
BHP Group	3.6	Objective Corporation	61.9
Mineral Resources	4.1	Woolworths Group	63.2
Lycopodium	4.2	Pro Medicus	65.7
Pinnacle Investment Management	4.3	Reliance Worldwide Corporation	76.4
Premier Investments	4.3	Technology One	132.8
ARB Corporation	5.3		

Table N
Dividend yield

Many investors buy shares for income, rather than for capital growth. They look for companies that offer a high dividend yield (the dividend expressed as a percentage of the share price). Table N ranks the companies in this book according to their historic dividend yields. Note that the franking credits available from most companies in this book can make the dividend yield substantially higher. The dividend yield changes with the share price. The figures in this table are based on share prices as of 4 September 2023.

	%
Platinum Asset Management	9.9
Woodside Energy Group	9.8
Magellan Financial Group	9.3
Elders	8.8
Grange Resources	8.7
Fortescue Metals Group	8.7
Accent Group	8.6
Lycopodium	8.0
Michael Hill International	7.9
Servcorp	7.5
PeopleIn	7.2
Enero Group	6.9
JB Hi-Fi	6.8
GWA Group	6.7
Harvey Norman Holdings	6.2
Nick Scali	6.1
Metcash	6.1
Rio Tinto	6.1
Super Retail Group	6.1
CSR	6.0
NRW Holdings	6.0
ANZ Group	5.8
BHP Group	5.7
Adairs	5.6
Nine Entertainment Co. Holdings	5.3
Iluka Resources	5.2
National Australia Bank	5.2
Fiducian Group	5.1
Beacon Lighting Group	4.6
Commonwealth Bank Australia	4.4
IPH	4.3
Macquarie Group	4.2
Santos	4.2
Telstra Group	4.2
Coles Group	4.2
Lindsay Australia	4.2
IGO	4.1
Medibank Private	4.1
ASX	4.0
Pinnacle Investment Management	3.9
Premier Investments	3.8
Smartgroup Corporation	3.8
Ridley Corporation	3.7
Wesfarmers	3.6

Baby Bunting Group	3.5
NIB Holdings	3.5
Reliance Worldwide Corporation	3.5
Monadelphous Group	3.3
Bapcor	3.3
Credit Corp Group	3.3
GUD Holdings	3.2
Lovisa Holdings	3.1
Supply Network	3.1
Data#3	3.0
Computershare	2.8
Jumbo Interactive	2.8
Woolworths Group	2.7
Collins Foods	2.7
Steadfast Group	2.7
Insurance Australia Group	2.6
Mineral Resources	2.6
Beach Energy	2.5
Codan	2.3
BlueScope Steel	2.3
Brickworks	2.3
Carsales.com	2.1
Seek	2.1
Hansen Technologies	1.9
ARB Corporation	1.8
IDP Education	1.6
Australian Ethical Investment	1.6
Netwealth Group	1.6
Clover Corporation	1.5
CSL	1.4
Johns Lyng Group	1.4
Aristocrat Leisure	1.3
Breville Group	1.3
Reece	1.2
Cochlear	1.2
PWR Holdings	1.2
Altium	1.1
Objective Corporation	1.1
REA Group	1.0
Technology One	0.9
Lifestyle Communities	0.7
Pro Medicus	0.4
Clinuvel Pharmaceuticals	0.3
WiseTech Global	0.2

Table O
Year-on-year dividend growth

Most investors hope for a rising dividend, and this table tells how much each company raised or lowered its dividend in its latest financial year.

	%
IGO	480.0
Accent Group	169.2
Woodside Energy Group	100.5
Beach Energy	100.0
Mineral Resources	90.0
Iluka Resources	87.5
Santos	70.7
Johns Lyng Group	57.9
Lindsay Australia	53.1
IDP Education	51.9
Clover Corporation	50.0
Lycopodium	50.0
Supply Network	50.0
Insurance Australia Group	36.4
Pro Medicus	36.4
WiseTech Global	34.5
Elders	33.3
NRW Holdings	32.0
Computershare	29.6
NIB Holdings	27.3
Aristocrat Leisure	26.8
Telstra Group	25.9
Clinuvel Pharmaceuticals	25.0
Premier Investments	25.0
Objective Corporation	22.7
Data#3	22.3
Carsales.com	22.0
Macquarie Group	20.6
Netwealth Group	20.0
National Australia Bank	18.9
Commonwealth Bank Australia	16.9
Australian Ethical Investment	16.7
CSR	15.9
Steadfast Group	15.4
Altium	14.9
CSL	14.1
Woolworths Group	13.0
Ridley Corporation	11.5
Super Retail Group	11.4
Reece	11.1
Cochlear	10.0
Servcorp	10.0
Lifestyle Communities	9.5
Medibank Private	9.0

	%
IPH	8.2
Technology One	8.0
PeopleIn	7.7
Nick Scali	7.1
Seek	6.8
Wesfarmers	6.1
Reliance Worldwide Corporation	6.1
Coles Group	4.8
Metcash	4.7
PWR Holdings	4.2
Brickworks	3.3
Pinnacle Investment Management	2.9
ANZ Group	2.8
Bapcor	2.3
Fiducian Group	2.0
Breville Group	1.7
Jumbo Interactive	1.2
BlueScope Steel	0.0
Collins Foods	0.0
GUD Holdings	0.0
Michael Hill International	0.0
Monadelphous Group	0.0
JB Hi-Fi	−1.3
ASX	−3.4
REA Group	−3.7
Credit Corp Group	−5.4
Lovisa Holdings	−6.8
Beacon Lighting Group	−10.8
Enero Group	−12.0
Smartgroup Corporation	−12.3
ARB Corporation	−12.7
GWA Group	−13.3
Fortescue Metals Group	−15.5
Hansen Technologies	−16.7
Platinum Asset Management	−17.6
Nine Entertainment Co. Holdings	−21.4
Harvey Norman Holdings	−33.3
Codan	−33.9
Rio Tinto	−34.6
BHP Group	−43.6
Magellan Financial Group	−51.6
Baby Bunting Group	−51.9
Adairs	−55.6
Grange Resources	−66.7

Table P
Five-year share price return

This table ranks the approximate annual average return to investors from a five-year investment in each of the companies in the book, as of September 2023. It is an accumulated return, based on share price appreciation or depreciation plus dividend payments.

	% p.a.		% p.a.
Fortescue Metals Group	52.4	Macquarie Group	9.9
Johns Lyng Group	47.3	NRW Holdings	9.8
Pro Medicus	46.4	Telstra Group	9.8
Mineral Resources	40.2	Premier Investments	9.5
Data#3	38.4	Accent Group	9.0
Objective Corporation	35.1	Computershare	8.4
Supply Network	32.4	Woolworths Group	8.4
Grange Resources	29.1	Fiducian Group	8.3
IGO	28.4	Coles Group	8.0
Lindsay Australia	27.6	Medibank Private	7.2
PWR Holdings	27.6	Pinnacle Investment Management	7.2
WiseTech Global	26.9	Aristocrat Leisure	6.8
Lifestyle Communities	24.6	NIB Holdings	6.7
Australian Ethical Investment	23.9	Beacon Lighting Group	6.6
Technology One	23.7	Michael Hill International	6.5
Codan	22.8	BlueScope Steel	6.3
Jumbo Interactive	21.8	Santos	5.6
Lycopodium	21.4	Woodside Energy Group	5.5
IDP Education	19.4	Cochlear	5.2
Nick Scali	18.5	National Australia Bank	5.0
Rio Tinto	18.0	CSL	4.3
JB Hi-Fi	17.6	Clinuvel Pharmaceuticals	4.1
Lovisa Holdings	17.0	Monadelphous Group	3.7
Steadfast Group	16.4	PeopleIn	3.7
Carsales.com	14.9	Elders	3.2
Collins Foods	14.7	ANZ Group	2.0
Netwealth Group	14.1	Nine Entertainment Co. Holdings	2.0
Breville Group	13.8	Seek	1.9
REA Group	13.4	Baby Bunting Group	1.8
ARB Corporation	13.1	Credit Corp Group	1.0
BHP Group	13.1	ASX	0.3
Altium	13.0	Iluka Resources	0.3
Enero Group	12.7	Bapcor	0.1
CSR	12.3	Servcorp	−0.3
Ridley Corporation	12.2	GUD Holdings	−0.4
Brickworks	12.0	Beach Energy	−1.4
Super Retail Group	11.7	Reliance Worldwide Corporation	−1.9
Wesfarmers	11.7	Smartgroup Corporation	−2.3
Commonwealth Bank Australia	11.4	GWA Group	−2.5
Reece	11.3	Adairs	−2.6
Harvey Norman Holdings	10.9	Insurance Australia Group	−2.6
Hansen Technologies	10.8	Clover Corporation	−5.2
IPH	10.6	Magellan Financial Group	−8.2
Metcash	10.6	Platinum Asset Management	−14.3

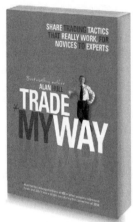

Best-selling author Alan Hull presents the complete sharemarket solution for novices to experts. Whether you're managing your portfolio, trading tactically on the sharemarket or investing in blue chip shares, Alan Hull explains the ins and outs of investing and trading in easy-to-understand and engaging language.

Available in print and e-book formats